000096

Picture Bride

and Related Readings

McDougal Littell
A HOUGHTON MIFFLIN COMPANY

Evanston, Illinois   *Boston*   *Dallas*

Acknowledgments

The Bancroft Library (University of California, Berkeley): *Picture Bride* by Yoshiko Uchida. Copyright © 1987 by Yoshiko Uchida. Reprinted by permission of The Bancroft Library (University of California, Berkeley).

Westernlore Press: Excerpt from *City in the Sun* by Paul Bailey. Copyright © 1971 by Paul Bailey. Reprinted by permission of Westernlore Press.

Houghton Mifflin Company: "Shikata Ga Nai," from *Farewell to Manzanar* by James D. Houston and Jeanne Wakatsuki Houston. Copyright © 1971 by James D. Houston. Reprinted by permission of Houghton Mifflin Company. All rights reserved.

Continued on page 315.

The editors have made every effort to trace the ownership of all copyrighted selections found in this book and to make full acknowledgment for their use. Omissions brought to our attention will be corrected in a subsequent edition.

Cover illustration by Gail Piazza.
Author photo: © June Finfer, Filmedia Ltd.

ISBN 0-395-77540-X

Contents

....

Selected Poems by Janice Mirikitani

Breaking Silence

For My Father

Clothes

The Heart of a Woman

Picture Bride

Yoshiko Uchida

*In memory
of those brave women
from Japan
who travelled far,
who endured,
and who prevailed.*

Chapter 1

1917–1918

Hana Omiya stood at the railing of the small ship that shuddered toward America in a turbulent November sea. She shivered as she pulled the folds of her silk kimono close to her throat and tightened the wool shawl about her shoulders.

She was thin and small, her dark eyes shadowed in her pale face, her black hair piled high in a pompadour that seemed too heavy for so slight a woman. She clung to the moist rail and breathed the damp salt air deep into her lungs. Her body seemed leaden and lifeless, as though it were simply the vehicle transporting her soul to a strange new life, and she longed with childlike intensity to be home again in Oka Village.

She longed to see the bright persimmon dotting the barren trees beside the thatched roofs, to see the fields of golden rice stretching to the mountains where only last fall she had gathered plump white mushrooms, and to see once more the maple trees lacing their flaming colors through the green pine. If only she could see a familiar face, eat a meal without retching, walk on solid ground and stretch out at night on a *tatami* mat instead of in a hard narrow bunk. She thought now of seeking the warm shelter of her bunk but could not bear to face the relentless smell of fish that penetrated the lower decks.

Why did I ever leave Japan, she wondered bitterly. Why did I ever listen to my uncle? And yet she knew it was she herself who had begun the chain of events that placed her on this heaving ship. It was she who had first planted in her uncle's mind the thought that she would make a good wife for Taro Takeda, the lonely man who had gone to America to make his fortune in Oakland, California.

It all began one day when her uncle had come to visit her mother.

"I must find a nice young bride," he had said, startling Hana with this blunt talk of marriage in her presence. She blushed and was ready to leave the room when her uncle quickly added, "My good friend Takeda has a son in America. I must find someone willing to travel to that far land."

This last remark was intended to indicate to Hana and her mother that he didn't consider this a suitable prospect for Hana who was the youngest daughter of what once had been a fine family. Her father, until his death fifteen years ago, had been the largest landholder of the village and one of its last *samurai*. They had once had many servants and field hands, but now all that was changed. Their money was gone. Hana's three older sisters had made good marriages, and the eldest remained in their home with her husband to carry on the Omiya name and perpetuate the homestead. Her other sisters had married merchants in Osaka and Nagoya and were living comfortably.

Now that Hana was twenty-one, finding a proper husband for her had taken on an urgency that produced an embarrassing secretive air over the entire matter. Usually, her mother didn't speak of it until they were lying side by side on their quilts at night.

Then, under the protective cover of darkness, she would suggest one name and then another, hoping that Hana would indicate an interest in one of them.

Her uncle spoke freely of Taro Takeda only because he was so sure Hana would never consider him. "He is a conscientious, hard-working man who has been in the United States for almost ten years. He is thirty-one, operates a small shop and rents some rooms above the shop where he lives." Her uncle rubbed his chin thoughtfully. "He could provide well for a wife," he added.

"Ah," Hana's mother said softly.

"You say he is successful in this business?" Hana's sister inquired.

"His father tells me he sells many things in his shop—clothing, stockings, needles, thread and buttons—such things as that. He also sells bean paste, pickled radish, bean cake and soy sauce. A wife of his would not go cold or hungry."

They all nodded, each of them picturing this merchant in varying degrees of success and affluence. There were many Japanese emigrating to America these days, and Hana had heard of the picture brides who went with nothing more than an exchange of photographs to bind them to a strange man.

"Taro San is lonely," her uncle continued, "I want to find for him a fine young woman who is strong and brave enough to cross the ocean alone."

"It would certainly be a different kind of life," Hana's sister ventured, and for a moment, Hana thought she glimpsed a longing ordinarily concealed behind her quiet, obedient face. In that same instant, Hana knew she wanted more for herself than her sisters had in their proper, arranged and loveless marriages. She wanted to escape the smothering strictures of life in her village. She certainly was not going to marry a farmer and spend her life working beside him planting, weeding and harvesting in the rice paddies until her back became bent from too many years of stooping and her skin turned to brown leather by the sun and wind. Neither did she particularly relish the idea of marrying a merchant in a big city as her two sisters had done. Since her mother objected to her going to Tokyo to seek employment as a teacher, perhaps she would consent to a flight to America for what seemed a proper and respectable marriage.

Almost before she realized what she was doing, she spoke to her uncle. "Oji San, perhaps I should go to America to make this lonely man a good wife."

"You, Hana Chan?" Her uncle observed her with startled curiosity. "You would go all alone to a foreign land so far away from your mother and family?"

"I would not allow it." Her mother spoke fiercely. Hana was her youngest and she had lavished upon her the attention and latitude that often befall the last child. How could she permit her to travel so far, even to marry the son of Takeda who was known to her brother.

But now, a notion that had seemed quite impossible a moment before was lodged in his receptive mind, and Hana's uncle grasped it with the pleasure that comes from an unexpected discovery.

"You know," he said looking at Hana, "it might be a very good life in America."

Hana felt a faint fluttering in her heart. Perhaps this lonely man in America was her means of escaping both the village and the encirclement of her family.

Her uncle spoke with increasing enthusiasm of sending Hana to become Taro's wife. And the husband of Hana's sister, who was head of their household, spoke with equal eagerness. Although he never said so, Hana guessed he would be pleased to be rid of her, the spirited younger sister who stirred up his placid life with what he considered radical ideas about life and the role of women. He often claimed that Hana had too much schooling for a girl. She had graduated from Women's High School in Kyoto which gave her five more years of schooling than her older sister.

"It has addled her brain—all that learning from those books," he said when he tired of arguing with Hana.

A man's word carried much weight for Hana's mother. Pressed by the two men she consulted her other daughters and their husbands. She discussed the matter carefully with her brother and asked the village priest. Finally, she agreed to an exchange of family histories and an investigation was begun into Taro Takeda's family, his education and his health, so they would be assured there was no insanity or tuberculosis or police records concealed in his family's past. Soon Hana's uncle was devoting his energies entirely to serving as go-between for Hana's mother and Taro Takeda's father.

When at last an agreement to the marriage was almost reached, Taro wrote his first letter to Hana. It was brief and proper and gave no more clue to his character than the stiff formal portrait taken at his graduation from Middle School. Hana's uncle had given her the picture with apologies from his parents because it was the only photo they had of him and it was not a flattering likeness.

Hana hid the letter and photograph in the sleeve of her kimono and took them to the outhouse to study in private. Squinting in the dim light and trying to ignore the foul odor, she read and reread Taro's letter, trying to find the real man somewhere in the sparse unbending prose.

By the time he sent her money for her steamship tickets, she had received ten more letters, but none revealed much more of the man than the first. In none did he disclose his loneliness or his need, but Hana understood this. In fact, she would have recoiled from a man who bared his intimate thoughts to her so soon. After all, they would have a lifetime together to get to know one another.

So it was that Hana had left her family and sailed alone to America with a small hope trembling inside of her. Tomorrow, at last, the ship would dock in San Francisco and she would meet face to face the man she was soon to marry. Hana was overcome with excitement at the thought of being in America and terrified of the meeting about to take place. What would she say to Taro Takeda when they first met, and for all the days and years after?

Hana wondered about the flat above the shop. Perhaps it would be luxuriously furnished with the finest of brocades and lacquers, and perhaps there would be a servant, although he had not mentioned it. She worried whether she would be able to manage on the meager English she had learned at Women's High School. The overwhelming anxiety for the day to come and the violent rolling of the ship were more than Hana could bear. Shuddering in the face of the wind, she leaned over the railing and became violently and wretchedly ill.

By five the next morning, Hana was up and dressed in her finest purple silk kimono and coat. She could not eat the bean soup and rice that appeared for breakfast and took only a few bites of the yellow pickled radish. Her bags, which had scarcely been touched since she boarded the ship, were easily packed for all they contained were her kimonos and some of her favorite books. The large willow basket, tightly secured by a rope, remained under the bunk, untouched since her uncle had placed it there.

She had not befriended the other women in her cabin, for they had lain in their bunks for most of the voyage, too sick to be company to anyone. Each morning Hana had fled the closeness of the sleeping quarters and spent most of the day huddled in a corner of the deck, listening to the lonely songs of some Russians also travelling to an alien land.

As the ship approached land, Hana hurried up to the deck to look out at the gray expanse of ocean and sky, eager for a first glimpse of her new homeland.

"We won't be docking until almost noon," one of the deck hands told her.

Hana nodded. "I can wait," she answered, but the last hours seemed the longest.

When she set foot on American soil at last, it was not in the city of San Francisco as she had expected, but on Angel Island, where all third-class passengers were taken. She spent two miserable days and nights waiting, as the immigrants were questioned by officials, examined for trachoma and tuberculosis and tested for hookworm by a woman who collected their stools on tin pie plates. Hana was relieved she could produce her own, not having to borrow a little from someone else, as some of the women had to do. It was a bewildering, degrading beginning, and Hana was sick with anxiety, wondering if she would ever be released.

On the third day, a Japanese messenger from San Francisco appeared with a letter for her from Taro. He had written it the day of her arrival, but it had not reached her for two days.

Taro welcomed her to America and told her that the bearer of the letter would inform Taro when she was to be released so he could be at the pier to meet her.

The letter eased her anxiety for a while, but as soon as she was released and boarded the launch for San Francisco, new fears rose up to smother her with a feeling almost of dread.

The early morning mist had become a light chilling

rain, and on the pier, black umbrellas bobbed here and there, making the task of recognition even harder. Hana searched desperately for a face that resembled the photo she had studied so long and hard. Suppose he hadn't come. What would she do then?

Hana took a deep breath, lifted her head and walked slowly from the launch. The moment she was on the pier, a man in a black coat, wearing a derby and carrying an umbrella, came quickly to her side. He was of slight build, not much taller than she, and his face was sallow and pale. He bowed stiffly and murmured, "You have had a long trip, Miss Omiya. I hope you are well."

Hana caught her breath. "You are Takeda San?" she asked.

He removed his hat and Hana was further startled to see that he was already turning bald.

"You are Takeda San?" she asked again. He looked older than thirty-one.

"I am afraid I no longer resemble the early photo my parents gave you. I am sorry."

Hana had not meant to begin like this. It was not going well.

"No, no," she said quickly. "It is just that I . . . that is, I am terribly nervous . . ." Hana stopped abruptly, too flustered to go on.

"I understand," Taro said gently. "You will feel better when you meet my friends and have some tea. Mr. and Mrs. Toda are expecting you in Oakland. You will be staying with them until . . ." He couldn't bring himself to mention the marriage just yet and Hana was grateful he hadn't.

He quickly made arrangements to have her baggage sent to Oakland and then led her carefully along the rain slick pier toward the street car that would take them to the ferry.

Hana shuddered at the sight of another boat, and

as they climbed to its upper deck she felt a queasy tightening of her stomach.

"I hope it will not rock too much," she said anxiously. "Is it many hours to your city?"

Taro laughed for the first time since their meeting, revealing the gold fillings of his teeth. "Oakland is just across the bay," he explained. "We will be there in twenty minutes."

Raising a hand to cover her mouth, Hana laughed with him and suddenly felt better. I am in America now, she thought, and this is the man I came to marry. Then she sat down carefully beside Taro, so no part of their clothing touched.

Chapter 2

They both looked straight ahead, but from the corner of her eyes Hana tried to observe Taro's face. He was not a handsome man, but his eyes were kind. He had a high forehead that blended into his baldness, a rather thick nose and heavy lips. Hana took special pains to look at his ears and was pleased that the lobes seemed large enough to hold a grain of rice, for that was a sign of good fortune. Her mother had told her to notice his ears and to report back on her findings without fail. She would be pleased to hear that his ear lobes were of generous proportions.

Hana folded her hands carefully on her lap and looked around, more and more aware of her conspicuous Japanese clothing.

"My clothes are not right," she murmured, tucking her feet with their white *tabi* and *zori* as far beneath the bench as she could. She held her *furoshiki* bundle close to her chest, but there was no hiding it or her clothes, and the curious stares of the people who sat opposite her were cold and unfriendly.

"I feel very much out of place," she whispered.

Taro nodded and understood. "Mrs. Toda will help you get some American clothing," he assured her.

In Oakland they boarded another street car and got off after a short ride. Hana followed Taro up the steps of the dingy gray house on Eighth Street where the Todas lived. It had been a long wet walk from the corner, for Hana, holding the umbrella so Taro could carry her bags, had found it difficult to share one umbrella and still not walk too close to him. Now she felt damp clear through and was shivering from the cold.

When the door opened, however, the sight of Kiku Toda quickly dispelled the gloom of the weather as well as her anxieties. Kiku was a warm friendly woman, who had obviously prepared for Hana's arrival by fixing her face and dabbing two circles of rouge on her cheeks.

"Come in, come in," she called brightly, and the smile on her round face widened with pleasure as she caught sight of Hana. "I've been waiting and watching for you ever since lunch."

She inspected Hana with a candid friendly gaze and nodded her approval. "Such a pretty young thing you've gotten from Japan," she teased Taro. "She doesn't even look twenty yet."

Hana blushed with embarrassment and Taro simply grinned as he removed his coat and hat and hung them with accustomed ease on the hall rack.

"It is so kind of you to have me," Hana said with a long bow. But Kiku scarcely listened to her formal words of greeting.

"Here, take off your wet shawl and coat. You must be exhausted after that long dreary trip. I can still remember how it was even though it's been five years since I came from Japan."

She led Hana quickly through the kitchen to a small room at the rear of the house. "Now take off your wet things. Would you like a hot bath? I can turn on the gas burner and have hot water in about forty minutes."

She didn't wait for Hana to answer, for although she had offered, she really wanted Hana to talk before disappearing for a bath.

Hana looked gratefully at the room that was to be hers. There was a small cot in one corner covered with a white cotton bedspread. A rocking chair was placed beside the single window that looked out on a weed-filled yard and beside it stood a high brown dresser covered with a starched white runner embroidered with pink daisies. A small braided rug lay beside the bed, but could not conceal the general disrepair of the floor boards.

"It isn't fancy," Kiku said, "but I thought it would be better than sleeping with nine other women at the Women's Home in one of the Japanese churches. That's where most single women stay until they get married."

"Oh, this is beautiful," Hana said quickly. "I have never before had the luxury of a room all to myself."

Kiku moved closer. "In America," she said, "everyone likes to have a room to himself with a key to lock the door. It's very different from Japan. They are very keen on privacy here. You'll see if you go out to do housework for a white family, and I expect you will, unless you help Taro at the shop every day."

Until that moment it had never occurred to Hana that she might go to work when she came to America. She intended, of course, to help Taro at his shop occasionally, but as the wife of the proprietor, she pictured herself sitting at the back of the shop knitting or crocheting in a comfortable chair. She had never once thought that she would go to the home of a white woman and do her housework for her. Taro was supposed to be a successful shopkeeper, and she had come to America to be a lady, not a servant. She thought fleetingly of the maid who had worked for them in Oka Village when life was generous and good.

"Is Taro San's shop going poorly then?" she asked.

Kiku hesitated. "I wouldn't say it is exactly prospering, but never mind, you'll soon see for yourself."

She flicked a speck of dust from the dresser and hurried out of the room, leaving Hana to muse on that bit of unsettling information.

"Make yourself comfortable and then come have some hot tea," Kiku called from the kitchen.

Hana folded her shawl and put it neatly at the foot of the cot. She wondered what Kiku had meant about Taro's shop. Perhaps he was not the successful merchant his uncle had made him out to be. It had sounded so hopeful and magnificent back in Oka Village, but suppose all was not as it had seemed. What could she do then? She had no money with which to return to Japan, and besides, she had promised to become Taro's wife. Hana shuddered and felt a chill pierce her heart. Not wanting to be alone in the small cold room with the sound of rain splashing at the window, she hurried after Kiku into the kitchen and asked if there was anything she could do.

At precisely five forty-five, Henry Toda came home from the bank.

"Ah, he is a banker?" Hana had asked when Taro told her where he worked.

"Not exactly, no."

"He is a teller or a clerk then?"

"No." Taro was silent a moment and then almost reluctantly, he murmured, "He is a janitor at the Bank of Italy."

"Oh, I see."

"*Tadaima!* I'm home!" Henry Toda called from the hallway. He was a large robust man who seemed to mirror the energy and cheer of his wife. Discarding his given name, Hisakazu, because it was impossible for a white person to remember, he had taken the name Henry and was called that even by his Japanese friends. He hurried into the dining room now with quick strides calling, "Where is the new bride? Has the new bride come?"

Waving aside Hana's deep formal bow, he took her hand in western fashion and told her how glad he was that she had come.

"Hah, you're a lucky one," he said to Taro, slapping him on the back and making Hana blush once more. Not knowing what to do or say, she simply looked down at her toes.

Kiku had made a special dinner of red bean rice, broiled sea bass and an egg custard with bamboo shoot and gingko nuts.

"These are the dishes I make best," she said proudly, and Hana marvelled at how five years could change a Japanese woman. If Kiku had been in Japan, she would have served her elegant meal demurring that she was a poor cook and disparaging her own efforts.

It was the first time since she left Japan that Hana was able to eat and enjoy a meal. Even more satisfying was the chance it gave her to sit opposite Taro and for the first time since their meeting, to view him squarely in the face. He looks like a good and kind man, she said to herself during the meal, and once when their eyes met, she had offered him a quick smile.

When dinner was over, Kiku and Henry went into the kitchen to do the dishes, leaving Hana and Taro alone. Determined to say something to indicate an interest in their future together, Hana said, "I have heard so much about your shop. I'm anxious to see it."

But Taro simply answered, "It is not so much to see. Besides, you will be spending much time in it in the days ahead."

He was silent for several minutes, as though searching for just the right words to say. "The day after tomorrow is Sunday and I do not work," he began. "Perhaps by then you will be sufficiently rested to go with me to our Japanese church. In the afternoon, if the sun is out, I could show you around Lake Merritt and the park."

"Of course, I would like that."

Taro rose then. "You must be tired and anxious to rest," he said thoughtfully. "I shall excuse myself now and come for you at ten-thirty on Sunday morning."

"Yes. Thank you. Goodnight."

Taro moved toward the kitchen, but paused at the doorway. "Take care of yourself," he said, and then he quickly thanked the Todas and left by the back door.

Chapter 3

Kiku confessed that she rarely went to church on Sundays because she couldn't bear to sit through Reverend Okada's sermons. She had a small Buddhist shrine in her living room, however, and occasionally lit incense there to pray for her ancestors.

"I guess I'm part-Buddhist, part-Christian and part nothing at all," she laughed. "But Taro is a fine Christian gentleman," she assured Hana, "and I'm going to see that he's proud of you at church this morning."

She pulled out an assortment of her own clothing and began to put them on Hana one by one. First she squeezed Hana into a stiff corset that she herself had outgrown.

"Is such an armour really necessary?" Hana asked dismally. But Kiku was determined. "How else will you keep up your nice silk stockings?" she asked. "And besides, a small waist is stylish."

She dressed Hana in a long sleeved white blouse with a lace jabot and a navy blue serge suit with a long full skirt. She pinned the skirt to take in an inch at the waist and stuffed cotton in the toes of the shoes that were a size too large. Then she put a hat of navy blue velours on Hana's head and secured it firmly with a long hat pin. "Always keep a hat pin handy," she warned. "You never know when you might need one. And Hana, when a strange man looks at you, don't ever look back into his eyes." Finally she put a leather handbag on Hana's arm and gave her a pair of white gloves to carry.

"There now, you look elegant," Kiku said, stepping back to survey her creation.

When Taro arrived, he seemed genuinely pleased at Hana's transformation. "You look like a real American lady," he said proudly, that being the highest compliment he could bestow.

As the long service at the Japanese church progressed, Hana wondered how much longer she could sit still. She took as deep a breath as the stiffness of the corset allowed and felt one of its stays dig into her diaphragm. She wondered how the other women managed to appear so comfortable and composed, and a faint sigh of protest trailed from her lips.

At last the bearded minister reached the close of his sermon and asked the worshippers to bow their heads in prayer. "Our dear Heavenly Father," he intoned, "bless these Thy children who have come from afar, leaving behind their native land to begin new lives in this land. Their hardships are many and they are not always welcome here. Help them, dear Father, to face their trials with courage and Christian love."

Hana lifted her head slightly to observe the minister's face. She wondered what he meant about their not being welcome. What trials were so difficult that his face should be contorted in pain as he spoke of them? She would have to ask Taro later. She glanced now to the other side of the aisle where he sat with the other men. There were some fifteen of them, their heads all bent reverently in prayer. Kiku had told her that some of the men worked in laundries or as cooks in cafes. One ran a cleaner's, another a grocery, another a shoe repair shop, and one was a tailor. She had also told her that Henry's good friend, Sojiro Kaneda, was a doctor. It was difficult to tell who did what, however, for today they were all wearing their best Sunday suits and high starched collars.

Hana found it rather pleasant to inspect the church

and its members while there were no staring eyes to see her. She looked about the small wooden structure with its rows of stiff brown chairs made endurable by the flowered cushions placed on each by the Women's Society. There was an old reed organ to the right of the pulpit with a single white chrysanthemum in one of its recessed cubicles. Hana lowered her head as she felt the woman next to her stir and caught her pocketbook as it slipped to her knees. She suppressed the beginning of a yawn with her gloved hand, wondering about this Father in Heaven to whom the minister prayed with such fervor. The Christian service was strange and totally unlike praying at the Buddhist temple in Oka.

Hana wanted to take one more look at Taro before the prayer ended. Just as she glanced toward him, however, she was horrified to find the young man next to him looking squarely at her. Hana immediately lowered her eyes, but it was too late. He had already seen her unseemly gesture and a flicker of a smile had crossed his face when their eyes met. Hana was embarrassed at having been caught in such a childish act and having to share the delicious wickedness of the moment with a total stranger. She felt her heart pounding under her corset, and she squeezed her eyes shut to make amends for her brief intransigence.

When the last hymn was sung and the benediction pronounced, the organist began the postlude on the wheezing organ. Pumping on the carpeted pedals, she had just produced a few full notes from the reeds when a tall dignified gentleman rose and interrupted the proceedings. Bespectacled and scholarly in demeanor, he wore a neatly pressed suit of black alpaca. Hana guessed at once that this must be Henry's friend, the doctor. He seemed older than either Henry or Taro for there was already a touch of gray at his temples. He smiled at Taro and said, "I believe Mr. Takeda has someone very special to introduce to us this morning."

Hana gasped. To be singled out for such attention so soon after her embarrassing lapse was almost more than she could bear. She looked down at the tips of her cotton-stuffed shoes and felt her face turn crimson. She wanted to vanish into the floor, but already she heard Taro rise and speak to the congregation. "I would like to introduce Miss Hana Omiya, who comes from Oka Village near Kyoto," he said quietly.

Hana heard the rustle of clothing as everyone turned to look at her in the back row. She knew she was expected to rise and acknowledge the introduction, but her knees nearly gave way. She clung to the chair in front of her and bowed toward the dignified gentleman who now smiled warmly at her.

"I thank you for your kindness," she murmured, "and I beg your kind indulgence in the future." She felt the jab of a corset stay and gasped as she awkwardly resumed her seat.

The women about her smiled and bowed in acknowledgement of her words. Soon the minister, his wife and all the women gathered around to greet her, asking about her trip, inquiring about her family in Oka Village. One woman drew her aside, informing her that she was a midwife and would be happy to assist her whenever the need arose. When, at last, everyone had spoken to her, they moved outside into the thin November sun.

Taro stood with the other men in front of the church and gradually made his way to Hana's side. He also steered toward her a tall, lanky man with an abundance of wavy black hair. He was far better looking than Taro.

"This is Kiyoshi Yamaka," he said. "He and I struggled together during our early years in America."

Hana recognized immediately the handsome face

she had encountered during the prayer and groped for something proper to say to excuse herself. But Yamaka quickly relieved her of further embarrassment.

"I hope you will be happy here," he said politely. "Taro is a lucky man." He had a disarming smile that made Hana relax, and he asked Taro if he could drive them somewhere.

"Yamaka is the only member of the church with an automobile," Taro explained with good-natured envy.

"But without a wife," Yamaka added. "I find the car a great convenience, but not very good company." He laughed and Taro laughed with him.

Much to Hana's pleasure, Taro accepted Yamaka's offer, inviting him to join them for lunch at a Chinese restaurant on Seventh Street. The gentleman who had made the announcement now came and touched Taro's elbow. Taro turned quickly to introduce Hana. "This is Dr. Sojiro Kaneda," he said, explaining that he was one of the early founders of the church. "Without him we would probably have no church. He is its life and strength." Taro spoke with grave earnestness and Hana could see that everyone treated Dr. Kaneda with the same deference they extended to the minister himself.

Dr. Kaneda took Hana's hand and shook it firmly. "Taro Takeda is a fine man and a good Christian," he said. "You are a fortunate young woman."

It occurred to Hana that he was the first person to tell her she was the lucky one rather than to speak those words to Taro. If this fine scholarly doctor thought so highly of Taro Takeda, then perhaps she truly was lucky. Hana murmured her thanks, bowing with each phrase she spoke.

"You will come to lunch with us too?" Taro asked.

Dr. Kaneda hesitated and glanced briefly at Yamaka as though questioning the wisdom of intruding on Taro and Hana's Sunday lunch. But Yamaka was already moving toward his car. "Come along, Dr. Kaneda," he said quickly. "We must help Taro celebrate."

"Well, a Chinese meal would certainly taste better than anything I could cook up in my dreary flat," he conceded and followed them without further protest.

"This is my very first ride in an automobile," Hana said delightedly as Yamaka cranked the motor and leaped into the driver's seat.

"Is it really? I am honored. My automobile is honored. I am at your service anytime you wish to be driven anywhere," he said expansively.

"Someday we will own a car too," Taro said, and Hana felt a rush of pleasure because he had included her in his hope. It was the first time since they met that he had referred even obliquely to their future together.

Yamaka did most of the talking during lunch, filling the awkward gaps of silence with tales of his early days in Oakland. "I almost killed myself the first week," he related. "I was only nineteen and hadn't the sense to say no to anything. Back home I never so much as held a mop or a broom," he admitted. "I wasn't even permitted to enter the kitchen or soil my hands with womanly work."

"It surely was another world for us," Taro agreed. "It scarcely seems real anymore."

"But can you imagine such a boy," Yamaka continued, "being sent by the Japan Employment Agency to do housework in an elegant white man's home? The first day I reported for work, the lady of the house gave me a bucket and a sponge and told me to wash all the upstairs windows inside and out."

Yamaka lit a cigarette and nudged Taro's elbow. "Did you ever wash upstairs windows during your first week in America?"

"No," Taro said, "but I did get fired twice, and each time spent the rest of the day in the park because

I didn't have the courage to go back to the Employment Agency. I nearly starved to death, and I decided then I'd go into business for myself as soon as I earned enough money."

The men laughed as they recalled their early trials and errors. "I remember the first home where I worked," Dr. Kaneda said, explaining to Hana that this was long before he had any patients. "The lady of the house asked me to peel some potatoes for supper, so I went down to her cellar, hauled up a fifty-pound sack and peeled every last one. I must have filled every pan in her kitchen with potatoes!"

"What ever did she do with all of them?"

Kaneda shook his head. "I never found out," he said, still laughing at the memory of it. "She told me to leave immediately and never come back."

"And your windows?" Hana asked Yamaka. "Did they ever get washed?"

"I did exactly as that gentle lady asked. I sat on the upstairs window ledge with my back against the sky, getting soapy water all over my only pair of work pants. Then, when I tried to raise the window with my soapy left hand and hold onto the sponge and the window frame with my right, I lost my grip and nearly fell backward a hundred feet into her cactus garden."

"Oh, no!" Hana gasped.

"I shouted so loud I think they must have heard me all the way down to Seventh Street." Yamaka wiped his forehead at the thought of it. "I thought in that brief moment I'd never live to see my beloved Japan again." He turned to Hana and grinned. "But you see, I didn't fall after all, and I will get back to Japan someday."

"Then you aren't going to stay here?"

"Oh, I will until I make enough money. Then I'll go back to Osaka and maybe open a small restaurant and find myself a nice wife."

"You could open a restaurant here," Taro suggested.

"And make Japanese dishes for poor starving rascals like me," Dr. Kaneda added.

But Yamaka shook his head. "A few thousand dollars wouldn't go far here, and besides, I don't want to spend all my life being a foreigner in an alien land, washing windows and mopping somebody else's floors."

Taro nodded. "There is that," he agreed, and suddenly the laughter of the day was gone. "Shall we be going?" he asked.

Hana quickly took a sheet of powdered paper from the small packet in her purse and dabbed her nose to remove the shine. The men rose and busied themselves with paying the bill.

When they went out onto the Sunday street, Hana was surprised to see so many men wandering about aimlessly. There were Chinese, Filipinos, Mexicans and Japanese standing in small groups talking and smoking or simply watching people pass by.

"Poor fellows," Taro said sympathetically. "Sunday afternoon is the loneliest time of all." At that moment, Hana understood for the first time Taro's own long years of loneliness.

The sight of the solitary men trying to warm themselves in the bleak sun seemed to depress Dr. Kaneda. "I think I'll go on back to church and work on the records for a while," he said. And shaking Hana's hand once more, he strode briskly away from them.

"He busies himself with work even on Sundays now that his wife is gone," Taro explained. "She died two years ago of tuberculosis. He's started a Japanese language school for children at church, to make up, I suppose, for not having any children of his own."

Yamaka saw the sadness cross Hana's face, and in an effort to distract her, he pointed across the street. "Look," he said, "there's Taro's shop, the only place in Oakland I'd consider buying my rice and white shirts."

Hana turned to Taro. "Your shop is here? On this street?" she asked unbelieving. The street contained only a succession of drab unkempt buildings—a Chinese meat market with smoked pork butts and rabbit carcasses dangling in the window, a noodle factory, a Chinese vegetable stand with its produce drying in the sun, and the faded shabby entrances of a few hotels and rooming houses.

"On week days the street is busier," Taro explained lamely. "It is quite different then, with people working in the shops. That was why I wanted to show you the shop on another day."

But Hana knew she would not sleep that night, not knowing more about the shop after having seen its shabby exterior. "Since it is so close, I think I'd like to see it now," she persisted.

Yamaka tried to make amends for having brought about an awkward situation. "You can see the shop anytime, Miss Omiya, but today I can take you for a ride to see the city of Oakland. Please let me do that for you," he urged.

Hana knew she should give in gracefully, deferring to the wishes of the men. She also knew it would be unseemly for her to press further, but she could not suppress her curiosity.

"Why couldn't we do both?" she asked. "Couldn't we see the shop for a moment and go for a ride too?"

Taro had known the woman he was about to marry was educated and bright. Now he learned with no little concern that she was determined as well.

"Very well then," he said, leading her to his shop down the street, past groups of loitering men whose eyes shifted quickly toward the welcome sight of a young Asian woman. He took a ring of keys from his pocket, unlocked the door and pushed it open. Hana could smell the dampness redolent with pickled radish.

"*Dozo*," Taro said with a slight bow. "This is my shop. Please come in."

Chapter 4

Kiku and Henry Toda usually spent most Sunday mornings in their sagging double bed instead of going to church. Henry was grateful that Kiku never required much coaxing or lengthy and tender ministrations before engaging in lovemaking. Like a man, she simply got down to the business at hand and performed her wifely duties with easy proficiency. Henry was quickly satisfied, and when he was through with her, Kiku demanded no further attention, but allowed him to turn over and go back to sleep. She would then get up and take a hot bath while a pot of coffee brewed on the stove.

It was then her greatest luxury to return to bed with the latest Japanese women's magazines, a box of creme-filled chocolate cookies and a steaming cup of coffee. She would settle back on two pillows, read, and gorge on cookies and coffee, completely savoring every moment of her Sunday morning ritual.

This Sunday, however, a restless prodding kept her from fully enjoying herself. She had already gotten up once to help Hana dress for church, and Hana's anxieties still haunted her, bringing back her own first days in America. She knew what it was to travel so far to marry a strange man. She knew too, that more often than not, the first meeting was a disappointment rather than a hope fulfilled, for no man was so foolish as to tell the whole truth about himself before marriage. He sent only the best photograph of himself, and a rosy view of the future based more on hope than on actual fact. Kiku knew more than one woman who had been led to believe her life in America would be one of comfort and prosperity. But often the landowner she had come expecting to marry turned out to be a poor dirt farmer who leased his land, and the car beside which he had posed for his photograph belonged not to him, but to his boss. The first months for many Japanese women were a cruel and bitter disappointment.

Kiku had been lucky to find a man such as Henry waiting for her. And she felt sure Taro would not have tried to deceive Hana in any way either. She had known him for many years now and always he had shown himself to be honorable and trustworthy. A woman could do worse than to marry Taro, she thought, even though he had not made much of his drab little shop. But Kiku sensed a deep inner fire beneath Hana's polite reserve, and she wondered if Taro might not prove to be something of a bore to her. Hana was still young and prettier than most, while Taro at thirty-one already seemed a middle-aged man.

"It is not the best match possible," Kiku murmured to herself. Unable to concentrate on her magazine, she got out of bed, dressed and swept the kitchen floor. When she was finished, she couldn't resist entering Hana's room. She looked about, not knowing exactly what she searched for, but hoping nevertheless to find some further clue to what Hana held in her heart. She found little to satisfy her curiosity, however, for the room was just as it was before Hana had occupied it. Her suitcases had been pushed beneath the cot and she had not placed anything into the dresser drawers that Kiku had emptied. Feeling a bit let down, Kiku left the room and thought about the wedding she must help plan for Hana.

Taro had said he wanted to have a fine, American-style Christian wedding. He wanted none of the stiff formality of a Japanese wedding with a doll-like bride, bewigged and so heavily encrusted with powder that the groom scarcely recognized her. Nor did he want any of the ritual of the Shinto ceremony.

"I want Hana to wear a long white dress with a veil and carry a proper bouquet," he instructed. "I expect she will need white shoes too, and all the things that go beneath the dress."

Kiku had nodded. "Leave it to me. I'll arrange everything," she had assured him. "I can sew a wedding gown for half the cost of the store-bought one and Toda can get your flowers wholesale."

"I've saved for the occasion," Taro explained. "You needn't skimp."

But Kiku warned him he would be glad he had listened to her. "There'll be the gift to the minister and the organist and the photographer, and a donation to the church. And then you'll want to buy her a ring, won't you, with maybe a little diamond in it? Then there's the reception. We could have cake and ice cream and sandwiches, instead of a big dinner. Believe me, Taro San, your money is going to slip through your fingers like sand from now on."

She further reminded him that Hana would need to be properly clothed from head to toe. "I'll see what I can salvage from her kimonos," she had said. "Maybe one or two can be ripped apart and made over into dresses."

Kiku sat at the kitchen table now and studied the wall calendar. It was November fifteenth. If she worked hard, perhaps she could have everything sewn and ready by the twenty-ninth. Of course there was Thanksgiving, and she would have to help Mrs. Davis with her turkey dinner. But in two weeks, she felt she could have Hana ready for her wedding. In fact, she would simply announce her intention to do so, for she knew it would not be good to put it off too long. If

Hana were given too much time to consider life with Taro, she just might find it impossible to enter into it at all.

Later that afternoon when Hana came home with Kiyoshi Yamaka and Taro, Kiku grew more determined than ever to proceed with plans for the wedding as quickly as possible.

"Here's a hunk of smoked pork for supper," Yamaka said, dangling his offering in front of Kiku. As she accepted his gift and welcomed him to stay for supper, she saw the excitement in his eyes and she observed Taro's silence. She saw too, the fragments of sadness in Hana's face.

Henry Toda brought out a bottle of *sake* at supper, but it was he and Yamaka who drank most of it and felt its rousing effects.

"Here's to the new bride," Henry said, his face flushed and glistening with sweat.

"To the beautiful young lady who has come to marry my most fortunate friend," Kiyoshi Yamaka said, raising his wine cup to Hana.

Taro raised his cup toward Hana and drank the small cupful in a single gulp. Hana giggled uncomfortably, not knowing what was expected of her.

"Go ahead," Kiku urged. "Have a little yourself."

Hana sipped her tiny cup of warm *sake* and felt it burn as it slid down her throat. "Thank you," she said, warmed by the sentiment as well as the wine. "Thank you all very much." It was difficult to believe that it was she whom they all toasted.

It wasn't until after Taro and Yamaka left and Henry was having his bath that Kiku found a few moments to talk to Hana.

"You had a nice time today?" she asked.

Hana nodded. "Oh yes, it was a most eventful day," she began. "It was my first visit to a Christian church, and there was lunch at a Chinese restaurant and then the lovely drive around the lake." She recited the day's activities like a dutiful child reporting to its mother. She paused a moment and added, "I also saw Taro San's shop."

"Oh. What did you think of it?"

"It was . . . well, it was very nice," Hana began, trying to find some kind words among the misgivings that raged inside her. She saw Kiku's questioning look, however, and suddenly abandoned all attempts at restraint and control.

"No, that's not true," she burst out. "It wasn't nice at all. It was drab and dirty and smelled of stale food. There were cobwebs and mice droppings in the corners, and the shelves were covered with dust. It's a wonder anyone would want to buy anything there." Hana swallowed, trying to blink back the tears.

Kiku put an arm around her. "You were expecting something a bit finer, I expect."

Hana nodded. Kiku's openness made it possible to answer her with shameless candor. "I thought he would have a large store on a fine street. I thought there would be American ladies and gentlemen coming to his shop to buy shirts and silks and thread." She paused, remembering the lonely men on Seventh Street. "Is it only people like those I saw today on his street who go there to shop?"

"The fine white American ladies and gentlemen have their own stores," Kiku explained gently. "They have no need to come to Seventh Street to buy pickled radish or soy sauce."

She turned Hana's face toward her and said gravely, "You're going to have to realize something important, Hana. We are foreigners in this country, and there are many white people who resent our presence here. They welcome us only as cooks or houseboys or maids. Why, even if Taro's store was twice as big and it was on the best corner in downtown Oakland, still his only customers would be the Japanese and the men on Seventh Street. Don't forget, we are aliens here. We don't really belong."

Hana recalled the minister's prayer that morning. "It isn't such a golden life here in America then, is it?" she said almost to herself.

"Just don't have too many big dreams and you're less likely to be hurt," Kiku warned. "You came to America to make Taro Takeda happy. Just remember that and don't expect too much from him or from America."

Hana listened carefully, and then, suddenly, she kicked off her shoes. "There, that feels better," she said. "I have never worn shoes all day. That is probably what made me feel so dismal."

"Are you sure?"

"I think so." Hana couldn't say any more, for doubts were already swirling inside her. She told herself she had been with Taro only two days and seen his shop only once. She must give herself more time before making judgments, but she couldn't help wondering if she could face the life that seemed to lie ahead. Yet what were the alternatives? She could beg Taro's forgiveness and break her engagement to him. She could wait a decent interval and perhaps marry someone else. Hana didn't dare let herself think who that might be. It was clearly impossible to renege on her promise, not only for Taro's sake, but for her uncle's. He would suffer a complete loss of face after having worked so hard to convince Taro's parents that she would be a good wife.

Kiku checked the water heater in the kitchen and told Hana there was enough hot water now for her bath. "Before you go," she added, "let me tell you what I've been planning today."

She sat down beside Hana and eagerly revealed her plans for the wedding. "I'm sure we could be ready in two weeks," she confided. "We'll talk to Taro San about it tomorrow, and I want to take your measurements so I can start your gown. Then we'll shop for some clothes for you, and you'll want to fix up his rooms so you can move right in after the wedding."

Hana nodded mechanically, realizing that she had momentarily nurtured a desperate delusion. It was quite apparent that she was fully committed. There were no alternatives after all.

"Thank you, Kiku San," she murmured. "You are very kind." Then she went quickly to her own room.

She had her bath in the strange bathroom where there was no area to wash herself before stepping into the tub of clean water. She thought with longing of the large pine tub at home where she could soak in hot water that came up to her chin. In winter that was the only place to get warm, and Hana recalled how she used to sit in the tub and dream until the maid was sent to haul her out.

A mass of troubled thoughts tumbled about in her head as she prepared for bed. Perhaps she had made a terrible mistake in coming to America. In her anxiety to escape the drabness of Oka Village, perhaps she had leaped too far and severed too many roots. Now, like a tree transported beyond its native soil, she must grope for life and sustenance in an alien land, to be cherished by a stranger whose love she feared and whose life must, in the end, become her own.

Hana held her hands together and murmured, "*Namu Amida Butsu*," as she had done so often at the temple back home, turning to the loving grace of Buddha. But tonight, the words brought little solace. She wrapped her hips in a flannel cloth, pulled her night-kimono close about her, and crept into the damp cold cot for her third night in the new country.

Chapter 5

Hana and Taro's wedding produced more excitement at the Japanese church than anything that had taken place all year. The women of the church spent extra hours after their own private labors going over every inch of the chapel with dust cloths and brooms, decorating the altar with white candles and vases of white chrysanthemums.

Hana made an enchanting bride in her white satin dress. Kiku had labored over it many hours, embroidering tiny white beads around the neckline to match the beads of the head piece. She carried a bouquet of white roses and wore a pair of satin slippers that were stiff and too tight. Hana had never worn such finery in all her life, and as she looked at herself in the mirror, she wondered at the strange woman who looked back at her with such dark solemn eyes.

Taro borrowed his striped pants and morning coat from one of the young students who lived in the men's dormitory behind the church. "It's as good as new," he informed Taro. "It was a going-away gift from my uncle, and the only time I wore it was when I went to apply for my first job."

Nervous as he was, Taro laughed as he put on the suit, recalling that its owner had been interviewing for a job as houseboy when he had worn it himself. The startled lady of the house had taken one look at this Japanese man dressed to the teeth in his striped pants and gasped, "My dear young man, I believe you've come to the wrong address. I asked the agency for a houseboy, not a diplomat."

Other pathetically comic tales swept through Taro's mind as he struggled with his tie. There were the men who had come to America not knowing one word of English. They had gone to cafes flapping their arms and cackling like hens to order eggs and mooing like cows when they wanted milk. They thought spittoons were used to wash faces.

What foolhardy souls we were, Taro thought, stepping back to look at himself in the mirror. We left behind everything that was familiar and dear to plunge into a foreign land like blind men rushing into a crowded street, hoping to get across. He thought of his own foolish mistakes during his early years in California when he had been humiliated because of his poor English. He had gone to high school for three years, then to night school, determined to learn the language of the land he intended to make his home.

Now here was Hana, who also had sailed far from home, trusting and full of hope, to become his wife. She was like a child coming to be led by a blind man. He felt anxious and fearful for them both, but was determined not to disappoint Hana. He would work hard and try to give her a good life. Perhaps one day they would have a family, and he would have enough money to rent a house on a proper street. He would see to it that Hana never regretted coming to America. He owed her at least that much.

When the minister asked whether he would love, honor and cherish Hana, Taro replied with a strong firm voice. Hana, on the other hand, scarcely understood what the minister said, even though he spoke in Japanese, and when he asked the same question of her, she had to be prompted to reply.

After the ceremony, a photographer stood with his head thrust under a black cloth to take a portrait of them.

"Please, Mrs. Takeda," he urged, emerging from his covering. "Relax a little so you do not appear so sad." Hana produced a flutter of a smile, and the photograph was taken.

Outside, Taro's friends waited in joyous, raucous confusion, and as Taro and Hana started for Yamaka's car, several men suddenly hoisted Taro to their shoulders, as though he were a portable shrine on a festival day. Shouting and laughing, they wove in and out among the well-wishers, finally flinging him in the car beside Hana with one last resounding cheer.

Taro was flushed with excitement, and as the car moved away he put a hand over Hana's. "Well, Hana," he said. "We begin our life together."

"May it go well," she murmured, and turned her head quickly so he would not see the tears.

The reception at the Toda home was a blur of smiling strangers to Hana, for they were all Taro's friends, and she knew only Kiku and Henry, Dr. Kaneda and Kiyoshi Yamaka.

Yamaka was mingling jovially, stopping to tell an amusing story that drew great spasms of laughter to one group, then moving on to another. At last, he stood next to Hana as she helped pass out pieces of the wedding cake.

"Well, Mrs. Takeda," he said slowly, as though to accustom both of them to her new title and status.

Hana kept her eyes on the cake. "You have had some wedding cake, Yamaka San?" she asked.

"I have," he confessed, "but I cannot resist having another from the lovely bride herself." As he took the plate from her, he became formal and solemn. "I hope you and Taro will be very happy together."

"Thank you," Hana said briefly, not daring to say anything more. She turned her attention to urging cake on another guest, and was grateful to find Dr. Sojiro Kaneda.

Dr. Kaneda smiled warmly as he accepted the plate she offered. "You are feeling a trifle nervous?" he asked, as he saw how her hand trembled.

Hana felt foolish. "I should remember I am not the only woman who ever became a bride," she said.

But Dr. Kaneda understood. "I know," he said. "I remember how it was for my wife. She was young and frightened too. And she never lived long enough to enjoy life in America." He stopped abruptly, realizing that this was not an occasion to speak of death.

"I was Henry Toda's best man at his wedding, you know," he said. "We came from the same town in Japan."

Hana tried hard to keep her mind on what he was saying. Although she had turned her back to him, she knew that Kiyoshi Yamaka was standing close by. It was impossible to ignore him, and when the reception was over, it was necessary to rely on him again to drive them to Taro's flat.

"It's only two blocks away," Hana protested as they made the arrangements. "We could easily walk."

But Kiku had laughed at her. It simply was not appropriate, she told her, for a bride and groom to walk away from their wedding reception as though they were going out to buy a loaf of bread.

"Besides," Taro had reminded her, "there will be your baggage. We must take all your things to my place."

So it was Yamaka who accompanied them to their new home and helped Taro carry Hana's bags.

Although Hana had spent several days sweeping and cleaning the three-room flat above the shop, its drabness was not easily concealed, for the furniture was utterly cheerless. The sitting room contained a large brown couch, an easy chair of simulated leather and a round table on which stood a glass hooded lamp. Hana had covered the table with a cloth crocheted by her mother, but somehow the delicacy of the cloth seemed only to emphasize the utilitarian ugliness of the table. A bookshelf in the corner contained some of Taro's old textbooks, two Japanese American dictionaries, a book on accounting and business procedures, some photograph albums, old magazines and a large box which contained Taro's stamp collection. A narrow kitchen opened off one side of the sitting room, and at the opposite end, a mud-colored curtain screened off the small bedroom.

Yamaka put down Hana's bags and surveyed the sitting room. "It looks better already," he commented. "A woman's touch surely makes a difference."

"You should avail yourself of that privilege too, Yamaka," Taro suggested. "You know it's not at all impossible."

Yamaka grinned. "As a matter of fact, I've been thinking of that very possibility lately," he began. Then seeing Hana's discomfort, he dropped the subject and prepared to go.

Hana, however, urged him to stay. "Please have a cup of tea with us," she invited. "Or perhaps you would prefer some *osake*? I could warm some in a moment. You've been so kind and we are most grateful."

She hurried to the kitchen which she had scoured the day before, and filled the kettle with water. She opened the cupboard to look for rice crackers and she juggled bottles of vinegar and oil searching for a bottle of rice wine. Somehow it seemed absolutely necessary to keep herself occupied and equally urgent to keep Yamaka there with them a little longer.

Yamaka, however, protested her sudden activity. "This is not the time to be entertaining guests, Mrs. Takeda," he said stiffly. "I am going now before your husband throws me out."

Before Hana could even come to the door to say goodbye, he was half way down the stairs. "I'll close the front door," he called. "Don't bother coming down."

"Thanks for your help," Taro called after him, as he closed the door to their flat. With Yamaka gone, a ponderous silence engulfed them, and Hana sat down wearily on the sofa.

Taro sat beside her. "Were you really so anxious to have Yamaka stay?"

Hana shivered. She wasn't prepared to discuss Kiyoshi Yamaka so soon after their wedding ceremony. "No, no, of course not," she protested. "It was just that he has done so much for us, I thought it only proper to offer him some tea."

She went on speaking of the kindnesses Kiku and Henry had extended them as well. "What shall we do to repay them?" she asked, intent on involving Taro in her thought. "Do you think we might buy them some fine gift for their home? Something Kiku has always wanted but can't afford to buy? Or should we take them to a very fine restaurant for dinner one evening? What do you think?"

But Taro wasn't listening. He was looking at her with a strange intensity she had never seen before. "Stop all that talking, Hana," he said, and drawing her gently toward him, he took her in his arms and kissed her.

"You are my wife now," he said slowly, as though explaining something to a child. "You belong to me and to no one else. Do you understand, Hana?"

"I understand."

He kissed her hard then, entering her mouth and holding her until she gasped for breath. Hana had never before been kissed by a man. She hadn't known what it would be like. Surprised, she wiped her mouth with the back of her hand. But now Taro took her by the hand and led her to their bedroom. Clumsily, he tried to hasten her disrobing, but she fled to the bathroom to undress alone. When at last she came to his bed, Taro was waiting and ready. In his eagerness, he probed her long before she was ready, assuaging the years of loneliness and longing by forcing himself with a fierceness that startled Hana.

"Don't . . ." she whispered, but Taro didn't hear her. She wanted to cry out to him to stop.

Why didn't somebody tell me it was going to be like this, she wondered, and then, suddenly, she stopped struggling and accepted the full urgency of his need.

Chapter 6

Taro stood in the middle of his shop and carefully surveyed the results of Hana's labors.

"It's a big improvement, Hana," he said with enthusiasm. "I think your coming was the best thing that has happened to this shop. I knew a wife would serve some useful purpose if I acquired one." He glanced at Hana to observe the effect of his humor and was pleased to see that she smiled with him.

"Of course," she answered. "Especially if the wife is as clever as I am."

They laughed together and felt the beginning of an ease in being husband and wife.

The week after the wedding Hana had concentrated on getting settled in the flat. She unpacked all her clothes and books and placed her possessions wherever Taro had made space for them. She made new voile curtains for the bedroom with Kiku's help, washing and ironing the others.

When that was done, Taro asked her to come down to the shop. Hana wasn't especially anxious to be harnessed to a succession of long days in his shop, but there was no way to refuse him. She had appeared one morning wearing a large cotton apron, with a thin towel wrapped around her hair to protect it from dust.

"Just what is it you plan to do?" Taro asked warily.

"Give your shop a thorough cleaning."

"I thought I'd first show you where everything is kept," Taro ventured.

But Hana was eager to get to the cleaning. She scattered damp tea leaves over the floor, sweeping the dust from every corner of the shop.

"I'll straighten out all the boxes on the shelves next," she announced.

"You must be careful not to mix the sizes and styles," Taro cautioned. He wasn't sure if she could read the labels and Hana saw his anxiety.

"Don't worry," she called as she climbed the step ladder. "I can read English. It was one of my best subjects."

She then proceeded to pull down every box she could reach. There were shirts and underwear, socks and collars, silk hosiery and aprons, and on the lower shelves, boxes filled with spools of cotton thread, darning wool, handkerchiefs, buttons, needles and an assortment of notions. Hana inspected the contents of each box with enormous interest and dusted everything with a large feather duster before returning it to the shelf.

Tackling the dirt and disshevelment of Taro's shop seemed to release the restless energy bottled up inside her, and as the shop improved in appearance, Hana began to relax and enjoy herself. After a few days, Taro stopped hovering over her and decided it was safe to leave her to her own devices while he worked on his books.

Hana worked next at scrubbing out the corner that harbored the Japanese foodstuff. There were sacks of rice, tubs of bean paste, bean curd cakes in vats of cold water, barrels of soy sauce and pickled *daikon* whose pungent smells filled the shop in spite of the wooden lids on their bins. Hana rather enjoyed the smell, recalling the market place in Oka Village with an intense nostalgia.

From the day Hana appeared in the shop, the customers seemed to increase. Any number of single men would drift in during the day to buy a pair of socks for fifteen cents or a handkerchief they didn't need, or ten cents worth of bean paste. Then they would linger to chat with Hana.

When Taro was there, they asked her about Japan and her voyage to America. But when Hana was alone while Taro went to the bank or the wholesalers, the men would stroll in and not even make a pretense of a purchase.

"Do you have the time, sweetheart?" they would ask. Or, "What's a pretty thing like you doing in this shabby old shop?"

Hana dreaded being alone and hated the hunger in their eyes as the men leered at her. She wished Taro could stay with her, but she knew she was most useful when she could free him for his errands. It was for this reason Taro had so painstakingly shown her where everything was kept and taught her how to count out change in American money.

Now, as Taro complimented Hana on the improvements she had made, he took a box of white knitting worsted from the shelf and told her she could have it to make a sweater for herself. As she joyfully inspected the wool, Taro told her of the trip he was about to take.

Reverend Okada and Dr. Kaneda had asked him to go with them to the farmlands near Salinas on a trip they both contemplated with missionary zeal. The minister wanted to tend to the spiritual needs of the Japanese farmers, while the doctor wanted not only to offer medical aid, but to advise the farmers of new agricultural methods he had read about in journals at the library. Both men felt keenly the plight of the hardworking farmers isolated from their countrymen in remote rural areas. They wanted Taro to go with them with Japanese food supplies, knowing those might provide more cheer than the comfort the two of them alone could offer. When they asked Taro to go with them he had agreed, then thought of Hana.

"You will be gone all day?" she asked anxiously.

"We should be back about supper time," Taro said. "Don't you think you could manage?"

"I suppose I could," Hana said tentatively, but she was also pleased that Taro felt he could leave her in charge of the shop. "Yes, I think I could," she said.

"Good. Then it's settled. We're going on Friday."

That morning, however, Taro didn't seem as sure of Hana's abilities as he had first indicated. "I've asked Kiyoshi Yamaka to stop by sometime during the day," he explained. "He told me he's off this afternoon. And then there's Kiku. Here is the telephone number where she's working today in case you need help."

He looked around the shop before he left, as though to reassure himself that all would be well. "Now be very careful," he warned.

"I will. You will please be careful too."

Hana helped Taro carry out his supplies to the car in which one of Dr. Kaneda's patients would drive them. As the men greeted her, she bowed to them and watched them drive off. Taro waved to her until they turned the corner.

About noon, Yamaka strolled into the shop. "Do you by any chance serve Japanese food here, madam?" he asked with a grin. "I would settle for a bowl of cold rice, if you'd give me a pickled plum and hot tea to go with it."

"Oh, Yamaka San," Hana said, melting into a smile of relief and pleasure. "I'm so glad to see you."

"Have you had any trouble?"

"No, no trouble. Only one customer came. He wanted a spool of black thread to sew on a button. I was so lonely, I almost offered to sew it on for him."

Yamaka looked serious. "You must never perform those tender chores for anyone now except your husband," he said. "A lonely man might mistake your kindness for something else."

"Yes, I thought of that. That's why I just sold him the thread and let him go."

Yamaka brightened. "I, however, shall gladly accept whatever you could give me for lunch, and I will know it is nothing more than the kindness of your gentle heart that prompts it."

Hana hurried to the small room in back of the shop where there was a sink and a hot plate. She always kept a kettle of hot water ready for tea, and she carried out the tea tray with her own lunch. She had packed some rice balls, a hardboiled egg and some pickled radish, which was all she had left after packing a lunch for Taro and his friends.

"My lunch is very simple," she apologized, "but you're welcome to half of everything, and there's plenty of tea."

Impulsively, she went to one of the shelves and took down a tin of broiled eel. "Here, we'll open this too," she said. "I know Taro would want you to have a proper lunch."

Yamaka pulled up a chair and sat opposite Hana at the counter while she peeled her egg. Breaking it in half, she dipped it in salt and offered it to Yamaka.

"*Dozo,* please have some."

Yamaka's fingers touched hers as he took his half of the egg, and for a moment, he looked at her with the same terrible intensity that had flooded Taro's face on their wedding night. He recovered quickly, however, and turned his attention to the food. "It's very nice having lunch with you like this," he said.

"Yes, for me too."

"Are you happy here in America . . . in your new life?"

Hana was silent a moment. "It is still all so new and strange for me, but Taro San is kind and patient. I hope to be a good wife to him."

Yamaka nodded, "Of course, that is how it must be."

They finished their lunch in silence, each of them dwelling on thoughts that could not be spoken.

Yamaka took out his cigarettes. "Will you let me smoke?" he asked. "Because if you don't, I shall have to go outside and loiter in front of the shop."

"I don't mind the smoke," Hana answered. "Please don't go outside."

"We're not permitted to smoke inside the church dormitory you know," Yamaka explained.

"Then what do you do?"

"It's no problem during the day, but at night I have to put my head in the fireplace and blow the smoke up the chimney."

Hana laughed at his wickedness. "The others too?"

"We take turns. Those poor wretches were so afraid of being thrown out of the dormitory, they'd sit on the back porch at night, wrapped in blankets, shivering as they had their secret smoke. But now, we stay inside and smoke all we please. It's just that we all have stiff necks in the morning."

"You are a rascal," Hana said, laughing. "I think you're teasing me. I don't think you do that at all."

Kiyoshi Yamaka leaned toward her and suddenly took her hand in his. "It is very good to see you laugh," he said gently. "I have watched you all this time and mostly you looked so sad and vulnerable. But I knew all along there was laughter inside you somewhere."

Hana drew her hand away. "Oh, Kiyoshi San," she said, using his given name for the first time. "This is quite impossible."

"I know that even better than you do. I want only your friendship, Hana. Nothing more. I swear."

Hana caught her breath. "If only it could have been

otherwise," she admitted, immediately astonished at her candor and filled with remorse at her easy words of infidelity. It had been so simple for Yamaka to strip her of her outer self, to reveal her heart as though he had removed her garments and seen her nakedness. "I wish . . ." she began, and tears gathered in her eyes.

"I wish too, Hana. Little Hana Chan," he murmured. "Please don't cry."

"If only we had met in Japan before . . ."

"You wouldn't have liked me," Yamaka insisted. "I was a completely unreliable fellow. My parents hoped I would become a merchant or a shopkeeper and settle down to lead a respectable life, but I wanted none of that. I wanted to see more of the world than our small string of islands. When I had a chance to go to Hawaii, I packed my bags and left without even telling my parents I was leaving. I sent them a letter from Yokohama the day my ship sailed, and they've never forgiven me."

Hana listened eagerly as Yamaka talked.

"I worked in the sugar cane fields of Hawaii for a while," he continued, "but after a few months, I grew restless and made my way to California. For the first few months I spent more time in the employment agency than anywhere else. I went out on calls from the farms and fruit orchards to pick cherries and peaches and lettuce and strawberries. Then finally, one day as I sat on the hard bench at the agency waiting for a call, I met Taro."

Hana nodded at the mention of her husband's name.

"He was waiting for a call for a houseboy or a cook. He told me they made $1.25 a day, and while it was scarcely man's work, it seemed better than bending all day in the hot sun. We waited together, and when the first call came, Taro let me have it. In fact, he even went with me because I didn't know the first thing about being a houseboy. He was going to high school too, to study English and bookkeeping. He used to tell me how the youngsters made fun of him, but he didn't give up. He helped me improve my English too. He was always generous about lending me his textbooks and helping me study. He's been a good friend to me, Hana."

Yamaka paused, but Hana was anxious to hear more. "Please go on," she urged. "Taro has never told me these things about himself, and I want to know more about you, too." It was as though a blurred image of both men were gradually coming into focus.

"There isn't much more. After a few more years, Taro had saved some money so he could borrow enough to go into business for himself, but I wasn't as careful. I like to smoke and drink and eat good food. When I saved some money, I wanted a car before anything else for the sense of freedom it gave me. But Taro saved, paid off his debts and finally, he was able to send for a wife."

Yamaka smiled. "Here I am, still drifting from one job to the next. But I'm a pretty good houseboy now and can cook a fairly decent meal. Someday, if I ever save enough, I'm going back to Japan, and then I'll settle down and look for a woman like you, Hana."

"And until then?"

"I will stay in Oakland, work hard and hope to see you and Taro often. I hope we can all be good friends."

"How old are you, Kiyoshi San?"

"Twenty-eight. And you?"

"Twenty-one."

Yamaka cleared his throat and poured himself another cup of tea. "Well, now you've heard the miserable tale of my life." And leaning back in his chair, he lit another cigarette.

As Hana watched him, she realized she had never

before talked with a man with whom she felt so completely at ease. She wanted to tell him that she would gladly work to help him save enough for a business of his own. She longed to tell him what joy she felt in simply being close enough to touch him.

For the first time since she had come from Japan, she felt intensely alive. She was aware of every breath and movement of her body and saw every detail of the ugliness that surrounded her in the shop. She could almost feel the texture of Yamaka's sweater, pulled over his rough blue work shirt. She observed his thin nose and sensitive lips and the strong brows frowning slightly over his brown eyes.

She felt as though the bindings of her body had been removed, and she was free at last to feel truly alive. Now she knew the real reason she had travelled across the ocean. It was to be here, in this place, at this very instant.

Suddenly, she reached out and clasped Yamaka's hands in both her own.

"You will always be my friend, Kiyoshi San," she promised, "for as long as I live."

And for that brief moment, Taro did not even seem to exist.

Chapter 7

Hana awoke at six o'clock to the happy thought that it was New Year's Day of the year 1918. It was a time for new beginnings and a time to be grateful. She held her hands together in remembrance of her family and her ancestors. She beseeched Buddha and Taro's Christian God to purify her soul at the start of this new year in her new life. She tried to hold on to the good thoughts, but too many other thoughts crowded them out. She quickly thrust aside her piety and hurried out of bed.

It was still dark and the room was silent except for Taro's deep even breathing and the ticking of the clock beside their bed. He would sleep for another hour, but Hana had work to do before her guests arrived for New Year's breakfast.

She hurried to the bathroom and lit the coal oil heater, looking up at the ceiling to see the circular pattern of lights cast from the vents. It was a friendly, comforting sight, and she always looked for it before erasing it with the kettle she put on top of the heater.

Shivering in the damp cold, Hana carried her clothes to the bathroom and dressed as close to the heater as she dared. Although she was trying hard to adapt to her new country, today she wanted to cling to the familiarity of her kimono which still felt more comfortable than her western dresses. She put on her best silk kimono with the scattering of peonies at the hem, and as she slipped into it, she remembered other New Years in Oka Village.

She remembered the sounds and smells that drifted from their dark kitchen as her mother and the maid prepared for the New Year feast. The best years were when her father was still alive and pounded the rice for the rice cakes himself. Hana and her sisters were always up long before he was ready, and having exhausted themselves throwing snowballs and building ice houses in the bitter cold, they would come into the steamy kitchen blowing on their frozen fingers and clustering near the large earthen oven.

When the special rice for *mochi* was steamed and fluffy, the maid would place it in a big stone mortar. Father would lift the heavy wood mallet to his shoulders and bring it thudding down on the mound of rice. The maid's task was to turn and reshape the mound between each blow, and as the mallet went up into the air, her hand darted in, escaping seconds before it came thudding down again. Pound and turn . . . pound and turn . . . "*Hai, hai . . . yoi, yoi . . . hai, hai . . . yoi, yoi . . .*" The children gathered around, chanting with them to the rhythm of their movement.

When the first batch of *mochi* was ready, Father would squeeze small pieces from the soft round mass and let each child have one to dip into a bowl of sweetened bean flour. Hana could recall even now the hot, sweet, sticky lumps of *mochi* which they could barely contain in their mouths. Gasping, blowing and squealing with delight, they sampled each new batch until they bulged like plump rice cakes themselves.

Hana smiled to herself as she remembered, wishing it were possible to store such happiness away to draw on when it was needed. But perhaps one was entitled only to such remembering as she was doing now and the fleeting moment of warmth it brought to her heart. Perhaps one could store only a few such joys in all of a lifetime, to be pulled some day from the pocket of memory. And who could tell but that someday in her old age, she might recall these very days of new beginnings with the same faint stir of happy memory she felt now.

Hana went to the kitchen to get on with her work. She washed some rice with a firm, practiced hand, swishing rhythmically, rinsing until the water ran clear. She added water to the first joint of her middle finger and put the pan on the stove to cook. Then she prepared the broth with a large piece of kelp and bonito shavings. It seemed strange to be performing such familiar tasks as though she were still in Japan when, in fact, she would soon be serving her first New Year's breakfast to her friends in America.

Taro usually had coffee, cereal and toast for breakfast, but Hana couldn't begin a day without rice and bean soup. When she had insisted that on New Year's Day they must have a proper Japanese breakfast, Taro had suggested they invite Kiku and Henry, Dr. Kaneda and Kiyoshi Yamaka to join them.

Slightly apprehensive at the thought of entertaining her first guests, Hana had spent the last three days preparing a variety of special dishes. She had already cooked a pot of sweetened black beans, a dish that supposedly brought a year of good health to those who ate it. Still lingering in the small kitchen was the aroma of the sweetened soy sauce in which she had cooked such delicacies as lotus and burdock root, bamboo shoot, dried mushrooms, fish paste, herring roe, taro root and such ordinary fare as chicken, carrots and celery. She had put them all in her tiered lacquer boxes to be stored until it was time to bring them to the table.

In another hour she would broil the whole sea bass and toast the rice cake squares for the broth so she would be ready when her guests arrived at ten-thirty.

Surrounded by the array of delicious food, Hana couldn't wait. She filled a bowl with cold rice, poured hot tea over it and ate it in quick gulps with slices of yellow pickled radish.

When Taro came to the kitchen for coffee, he found Hana flushed and excited, humming as she prepared the fish for the broiler. He was pleased to see that she looked almost as she had the day she arrived from Japan.

"You look very pretty in your kimono," he told her. "I'm glad you decided to wear it today."

"It just didn't seem right not to," Hana explained. "I hope Kiku won't think I am being too Japanese."

"But you *are* Japanese. You needn't be otherwise."

"It's just that she tells me so often I must adapt to American ways. She says I must learn to look like an American and speak better English too."

Taro put a finger under her chin. "You please me exactly as you are, Hana. There will be time enough to become Americanized. Take your time with it."

Kiku and Henry Toda were the first to arrive, bursting into the quiet of the flat with a torrent of talk. "Happy New Year! Happy New Year! May good fortune be yours this year," Henry called out effusively.

Hana was still too bound by Japanese amenities not to remove her apron, smooth back her hair and bow in a formal greeting. *"Shinen omedeto gozai masu,"* she said. "Our deep thanks for the kindnesses of the past year. Please favor us with your continued kindness in the coming year."

Henry raised a hand to stop her. "Come, come, Hana," he protested. "You need not be so formal with us. After all, we are old friends now, and remember you are in America, not Japan."

Kiku poked her husband to silence him. "It's the way she has been brought up. She is a lady and not an uneducated dumpling like me. You should be proud to be addressed in such a fine manner."

She smiled at Hana then, and exclaimed over her slim gracefulness. "You do look beautiful in a kimono," she said. "I believe you look better in that than in your corsets and dresses, in spite of all I've said."

Hana was relieved not to be reprimanded for reverting so soon to her past and to find Kiku in such a fine expansive mood. Kiku looked around the flat and noticed the two new prints that hung on the walls. She saw, too, the small Japanese dolls and figurines on the bookcase and the two new vases, one of which contained a branch of budding plum. A bowl of fresh fruit stood in the center of the table, surrounded by six individual black lacquer trays bearing the finest china from Taro's shop. Kiku was pleased to see Hana's feminine touches everywhere and to find that Taro himself had blossomed with a new warmth generated by his happiness.

"Sit down, sit down," he urged as he took their coats and hung them on the rack. "Hana, bring some hot tea. Or maybe Henry would rather have some *sake*. Would you?"

But Henry was content to sink into the easy chair and talk. "It is very gratifying to be a guest in your home, Taro, and to see you happily settled with a good wife and the comforts you deserve. You are the proprietor of a prospering shop, you are a fine Christian gentleman and a good American. You should be pleased and proud, and doubtless your parents in Japan are pleased and extremely proud indeed."

Taro surmised that Henry had already warmed himself with *sake* before he came, for he couldn't seem to stop the words that flowed from his mouth like water from an open tap. He required no reply from Taro, but simply wanted a silent ear into which he could pour his noble New Year's sentiments.

He was stopped only by the arrival of Dr. Kaneda,

who still spoke the proper words of a formal New Year's greeting with a courtly bow. He also brought a box of chocolates in fine American fashion, saying, "This is for you, Mrs. Takeda, with my good wishes for the coming year."

Hana had never before received a box of chocolates. She poured out her gratitude, bowing repeatedly as she thanked Dr. Kaneda for his thoughtfulness.

Kiyoshi Yamaka arrived shortly after, his nose and ears red from the cold, his eyes dark and alive. "I had to walk over," he explained, thrusting a bottle of wine at Taro and shaking off his coat. "I couldn't get my car started no matter how hard I coaxed it. It behaved exactly like a stubborn woman."

Yamaka did not see Hana until she appeared with the tray of tea. She looked so frail and delicate in her kimono, he instinctively rose to help her, but almost at once, Taro moved to assist her, and Yamaka quickly resumed his seat.

They sat at the table with its linen cloth, eating, talking and drinking until well into the afternoon. Hana glowed with pleasure, for her New Year's feast had been excellent. Even Kiku, who was not easily pleased, had praised Hana for the delicacy of her flavors.

No one except Hana herself knew, however, that her greatest pleasure came in having Kiyoshi Yamaka there to eat what she had prepared with such care. During all the days she had shopped at the Chinese groceries and fish markets and selected the finest canned goods from Taro's shelves; during the time she worked in her kitchen chopping and cooking, she had thought not so much of Taro, but of Kiyoshi Yamaka and of the pleasure she would give him. She had thought of all the twenty-five cent rice and curry meals he had eaten at grimy restaurants and the miserable meals he had dredged up for himself at the dormitory. She wanted to lavish on him today the most elaborate and delicious dishes she knew how to prepare.

Only she knew that she was thinking of Yamaka as she put on her best silk kimono, and it was for him she had pinched her cheeks and bitten her lips to bring out their color. She tried hard not to glance too often at him during the meal, but he had taken the chair to her right, and gathered as they were around the small table, it was impossible not to be aware of his foot so close to hers or the occasional brushing of their elbows.

Everyone was growing flushed and garrulous from the warm *sake*. Hana had sipped one cupful, but it was not the wine that fed her excitement. She laughed and chattered more than she had done since she came to America.

Yamaka told the story of the Japanese student who, on his arrival, had been invited to stay in a white man's home. Confronted for the first time by a bath tub, he washed and rinsed himself before getting into it as he did in Japan, splashing water all over the linoleum floor. When the water began leaking through to the first floor, his startled hostess rushed to the bathroom door, shouting at him to turn off the water.

"The poor devil was so alarmed," Yamaka concluded, "he came running out of the bathroom stark naked, causing his hostess to faint dead away. Of course, he was never invited to that home again."

Hana rocked with laughter. "Oh, such a story," she gasped, and absently put a hand on Yamaka's arm. As she did, she felt his hand rest lightly on her thigh. She quickly lowered her own hand to push it away, and as she looked up, she caught Henry Toda's eye. In an instant, she knew that he understood everything. He was drunk, but still there had been a flash of comprehension in his glazed eyes and he blurted, "Ha,

Yamaka, you rascal. You've always had a way with women!"

Hana saw Kiku poke Henry under the table. She also saw a look of both compassion and concern on Dr. Kaneda's face. He began to sing a mournful Japanese song, "*Shika ra rete . . .*" closing his eyes as he reached for the high notes.

Did they all know then? All of them? Even Taro?

"I think it's time we were going," Kiku announced firmly. "We've stayed all day enjoying breakfast, but tomorrow we must get up early and go to work again." As she prodded Henry from his chair, she looked at Yamaka. "Come on," she urged. "You too. You need some exercise after all that food."

Dr. Kaneda rose quickly to support Kiku's suggestion, and quite abruptly the festivities came to an end.

"This has been a day to remember all our lives," Dr. Kaneda said graciously, bridging the awkward moment of leavetaking. He provided the proper words and gestures often lacking at Japanese gatherings, for their ways were not those of casual banter, and silence was often the only response even to a happy moment.

"It has been a wonderful day for me," Yamaka said, shaking hands with both Taro and Hana.

When the guests had gone, a burden of silence filled the flat. Hana found it especially oppressive because the gaiety that preceded it had been so intense, and because she feared her feelings for Yamaka had been revealed to everyone. She hurried to the kitchen and boiled water for the dishes, scraping and stacking them, as she busied herself with the task of cleaning up.

If Taro noticed anything or thought that Henry Toda's remark was anything more than a meaningless remark brought on by an abundance of *sake,* he said nothing and revealed no anger. He emptied the ash trays and rearranged the chairs as he straightened up the sitting room. Then he came to stand at the kitchen door, watching Hana prepare the soapsuds to wash the dishes. He stood silently for several minutes, and when he spoke at last, he simply said, "Hana, I would like to have a child."

Chapter 8

Although the city still wore the bleak face of winter, a few quince and magnolia had begun to bloom, and the trees bore a faint breath of new green. The days were noticeably longer and the air was alive with the promise of spring. Hana felt within herself, too, the faint stirrings of new life and thought perhaps there was a child. She had not spoken of it yet, however, to Taro.

The early arrival of spring in California delighted her, for the letters from Japan still spoke of the snow and cold. It was only the beginning of March and yet she had discovered a few violets flowering in the narrow lot behind the shop.

One day Taro returned from an errand carrying a bouquet of freesias. He simply left it on the counter beside the cash register for Hana to find, and her first knowledge of them was their sweet fresh scent that flooded the corners of the shop.

"They smell wonderful," Hana cried happily. "What can I put them in?" And she rushed upstairs for a proper vase, completely forgetting to get Taro his cup of tea.

Taro watched her go with an indulgent smile and went to the back room to boil some water. After all, it was a small thing to make his own tea and he preferred that Hana have this brief moment of joy. Besides, he wanted her to be in a good mood when he told her of another trip to the farmlands with Reverend Okada and Dr. Kaneda.

Hana seemed apprehensive when he mentioned the trip. "Will you be gone all day again?" she asked.

"About the same as before, I think. But you are more experienced now. You shouldn't have any trouble, do you think?"

Hana shook her head. "I can manage. Don't worry."

Taro didn't say he would ask Yamaka to look in on her this time, but Hana knew she would tell him herself. She was careful not to nurture an impossible hope, but having some time with Yamaka seemed a harmless pleasure she couldn't deny herself.

Kiyoshi Yamaka made an effort not to visit them too often. Still, he and Taro were friends and each Sunday he drove them home from church, staying to lunch with them at their flat or at one of the Seventh Street cafes.

Always Hana was discreet so her pleasure in being with Yamaka wasn't apparent to anyone, and he was careful as well. If Taro knew the three of them were treading a precarious passage, he said nothing. In fact, as Hana suspected he might, Taro himself mentioned his forthcoming trip to Yamaka.

"If I have any time I'll try to stop by," he said casually, but he didn't promise.

Taro, Dr. Kaneda and Reverend Okada left early one Monday morning, each of them taking his special form of solace and knowledge. As they neared the farming communities they saw endless fields of lettuce planted in neat, even rows. Taro always marvelled at the sight.

"They work so hard, the Japanese farmers," he mused, "from sunrise till sunset, seven days a week. I suppose that's why they can sell their produce for less than the white farmers."

"And thereby incur their wrath up and down the state," Dr. Kaneda added. "As long as we are an economic threat, we are going to be hated. It's as simple as that. And yet why should our farmers be hated for being frugal and working hard to make an honest living? Even every evidence of their Japaneseness is despised." He was thinking of the barrels of soy sauce left strewn in some of the empty yards.

As the car rumbled over the unpaved dirt road to the first farm, Taro glanced at his pungent Japanese foodstuff, so offensive to the white man's nostrils. Was he really helping them become assimilated and accepted, which was for him, too, the ultimate goal? Still, Taro was pleased to bring some pleasure into the lives of these lonely hardworking people. He had seen their leathery sun-browned faces and their calloused hands. He had seen the women bending in the hot sun to the same backbreaking chores of planting, weeding and harvesting as their men. Often it was only land discarded as unarable that the Japanese farmers could lease, and it was by their patient, constant labor that the land became fertile and productive. They should feel proud of that, Taro thought.

The last time he had come, he'd found the women making flour and water dumplings because they had no rice, eating them with pickled cabbage pressed with stone weights.

One woman told him she lived only for the day when they had enough money to return to Japan to see their children again. "They are not with you then?" he had asked.

"They have been sent to their grandparents in Japan to free me to work in the fields beside my husband. I'm not the only one. Others have had to do the same." Her eyes filled with tears as she added, "I hope they still remember me."

If in such a barren existence they could not even eat the food they craved, Taro thought, they were no better than animals. So he had promised to return again with more supplies, and he had come eagerly, even though it meant leaving Hana alone for another day. He had felt a vague uneasiness about asking Yamaka to look in on her, but he believed Hana to be faithful and was determined not to seek evil where it did not exist. Now, as they neared their destination, he gave no further thought to Hana.

Taro sold all his foodstuff at cost, with no profit to himself.

"I didn't ask you to come to make a charitable gesture, Mr. Takeda," the minister said, watching Taro dispose of his stock with no concern for making money. "I hoped there would be a little profit in the venture for you now that you have a wife to support."

But Taro didn't mind. "Life is not just a matter of making money," he answered. "I will sleep better tonight for having done this."

Sojiro Kaneda, too, had closed his office for the day because he felt this was something he had to do. "What use is my knowledge if I do not share it with those who need it most?" he asked.

So Taro left his food, Dr. Kaneda his knowledge and medicine and Reverend Okada his tracts and prayers. The men returned to Oakland feeling fulfilled and satisfied, each in his own way.

It was past eight o'clock when Taro returned to his shop, and Hana had already locked up and gone upstairs. Taro felt the dust of the road on his face, and his back ached, but he couldn't resist a quick look around his shop to make sure everything was properly locked. He had just checked the cash register and observed that Hana had remembered to empty it, when one of the church women came in.

"Good evening. I was just about to lock up."

"Well then, I'm glad I came just in time," the woman said breathlessly. "I just need a little pickled radish and some bean curd cakes." She continued to talk as Taro wrapped her purchases.

"I came by at noon today, but your shop was closed," she said, "and I was afraid you might be ill, until I remembered Reverend Okada saying you were going out to the country today. Then I wondered why your wife wasn't here, and thought maybe she was taken ill. I almost rang the bell to your flat, but thought it best not to disturb her."

The woman looked at Taro, watching for a sign that might reveal some interesting fact she could disseminate later. She wasn't the only one at church who thought Taro Takeda's young wife was too high-spirited and attractive to be content with the placid shopkeeper. But Taro told her nothing more to feed her curiosity.

"I'm sorry you had to come twice," he said calmly. "I told Hana to close up at noon and have her lunch upstairs today." Handing the woman her purchases, he then eased her out and locked the door. As he made his way upstairs to their flat, he could smell fried shrimp and knew that Hana was preparing his favorite dish.

"*Tadaima*, I'm home," he called.

"Did you have a good trip? Were the farmers glad to see you?" Hana came from the kitchen holding her flour-covered hands in front of her so she wouldn't soil her apron. "I'm making fried shrimp for you."

"Yes, I smelled it."

Instead of his usual grin of pleasure, Hana saw Taro sink wearily into the easy chair.

"Maybe you'd like a bath first. I can keep the shrimp hot." She looked at him anxiously, but there was no response to her concern.

"No, let's get on with supper. I'll just wash up."

It wasn't until they sat down to eat that Taro spoke his mind. "How did it go at the shop today?"

"Fine. There were hardly any customers, but I did sell one shirt and a pair of socks."

"Did Yamaka come?"

"Yes, for a short while."

"When?"

"About noon, I think it was."

"And he ate with you?"

"Why yes. I thought it only polite to offer him some lunch since he was kind enough to stop by."

"Where did you eat?"

"I didn't have enough in the shop, so I asked him upstairs to help me finish last night's chicken. Wasn't that all right?"

"And you closed up the shop?"

"Only for a short while, Taro. I couldn't leave it unlocked and unattended."

"Ah, Hana," Taro said with a long sigh. "That was very unwise and indiscreet of you. One of the church women came and found the shop closed. She was careful to point that out to me just now."

"But Taro, we just ate lunch and went right down in half an hour. I wanted to heat the chicken and I couldn't do that in the shop. Truly. Please believe me."

But Hana saw the doubt in his eyes. Taro simply looked at her and said in a voice so low she could scarcely hear him.

"I know you have feelings for Kiyoshi Yamaka that you do not have for me."

"Oh no!" Hana cried out. Seeing the pain in his face, she felt a remorse that overwhelmed her.

It was true that when Kiyoshi Yamaka had come to see her, she wasn't sure what she would do. When they were alone in the flat, he had taken her in his arms and kissed her with such hunger that she had almost lost control. But when he undid the buttons of her blouse and reached for her breasts, she knew she must stop him. Surrounded by Taro's possessions, she couldn't defile his home by such a deliberate act of infidelity. "We cannot do this to Taro," she had said and sent Yamaka home.

The fact that she had successfully curbed Yamaka's passion as well as her own seemed somehow to purge the guilt that pricked at her so constantly. Although unfulfilled, Hana had felt pleasantly self-righteous after Yamaka's departure, and she further nourished this state by preparing Taro's favorite dish.

Now, however, she knew that Taro did not believe her. She had lost his respect and trust, perhaps causing the loss of one of his closest friends. Whatever love Taro might still have for her would now be tempered by doubt. Their marriage, she knew, might never again be the same. Hana wanted to weep.

"Please believe me, Taro," she begged.

But Taro left the table, his dinner only half eaten, and Hana felt a chill run through her body as she heard the door slam behind him.

Chapter 9

It was late October, and the terrible war in Europe seemed at last to be drawing to an end. Still, Hana thought, it was as though God did not intend man's suffering to end, for now the world was engulfed in an epidemic of deadly influenza that killed almost as surely as man's bullets.

Hana's thoughts drifted back to herself and to the child that moved within her. She rubbed the bulge of her body gently and whispered, "Please be a boy. Please try."

Since she had once disappointed Taro so deeply, she wanted to present him with a son as a way of making amends. She knew, however, that the child could only be what it already was, and brushing aside her foolishness, she rose to make some tea. A cup of hot tea always revived her, and today she had the silly notion that it would warm her unborn baby as well.

As she sat indulging in pleasant half dreams about her child, there was a knock at the door. It was Kiku Toda, laden with a supply of old Japanese magazines for Hana. She also carried a large *furoshiki* bundle containing her apron and some towels.

"I'm on my way to church to do what I can," she said, putting down the magazines.

For the past two weeks, cases of influenza had mounted so drastically that hospitals were overflowing and could take no more patients. Schools and churches had been converted into temporary hospitals, and now their church, too, was filled with ailing Japanese.

"How are they, all those sick people?" Hana asked.

"They just keep coming and coming . . . so many of them, and they're all so dreadfully sick with temperatures of 104 and 105," Kiku said. "There really isn't much we can do for them except cool their heads with compresses and give them aspirins and enemas. Poor Dr. Kaneda and Reverend Okada have been working night and day."

Just yesterday Dr. Kaneda had spoken of losing two people. Hana shuddered as she thought of them.

"You must be very careful," Taro had warned her, "not only for your own sake, but for the baby's." So although she wanted very much to help, Hana had stayed away from the church to guard against infection. She washed her hands whenever she came home from errands and kept a good distance from customers when she was in the shop.

Still she had an uneasy feeling that it was only a matter of time before the terrible illness struck and enveloped her as well. After all, she deserved no immunity. She deserved to suffer with the most wicked. But she knew that life's judgments were never meted out with such grand simplicity; that it was often the decent who suffered most, while the miscreants lived a long, successful life. No doubt she would live to be eighty-eight.

The following morning, Kiku came again. This time she brought no magazines and there was no cheer in her voice. Pale and drawn from lack of sleep, she did not sit down or accept Hana's offer of tea. She simply told what she had to tell in her usual direct manner. But today her voice was touched with compassion.

"Sit down, Hana," she urged. "I came to tell you that Kiyoshi Yamaka is very ill."

Hana gripped the edge of her chair. "He has caught this influenza?"

"He's had it for several days, but he was foolish

enough not to stay in bed. Now he is desperately ill."

"But he will recover, of course."

"Dr. Kaneda told me last night that he has developed pneumonia, and that can be dangerous. It might be bad, Hana."

Hana sat still, trying to understand and accept the words she had just heard. It had been a long time since she had seen Kiyoshi Yamaka, for Taro had made it clear he no longer wished to have Yamaka visit their home. He even refused to ride home with him after church. So Hana could speak only briefly with Yamaka after church services, or when he came to the shop for some small purchase.

It had taken Taro many weeks to forgive Hana, and she was still not sure whether he really believed her. But at last, Taro had accepted what happened with the same fatalistic shrug that enabled him to accept much in life that might have embittered another man. Hana, for her part, was determined to be a good and loyal wife.

In the instant she heard of Yamaka's illness, however, Hana forgot every good intention of the past.

"Kiku, I must go to him," she said.

"You'll be risking both yourself and the child," Kiku warned. "You know Taro wouldn't approve."

But Hana was already getting her hat and coat. "I can't help it," she answered. "I must go see Kiyoshi San. If anything happened to him and I hadn't gone, I would never forgive myself."

Kiku understood and didn't try to stop her. "Maybe you shouldn't mention your going to Taro."

At that moment, however, Hana didn't care whether Taro found out or not. She only knew she must see Kiyoshi Yamaka and make him get well.

The sharp bitter smell of antiseptics and medicine struck Hana as she entered the church, and the minister's wife gave her a gauze mask to cover her mouth and nose. Reverend Okada came only to greet her and then moved on quickly to comfort the sick.

There was a quiet stream of activity as women wearing aprons and face masks moved among the patients, changing a cold compress, taking a thermometer from dry cracked lips, giving a sip of water or removing a bed pan. Occasionally, a long faint moan would drift from an aching, fever-ridden body.

Kiku took Hana's hand and led her to Yamaka's bed. There was no need for Hana to make a pretense of having come to help. The women nodded to her and seemed to know why she had come. She knelt beside Yamaka and took his hand in hers.

"Kiyoshi San," she murmured. "I'm here."

His hand was burning and seemed devoid of life. Hana wiped his forehead with a fresh cold cloth. Still he did not open his eyes.

"You're going to get well, Kiyoshi San," Hana murmured. "You're going to be strong and well again." Finally, she begged him, "Please try. Try hard to get better."

When he finally opened his eyes and saw Hana, he smiled weakly. "You know," he said, his voice barely audible, "in my next life I'm going to be a bird . . . I'm going to soar in the sky . . . and never have to hold a broom . . . or wash a window . . . or . . . love the wrong person . . . Hana."

Hana put a finger on his dry lips. They were cracked and bleeding. "Oh, Kiyoshi San," she whispered bending closer. "You must rest now and save your strength."

"There's nothing left to save, Hana," he murmured.

Hana felt someone standing behind her. It was Dr. Kaneda, his white coat rumpled and soiled, his sleeves rolled up to his elbows, his stethoscope hanging limply on his chest. His eyes were sunken and bloodshot. His shoulders sagged with exhaustion.

"He must rest now, Hana," he said gently, helping her to her feet.

"I'll come again tomorrow," she promised, holding Yamaka's hand in both her own. "You'll be better tomorrow."

"Dr. Kaneda, he will be better tomorrow, won't he?" she asked desperately.

But Dr. Kaneda only said, "I'm doing everything I can for him, Hana. Go home now and pray for him."

Hana didn't know how she got home. She had simply moved one foot in front of the other, feeling the heaviness in her womb, thinking only of Kiyoshi Yamaka and praying to Taro's god.

"Please spare him," she prayed as she walked. Please just save him and I shall never cause Taro another moment's grief, ever. Please forgive Kiyoshi San. Forgive me . . . I promise. . . ." What could she promise? To stop loving Kiyoshi Yamaka? To love Taro more? Her words died away before they were even uttered.

When Taro came home for supper, Hana told him what she had done. "Yamaka San is very ill with influenza," she explained. "Kiku thinks he is dying, and Dr. Kaneda couldn't promise that he would live."

Taro was silent for a moment. Then he put on his coat. "I must go see him," he said. "Don't wait supper for me."

"I'm glad you're going," Hana answered, and as he hurried out the door, she called, "Pray for him."

Hana broke a plate as she was washing the supper dishes. It was a bad omen. She got some glue and tried to piece it together. If I can fix it then Kiyoshi San will live, she told herself. But the plate fell apart even before the glue could dry.

It was Dr. Kaneda who brought the news to them the next morning. He had walked from church where he had been up all night watching over his patients. His eyes were red-rimmed and his voice hoarse from fatigue. "We lost Yamaka early this morning," he said sadly. "Reverend Okada was at his side too. Just before the end, he asked that his car be given to you, Taro." He paused, took a deep breath and added, "It was a peaceful end, as though he were relieved of a great burden and just drifting off to sleep. He is at peace now."

Taro made it easy for Hana. "We've all lost a good friend," he said quietly. "I'll go back to church with you, Dr. Kaneda, to make funeral arrangements." The two men left quickly so Hana would not have to cry in front of them.

When they were gone, Hana sat at the round table and buried her head in her hands. She wept uncontrollably, her sobs shaking her entire body so she jarred even the child she carried.

"Why were you so careless with your life?" she cried in anger and grief. "Why couldn't you have lived long enough to fulfill your own dreams?" Kiyoshi had slipped away from her in such a short trembling space of time. She wondered if Reverend Okada had been with him long enough to help him prepare his soul for death.

"Why did you let him die?" she asked Taro's god. And then she blamed herself for not having been more watchful of him. If she and Taro had seen him more often, they might have told him to be more careful of his health. It was my fault, she thought bitterly.

Hana did not know how long she sat there weeping. When she went to wash her face, her eyes were so swollen she scarcely recognized herself. She washed her face with cold water, then lay down with a cold towel over her eyes. She lay there an hour, or perhaps it was two. Finally she got up, reprimanding herself for her shameless lack of discipline. Her own mother did not shed one tear in front of them when her father had died, and Hana was ashamed that she did not have as much control. As she combed her hair and powdered her nose, the one aching, devastating thought that consumed her was that she would never see Kiyoshi Yamaka again.

Three days later, as Hana washed some clothes in the bath tub, she couldn't stand up. She grasped the edge of the tub and tried to raise herself, but a sharp pain in her back and an overwhelming dizziness forced her back on her knees. She was still kneeling there, her head against the tub, when Taro found her at noon.

"Hana! Is it the baby?" he asked.

"No, it's just . . . I can't get up." Then she slumped to the floor. Taro carried her to bed, called Dr. Kaneda and then asked Kiku to come. He felt Hana's forehead and knew her temperature was soaring. When Dr. Kaneda came, he quickly confirmed Taro's suspicions.

"Hana has contracted influenza," he said gravely. "Her temperature is over 105. Cool her head with cold compresses and give her aspirin with plenty of water every four hours."

"I'll stay with her," Kiku offered, and she urged Taro to return to his shop.

"Go, go," she admonished, for she could see that his anxiety was doing nothing but sapping his strength. "Hana is going to be all right, and you're better off going about your business." He finally left when Kiku promised to call if Hana needed him.

Hana was quite sure she was dying. She had such a throbbing pain in her head, she could not bear even to move her eyeballs. The slightest movement sent sharp pains shooting through her head. She felt as though she were burning up inside a hot oven, and yet she was consumed with uncontrollable chills that made her teeth chatter and convulsed her entire body.

Sometimes she thought she was back in Japan. She thought it was her mother who sat beside her putting cold compresses on her head and moistening her parched lips. Once at dusk she had called to her, "Oka San . . . Mother . . ." But her mother didn't answer. Once she thought she saw Kiyoshi standing beside her. Relieved that he had not died after all, she opened her eyes with the greatest of effort, but the man turned out to be someone else. Who was this man who hovered beside her looking so sad? And then she remembered. It was Taro, her husband. The man she had crossed an ocean to marry. And in her delirium she asked why he wasn't out in the fields harvesting rice with the others.

"Help them, before the rains come," she urged. And then she was floating away from him in a raft, protesting all the while that she was too heavy and would sink because of the great burden she carried in her womb.

Dr. Kaneda came to see Hana whenever he could leave the sick whom he tended at church, and finally, one morning, Hana's temperature broke. "She's going to be better now," he told Taro, "but she will still be very weak." So Kiku continued to come each morning to cook a pot of rice gruel and to be with Hana until Taro could come upstairs.

After three weeks, Hana was able to get up, but could take only a few steps. And although she had passed through one crisis, she felt a strange premonition that something worse was yet to come. It was as though the illness were only a prelude, that she still had not been properly punished for her improper love.

I deserve whatever may come, she said to herself. I have hurt and humiliated my good husband and I let Kiyoshi San die. It is all my fault . . . everything. And she waited, consumed with guilt and dread for what was still ahead.

"You are feeling the usual depression that follows the illness," Dr. Kaneda explained as he observed his wan, forlorn patient. "When the sun is out in the afternoon, go sit in its warmth for a few minutes. The fresh air will be good for you."

The next day Taro helped Hana put on her heavy coat, and she crept slowly down the steps leaning heavily on his arm. He put a chair outside in front of the shop where Hana would be sheltered and yet get some sun. She sat very still, taking deep breaths of fresh air into her sickly body, hoping the baby soon to face the world would benefit as well.

Taro was busy with a customer when Hana began to feel cold. She stood up slowly and walked carefully to the door. Telling herself that she must be very careful, she grasped the railing and slowly started up the stairs to the flat. Half way up the narrow staircase she was overcome with dizziness. She paused to put a hand to her eyes, then reaching out again to grasp the railing, she caught only air. She fell backwards with a desperate cry and fell in a heap at the bottom of the steps.

Hana scarcely remembered what happened next. She knew only that the baby was coming and that she needed help. She heard herself screaming, and she heard Taro tell her he was calling the midwife.

Hana sank then into a hazy morass of piercing, agonizing pain and long lapses of delirium, in which she dreamed endless wild red dreams. Finally, toward evening, she gave birth to her first child, a premature infant who did not even live long enough to utter one small cry.

Hana knew when she saw Taro's face that something was wrong.

"The baby?" she asked softly.

"It was a boy," Taro answered, and then he put his head on her hand and wept like a child.

Chapter 10

1920–1921

"Good news, Hana!" Taro called as he came in.

Hana knew by the way he had bounded up the steps and flung open the door that he was excited. She quickly put a finger to her lips to caution him about the baby.

"She's asleep," Hana whispered.

The child, at six months, was still sleeping erratically, not napping when she should and falling asleep at the most inconvenient moments. She was also hopelessly spoiled, often crying for no reason than to be picked up and coddled. However, Hana could not restrain the extravagance of love that Taro lavished on his infant daughter, and she herself found release in a similar outpouring. It was as though the two of them unburdened on the tiny creature the affection they could not seem to show one another.

Taro lowered his voice. "I think I've finally found a house we can rent," he whispered. "It's in a residential area and there's a school close by." Actually, the neighborhood was beyond his means, but he had extended himself for the sake of their child.

"You're quite sure it's all right for us to move in?"

By now Hana was well acquainted with the anti-

Japanese sentiments that burgeoned throughout the state. Too many times Taro had come home discouraged and dismayed at having been refused a house because he was Japanese. The landlords had various ways of letting him know. "The house has just been rented," they would say, or, "I don't think you would care for this particular house."

It was difficult for Hana to understand why they should be so despised. She had been both puzzled and vexed when Taro had told her about the Gentlemen's Agreement, concluded by Theodore Roosevelt and the Japanese government ten years before her arrival, that prevented Japanese laborers from emigrating to America.

Hana had frowned. "But that doesn't seem a very gentlemanly thing for such a big country to do to a small country like Japan. There is so much room here."

Hana could scarcely comprehend the vastness of the United States. She would study a map, trace her finger across the breadth of the country, and then compare it with the meager droplets of land that was Japan. She could not understand the hatred and fear of such a giant land.

Taro explained that the problem was economic. "When the white men felt that we Asians were threatening their jobs, then words like 'yellow peril' began to appear in newspapers, and legislators passed laws discriminating against us."

"Peril?" Hana asked incredulously. "We Japanese are a peril to this enormous country?" It was beyond belief.

Taro enjoyed educating his wife to a more complete knowledge of the world.

"Do you know we Asians cannot own land in California, even if we have the money to buy it? There is a law called the Alien Land Law that prohibits it."

"But you are a responsible and law-abiding citizen."

Taro interrupted, "I may be responsible and law-abiding, Hana, but this country will not allow me to become a citizen because I am an Asian. That is the law of this land, too."

"Ah, they hate us so much?" Hana wanted to hear no more. It didn't matter so much for her or Taro, but she did not want her child to be hated simply because she was a Nisei—a second-generation American of Japanese ancestry.

"Well, our child is an American citizen, Hana, even if we cannot be," Taro comforted, "and we will give her a fine American name." He selected the name Mary because it was honest and forthright.

"Mary Takeda." Hana tried the name on her tongue many times. "That is a good name," she agreed, "but couldn't she have a Japanese name as well?" Taro wanted that, too, so they called her Mary Yukari.

Hana wondered now about school. "Will Mary be treated all right, do you think?"

"I can't be sure," Taro admitted. "But maybe by the time she's old enough to start school things will be better."

He hadn't told Hana that there had been a time when all the Japanese American children in San Francisco had been forced to attend a segregated school for Asians. He prayed that would never happen again, and went to the bedroom to look into the crib.

His daughter lay with her small pink fists curled tight and raised on both sides of her face. She had a tuft of black hair, and he reached down to feel its softness, sniffing the sweet baby smells of powder and oil.

"Mary Yukari, you are a good child," he whispered tenderly. "And I know you are *my* child. Hana's and mine."

The house Taro managed to rent was a modest brown shingled bungalow, but for Hana it seemed a mansion. It afforded such luxuries as two bedrooms, a full kitchen, a fireplace in the living room, and a separate dining room with built-in cupboards. She looked forward to furnishing it properly and making it the kind of home Mary would be proud of. Now she could entertain their friends more often and also take her turn in inviting the Church Women's Society to meet in her home.

Shortly after the death of her son, Taro had asked Hana to be baptized as a Christian and become a member of his church. Hana agreed mainly because she felt it her duty to do so. Each Sunday she accompanied Taro to the services, spoke politely to Reverend Okada and his wife, and mingled with the women. But she felt none of the closeness to any of them that she felt toward Kiku, who was half-heathen.

For many months after Yamaka and her infant son died, Hana had felt only anger and resentment toward Taro's God. But she felt, too, that she deserved His wrath. Finally, one Sunday as Reverend Okada preached that theirs was a God of love and forgiveness, she realized that her salvation lay in being forgiven by this God. She went to the Bible Study classes on Sunday mornings and flung herself into absorbing a knowledge of her new faith with an intensity the minister found most commendable.

"Never forget," he said, as she appeared pale and eager at her first class, "Jesus Christ is always at your side." And he read to her from the book of Matthew. "Come unto me all ye that labor and are heavy laden, and I will give you rest."

The words were strangely comforting, and Hana clung gratefully to them, copying them in her notebook and underlining them in the Bible Taro had given her. At last, she had found an avenue toward renewing herself. Having become more active in the church, she had long wanted a home in which she could invite the Women's Society to meet.

One week after they moved into their new home, four white men whom Hana didn't recognize came to call.

"Good evening, is your husband at home?" one of them asked.

Hana tried to explain that Taro was at a prayer meeting at church, but the words jammed in her throat and her English came out in broken spurts.

"She doesn't know anything," one of them said.

"Tell your husband we'll be back at seven tomorrow night." The men had not bothered to remove their hats, and their words, although harmless enough, seemed to carry ominous overtones.

Hana shivered and bolted the door after them. Their mere presence on the porch seemed a threat to her child, and she hurried to the bedroom to look in on her.

"It's all right, Ma Chan," she said. "It's all right." She repeated the words over and over until she succeeded in calming herself.

Hana saw a flicker of concern cross Taro's face when she told him of the callers, but he said nothing. Promptly at seven the next evening the doorbell rang.

"You need not come out to meet them," Taro told Hana, and he went to the door alone.

"Please come in," he said. The four men filled the living room with their large physical presence and the smell of cigars.

"We represent the people of this block," one of them began. "We'd like to have a talk with you."

"Yes. Please sit down."

The men glanced around the living room which Hana had taken great pains to decorate properly. A new flowered rug lay on the floor, and fresh white curtains that Kiku had helped Hana sew hung at the windows. The first tight buds of the flowering peach in their yard had begun to swell, and knowing there would be callers, Hana had arranged a spray on the mantel.

"We'll come right to the point," a tall red-headed man said without bothering to sit down. "There've been some complaints from the neighborhood about having Japanese on this block."

Taro caught his breath. "I see. Can you tell me who it was that complained?"

"Just some of the neighbors."

"What is it we have done to offend them?"

"Well, nothing specific."

Taro looked at each of the men in turn and tried to keep his voice steady. "Gentlemen," he began. "My wife and I looked many, many months to find a home where we might raise our daughter. When the owner said there would be no objection to our moving in here, we trusted him. It was a dream come true for us. We have already spent much time and money to make this house our home. And now, you would ask us to leave?"

Taro dared not stop before he finished all he wanted to say, "I should like to meet those neighbors who object to us," he said. "Is it any of you gentlemen?"

The men looked uncomfortable. "We're just here to represent them."

"Then please invite them to come talk to me. If they can tell me why we aren't desirable or why we do not deserve their respect, I shall consider their request. I am the proprietor of Takeda Dry Goods and Grocers on Seventh Street and I would be happy to have them visit my shop as well."

The men glanced uneasily at one another and had

nothing more to say. "Very well then," their spokesman said abruptly. "We'll inform them to that effect."

They moved to the door, and as they left, the last of them paused a moment and shook Taro's hand. "My name's Johnson," he said furtively, then he hurried out after the others.

The moment they were gone, Hana came from the kitchen where she had stood at the door watching through the crack, listening to every word.

"Will there be trouble?" she asked anxiously.

"I hope not," Taro's voice was heavy now with weariness. "I'm not going to give up our first real home without a fight."

"At least they didn't stay long," Hana said, and put away the broom she had stood, bristle-end up, with a dust cloth over it.

"What in the world was that for?" Taro asked curiously.

Hana's laughter was tinged with embarrassment. "The maid used to tell me when I was a child that setting up a broom like that would send an unwanted caller home quickly."

"Hana, you are still a child," Taro laughed, brushing a light kiss on her cheek.

"I'll do it again when the others come," Hana answered, wondering how long it would be before they appeared.

As Hana lay in bed, she recalled again the scene that had taken place in their home that night. The four enormous white men towering over Taro, suggesting that he move his family out simply because they had Japanese faces.

How calm and dignified and strong Taro had been, never faltering as he spoke. How reasonable his request that the objecting neighbors present themselves to him, Hana thought. Of course that was the only honorable thing for them to do. Taro had shown no anger or resentment, and in the end, the four men had gone off quietly like chastised children. And hadn't one of them even offered a hand of friendship before he left?

Hana felt proud of Taro and wanted now to tell him so, but he was already asleep. "It is because you are a good person that sleep comes so easily to you," Hana said softly.

She lay back, letting her mind drift toward those she held close, the living and the dead, in Japan, in Oakland and in Heaven. She tried to pray for each of them, but as she murmured their names, concern over the neighbors who hated them, and thoughts of the laundry to be done in the morning and of the supplies she needed intruded, and Hana fell asleep thinking that God had probably stopped listening to her incoherent ramblings.

In the morning, with the baby's needs to be met and the day's regimen to be followed, Hana never spoke of her pride to Taro. And so, never hearing the words that would have given him such joy, he went off to another day at his shop on Seventh Street.

Chapter 11

The objecting neighbors never appeared to voice their complaints. Taro never learned who they were, but he had more than a faint suspicion that the four men who had come had cloaked their own prejudice behind unnamed neighbors.

Taro was determined, moreover, to give them no cause for ever renewing their demand. He bought a second-hand lawn mower and cut his lawn each week without fail. He planted roses and pansies and petunias in front of the house and instructed Hana to keep the garden neat and watered. On no account, he told her, was she ever to litter their yard with telltale signs of Japanese occupancy, such as the soy barrels that offended the neighbors of the farmers.

"We are on trial, Hana," Taro explained gravely. "The way we live and comport ourselves may some-day affect the way the second generation Japanese Americans, Mary and her friends, are treated in this country."

Hana became so fearful of offending her neighbors, she was even careful about where and how she hung her laundry. She wondered if they objected to the diapers that fluttered on her line each day, and she took pains to hang any undergarments out of sight from their neighbors' windows.

In the weeks since they had moved into their new home, neither of their immediate neighbors had spoken to her. They somehow managed to hang their wash before or after Hana appeared in the yard to hang hers, and neither had come to call.

On days when the sun shone, Hana would take Mary out in her carriage and walk around the block. If she met anyone, she quickly lowered her gaze, fearing she would receive only a hostile glare if she dared look up. She admired the gardens and the neat bungalows, seemingly inhabited by beings who never materialized. Carefully boxed into their antiseptic houses, the men, she presumed, emerged only to go to work and the women appeared when they had errands to run.

In this neighborhood, there were no runny-nosed, dirty-kneed children running about in the dirt with bare feet. There were no outdoor pumps where aproned women bent to wash their clothes, crying babies strapped to their backs. There were no outdoor stalls laden with vegetables of the field or salt fish or baskets of tea or dried kelp from the sea. There was no gathering place for the people of the neighborhood, where one could listen to the sounds of laughter and talk or hear the busy scraping of wooden clogs on pebbled paths.

Clusters of yellow rape would be blossoming now in Oka Village, Hana thought, bordering the sharp green of the rice paddies like gaudy gilt frames. There would be workers in the rice paddies, bending to their perpetual battle with the weeds, and there would be crows wheeling in the wide open sky. Everywhere there would be familiar faces who would call out friendly greetings.

"But that is exactly what I fled," Hana would tell herself, "all those familiar faces who knew me too well." And she would be glad she was not standing ankle-deep in the cold slime of the paddies, to become one day a bent old woman with wrinkled brown skin.

With the arrival of their child, Hana could no longer help Taro in the shop, and it astonished her to realize that she missed the dreary place. At least there she saw an occasional person to whom she could speak in a tongue that did not frustrate her as did English.

When, one afternoon, Kiku Toda appeared at her front door, Hana welcomed her with a cry of delight.

"What a nice surprise, Kiku. Aren't you working today?"

Kiku explained that Mrs. Davis didn't need her today. Then she added, "That's not really so at all. I told her I couldn't come."

Sensing there was something on Kiku's mind, Hana urged her to sit down while she put on a kettle for tea. But Kiku followed her into the kitchen and spoke quickly of what troubled her.

"Hana, I must either leave Toda or move with him to the country to raise grapes."

Hana whirled from the stove. "What?"

"Toda has lost his job at the bank," Kiku said briefly. "They just told him his services were no longer needed and that he wasn't to come back any more."

"*Mah!*" Hana was too stunned to say more.

"Now Toda says there's nothing to be done but to go to his cousin's farm in Livingston and help him grow grapes."

"But surely there must be other jobs for him here."

"Toda's had his fill of demeaning work. He doesn't want to be a janitor anymore and says it's time he got back to the soil where he belongs. If I don't go with him, he is going alone."

Hana had to sit down. She couldn't bear the thought of not having Kiku nearby. "Why won't he even consider looking for something better here?"

Kiku sipped the tea that Hana offered her. "Well, that's a long story, but I'll tell you if you like."

In all the times they'd been together, Kiku had never told Hana how it was when she first came to America. Hana leaned forward now, eager to hear.

"When I first came to become Toda's bride," Kiku began, "he was working as a cook in a cafe. As soon as I arrived he wanted to move out to the country and find some land to farm, for that was what he knew best. But I wouldn't let him. I had always lived in a city and I wasn't ready to bury myself in a farm with no running water and an outhouse in back. I hadn't come to America to live like that. I insisted we stay in Oakland. In those days, I was even more stubborn and strong-willed than I am now," Kiku admitted with a wry smile. "So Toda agreed to stay in the city if I would bear him some sons who would grow up to carry on his family name. He stayed on as a cook, then he became houseboy, and finally a janitor at the bank."

Kiku was silent a moment and then looked at Hana. "Toda has already wasted ten years in Oakland. Today he is almost forty, he has no job, he has no land, and he has no sons. I've been quite a wife, don't you think?"

Hana reached out to touch Kiku's hand. "All of us have failed in one way or another," she said. "Probably I even more than you." It depressed her to watch Kiku turn herself inside out like this, unravelling her outer self to expose her vulnerability.

But Kiku soon straightened and regained her assurance. "Well, the Osaka city woman is about to find out what it's like to become a farmer's wife."

"You mean you have already decided?"

"I suppose I have. From now on, I'll be getting up in the dark to light a kerosene lamp and fetch water from the pump. I'll feed the chickens, harvest grapes, shiver in a cold, stinking outhouse, and who knows," she added, "maybe I can even give Toda his blasted sons."

"I'll miss you, Kiku."

Kiku sighed and rose to leave. "When the baby is

older, you must come visit us. It won't be hard with the car."

"Taro still doesn't drive as well as Yamaka San did," Hana said slowly. It had been a long time since she had even mentioned his name to anyone, but with Kiku it was possible.

Kiku looked hard at Hana and said firmly, "Hana, it is time you forgot the past. Let the dead rest in peace and live for the present."

"I know," Hana answered. She knew Kiku was right.

With Kiku gone, Hana turned more and more toward the Japanese church for friendship and comfort. She was elected treasurer of the Women's Society and was pleased they felt her capable of holding such a responsible position.

When the superintendent of the Sunday School came to call on her one afternoon, she assumed he had come to discuss something of mutual concern about the church. Actually, he was not one of Hana's favorite people. His stoop made him appear older than he was, and the thick lens of his glasses gave his eyes a distorted look that made Hana uncomfortable. He ran a nervous hand through his thinning hair and sat down on the edge of the sofa.

Hana put on some hot water for tea, and when she returned to the living room, she found the superintendent pacing nervously about the room, peering at the books in the bookcase and stopping to riffle through a magazine.

"Is your wife well?" Hana inquired.

"Yes, yes, quite well. And your daughter?"

"Mary is growing and getting fatter each day."

"Good. And your husband, his shop goes well?"

"Yes, although he is busier now that I can no longer help him."

Hana began to share the superintendent's uneasiness and couldn't bear to sit another moment exchanging these meaningless pleasantries.

"Is there something troubling you?" she asked at last. "Can I help you in any way?"

The man gripped his hands together until the knuckles were white. "Well, yes, Mrs. Takeda. The reason I came today is . . . you are the treasurer of the Women's Society, are you not?"

"Yes, I am."

"Yes. Well, I wondered about how much money you have in your treasury?"

It seemed a strange question, but not altogether improbable as he also was responsible for the Sunday School's funds.

"I'll get my notebook and see," Hana said, rising to go fetch her records. She kept the notebook, along with the money, hidden beneath the silk stockings in her bureau drawer.

"We have twenty-five dollars and fifty cents," she announced with some pride.

The superintendent seemed to find this heartening news, and he smiled for the first time. "Splendid," he said, as he wiped the steam from his eye glasses. "Now Mrs. Takeda, I would like to borrow your money for a few weeks." Seeing Hana's reluctance, he assured her it had been done before. Then he tried another tack. "You know Mr. Kenji Nishima, the seminary student who lives in the church dormitory?"

Hana nodded. She remembered well the earnest, scholarly young man who occasionally gave the Sunday sermons.

"He is my assistant, as you may know, and he cannot buy material for the Sunday School if we do not borrow the money before Sunday."

Hana thought of the Sunday School children sitting in their drafty rooms with no materials to use. "You say this has been done before?" she asked.

"Yes. After all, we are one church family and must help each other in times of need."

In the end, it was impossible for Hana to refuse. She went to her room, took the twenty-five dollars and fifty cents from its silken nest and put it in an envelope. "For the Sunday School," she wrote on it, "a loan from the Women's Society."

The superintendent was so effusive with his thanks that it never occurred to Hana to get a receipt. He rose hastily, not even waiting for the tea. He grasped Hana's hand and shook it firmly. "I am more grateful than you will ever know," he said.

As Hana watched him go down the front steps, she was convinced that her decision had been quite right and proper.

Chapter 12

Hana looked down at Mary cradled in her arms inside the pink blanket and found it impossible to concentrate on the minister's sermon. Across the aisle, she noticed Taro stealing frequent glances in her direction as Mary uttered her small infant sounds. He was smiling in spite of himself, then made a visible effort to rearrange the expression on his face to a properly reverent one. But Hana didn't even bother to do that. She simply wrapped her child in a loving gaze and emerged from her maternal reveries only when it was time to rise and sing the closing hymn.

After the hymn, Dr. Kaneda rose to make his usual announcements to the congregation. Today he seemed uneasy, and clearing his throat he said, "I am afraid I have some disturbing news to announce this morning. The superintendent of our Sunday School, who served us so faithfully for five years, has left very unexpectedly for Japan."

A murmur of dismay sifted through the chapel as Dr. Kaneda paused. "He informed none of us of his plans," he continued, "and no one knows why he left in such haste. I would like now to call on Mr. Kenji Nishima, who assisted him in the Sunday School. He will read us the note the superintendent left."

Hana gasped. Only last week, the man had come to borrow money for the Sunday School, and not once had he mentioned his intention to return to Japan. She waited anxiously to hear the contents of the note.

Kenji Nishima adjusted his glasses and began to

read in a thin, taut voice. "My dear Nishima," the note began. "I must ask the members of the church to forgive me if they can. My burdens have become too heavy to bear. I am now so much in debt, I am defeated, penniless and desperate. I have no recourse but to return to Japan and have used the Sunday School funds to buy steamship tickets for my wife and myself. I leave you in shame and disgrace. May God forgive me. Please find a way to restore the money to the Sunday School treasury."

Kenji Nishima's voice sank to a whisper as he read the last words, and his hands trembled as he sat down. In the stunned silence, Hana heard her own voice cry out, "And he borrowed all of the Women's Society money from me. He has taken that as well. Twenty-five dollars and fifty cents!"

Voices of shock and indignation circled the congregation. How could the mild-mannered superintendent do such an outrageous thing? How had he gotten himself into such trouble? Had he been gambling? Or drinking?

Reverend Okada was the first to recover his wits. Silencing the people, he prayed for the absconded superintendent and his wife, and asked the church members to find it in their hearts to forgive him and pray for him too.

Pray for him, indeed, Hana thought indignantly. The miserable man had lied and had deceived her. And to think he was her own countryman and a Christian at that.

The moment the service ended, Hana hurried to Dr. Kaneda's side. "I will repay the Women's Society money, of course," she said, although she hadn't the faintest idea how she would do it.

"Don't worry, Hana. We'll discuss this at the deacon's meeting. We'll find a way to cover the loss. In the meantime, do as the good Reverend suggests.

Pray for the man."

Hana felt a tap on her shoulder. It was Kenji Nishima, solemn and pale. Beads of sweat stood out on his upper lip. "Mrs. Takeda, I feel responsible for the superintendent's acts. I will do my best to repay the Women's Society."

"Oh no," Hana objected. "I am the one who made the mistake of trusting the man. I will worry about the women's money, and the church will see to the Sunday School funds. None of this should be your task."

But the young man seemed overcome. He went from member to member, bowing and apologizing, assuming the superintendent's disgrace as his own.

As they drove home from church, Taro and Hana could talk only of the startling occurrence. "I should never have given him the money," Hana said over and over. "I am responsible. I must pay it back myself."

"We'll find a way," Taro said quietly. "We can set aside a little each month."

Hana wanted to cry. She knew business in Taro's shop had slipped badly. The furnishings for their house had consumed his meager savings and the monthly rent was twice what he had been paying for the flat. In addition, there had been all the extra things for the baby: the crib, the buggy, milk bottles, diapers, and whatever clothing Hana hadn't made.

Hana had learned how to make a can of salmon last for two days by saving the liquid and using it to cook turnips the next day. She had learned to be frugal and indulged in no secret extravagances as Kiku had. Still, there was barely enough money for necessities, and now because of her stupidity, she had added another burden to Taro's increasing load.

"I'm so sorry," she said, grateful that he had not rebuked her for her lack of judgment. Now, for the first time, she contemplated the possibility of doing housework in a white home. One of the last things

Kiku had given her was the phone number of Mrs. Ellen Davis. "If you ever want to do housework," she had said, "you couldn't find a nicer person."

For several days, Hana grappled with the idea of going to work, taking it from her mind, examining it from time to time as she might observe a trinket. Unlike a cherished object, however, the thought of going to work brought no pleasure and seemed to offer nothing besides money and a new series of problems to complicate her life. She would have to learn to cook American food properly, and she would have to accustom herself to being a servant. That would be the hardest part, to make herself subservient to another woman—a white woman. And what would she do with Mary? In America, women did not go about their work with babies strapped to their backs, and Hana refused even to consider the solution many other women had taken. She would never send Mary to Japan to be brought up by her mother, even though the child could learn the amenities of Japanese life.

One morning Hana finally made up her mind, and having done so, wanted to tell Taro about her decision. Dressing Mary in her crocheted jacket and hat with the blue ribbon, she left the house and took the streetcar to Taro's shop.

Taro observed her entrance with startled pleasure. "What are you doing down here?" he asked.

"I came to tell you I've decided to go to work," Hana stated flatly. "I'm going to phone Kiku's Mrs. Davis and ask if I can do housework for her."

"Sit down, Hana," Taro directed. "Tell me calmly if that is what you really want to do."

Hana thrust the baby in Taro's arms. "I may not be able to earn very much," she said, "but I can help with the rent, and I can help pay back the Women's Society money."

Taro looked down at the child in his arms. "And

what do you plan to do with Mary?"

"I've thought it all out," Hana explained. "I'm going to tell Mrs. Davis that I must bring my child with me. If she's as kind as Kiku said she is, I'm sure she'll let me."

By now Taro knew Hana well enough to know that once she made up her mind, she could not be dissuaded. Besides, he felt it might be good for her to get out and meet new people.

"Very well then, Hana," he said. "It is decided."

Wanting to show some support for her resolve and to send her home with a present, Taro pulled a long, yellow, pickled radish from a barrel of bean mash and wrapped it in newspaper. He knew Hana liked nothing better at the end of a meal than pickled radish with rice and hot tea.

Hana felt enormously pleased with herself as she waited for the streetcar to return home. Taro had not objected to her decision, and in fact, had seemed pleased. She smiled at the conductor as she deposited her nickel in the fare box and found a seat next to a window. At each stop, as passengers came on board, one would sit next to her for a few minutes and soon move to another seat. Hana thought nothing of it until the conductor came back to speak to her.

"Madam, I believe whatever you're carrying in your bundle has begun to spoil. Would you mind moving to the rear of the car?"

In a terrible flash Hana understood it was the smell of the pickled radish that was sending everyone away from her. Its odor was pungent enough to permeate her house. Of course, now the entire street car must be reeking with it. She was so accustomed to its smell, it bothered her no more than the smell of roast beef would bother a white person. She had been so consumed with her own thoughts, she had forgotten all about her redolent bundle.

Flushing crimson, she murmured, "Oh, I am so sorry. I will get right off." Clumsily gathering Mary in one arm and her bundle in the other, she hurried from the streetcar, almost stumbling at the curb in her haste to get away. She didn't dare look back, for she was sure everyone inside must be laughing at her.

Keeping her eyes straight ahead, she hurried down the street. She walked two long blocks before she realized she was still more than thirty blocks from home.

Shifting Mary from one arm to the other, Hana walked until her legs felt wooden and her arms grew numb. She glanced longingly as one streetcar after another clanged down the street, passing her by. But she dared not get on another one as long as she had her pickled radish, and it never once occurred to her to abandon it in the gutter.

By the time she reached her own street, Mary was cross and wet and wailing. Close to tears herself, with sweat trickling down her face, Hana staggered home with the screaming baby and the offensive pickle to find a well-dressed white woman ringing her doorbell.

She turned as she heard Hana approach and smiled from beneath a large ribboned hat. "Good morning. I am Mrs. Johnson. I live down the street."

Hana didn't know whether to laugh or cry. She had waited so many months for one of her neighbors to call. Now when she was least prepared, when she had been humiliated and embarrassed and was close to exhaustion, Mrs. Johnson, with her hair neatly marcelled, wearing white gloves and her Sunday hat, had come at last to call.

"I believe my husband has already met you," Mrs. Johnson said as she stepped inside. "He came with a rather unpleasant request some time ago."

Hana remembered the four men and recalled the one who had paused to shake Taro's hand. "Ah yes," she said. "Your husband must have been the kind one."

"Do go put your child down and take off your hat," Mrs. Johnson suggested. "I'll wait for you here." She sat down carefully on the sofa.

Hana put Mary in her crib, threw the pickle out on the back porch and put on the kettle for tea. She wondered what she could serve Mrs. Johnson. At the same time she tried to put together in her mind the proper words to tell Mrs. Johnson how welcome she was. If only she could tell her what she had just been through, Hana thought, but there weren't enough English words in her weary head even to begin. Hana simply wiped her face with a handkerchief and hurried out to entertain her first white woman caller.

"I am so happy you came," she said. And she truly meant it.

Viola Johnson stayed only long enough to have some tea and to tell Hana that she meant to call long ago. She spoke slowly and raised her voice, as though Hana might be deaf or stupid or both. She explained that her husband was in insurance, that she had a son, six, and a daughter, four, and that she never had enough hours in the day to do all she'd like. Then, as she rose to leave, she asked Hana whether she knew of someone who might do housework for her.

"I suppose you don't do any day work yourself, do you, my dear?" she asked.

So that was why she had come to call. Hana stood tall and looked Mrs. Johnson straight in the eye.

"No, madam, I do not," she answered fiercely. "I am the daughter of a *samurai*." She would never work for a woman who looked upon her only as a maid.

Hana thus managed to preserve her pride, but Mrs. Johnson left uncomprehending and puzzled, for she had never heard of a *samurai,* and had no idea what Hana meant by her remark, nor why she had seemed so offended.

Chapter 13

Hana liked Ellen Davis from the moment she met her. She was a tall, large-boned woman with graying hair waved softly and pulled back into a french knot. There was a regal air about her that reminded Hana of the Empress, but there was also a warmth to her that invited friendship. She was completely understanding of Hana's problem with Mary.

"Of course, bring her with you," she assured Hana. "I'll bring my son's old play pen down from the attic, and you can keep an eye on her while you work."

Mrs. Davis lived in a large two-story house on a hillside overlooking Lake Merritt. Her husband was a surgeon and they had one son, Victor, who was fifteen. Ever since Kiku had gone to Livingston, Mrs. Davis had been looking for someone to take her place.

"When Kiku told me about you, I hoped so much that you would call," she said to Hana, and she grasped her hand as though she were greeting an old friend.

Hana had some misgivings as Mrs. Davis showed her through the house. It seemed enormous to her, for on the second floor alone there were four bedrooms and two baths. She glanced uneasily at all the windows, remembering Kiyoshi Yamaka's story, and was determined to refuse firmly if she was asked to wash them.

Hana agreed to work for Mrs. Davis every Thursday and Friday from nine until four o'clock. She would clean the house, do the laundry and ironing, and help start dinner.

On her first day, Mrs. Davis offered her some coffee when she arrived, but Hana wanted to get on with the cleaning. She settled Mary in the play pen, put on her apron, and asked for some wet tea leaves.

"Tea leaves?"

"Yes, to keep down the dust when I sweep."

"Then you've never used a vacuum cleaner?"

"No, I can clean very well with a broom."

"Well, Hana, I think you'll find the vacuum cleaner very useful," Mrs. Davis said, and proceeded to show her how to use it. Hana grasped the handle of the monstrous machine with its hideous whine, gritted her teeth and set grimly to work.

Mrs. Davis had been married for over twenty-five years, and the accumulation of those years was apparent everywhere. There were countless family portraits in gilt frames throughout her room, and Hana glanced at them, finding Ellen Davis in each, as she matured from a beautiful young bride to a gracious matron.

Hana sighed as she looked at Mrs. Davis's desk. It was strewn with books, papers, fancy paperweights, an inkwell with feathered pens, piles of clippings, baskets of letters, and small containers filled with clips and rubber bands. It was obvious Mrs. Davis had an abundance of friends and a voluminous correspondence.

Hana surveyed the room, wondering where to begin. Even the floor was not spared of clutter. Beneath her bed were large storage boxes and beside it was an assortment of slippers and shoes. Hana plunged into the cleaning as though she had been thrown into a lake and had to learn to swim. She struggled with heavy furniture as she pushed the bulky vacuum cleaner into inaccessible corners, and she held her breath as she dusted the delicate bottles and vases and frames that crowded together on the dresser.

Hana was relieved to move on to Dr. Davis's room, for his was as spartan as hers was baroque. His desk was cleared of everything except a writing pad and a lamp, his dresser held only his brush and comb, and his slippers and shoes were deposited neatly in the closet.

"Bless you, Dr. Davis," Hana said, grateful for his orderly habits, cleaning his room in half the time it had taken to do Mrs. Davis's.

Victor's room did not speak to Hana of its occupant with the clarity of his parents' rooms. There was a surface air of order, but on examining the bed, Hana saw that the spread had been hastily pulled up to conceal a rumpled mess beneath. One slipper was under the bed, while its mate was tossed into the closet. His desk was laden with school books and papers, but they had been arranged in neat piles. His bookshelf held a large collection of model ships, many of them on the verge of collapse.

"You are probably a good boy," Hana murmured, and she returned the vagrant slipper to its mate, straightened up his bed, and was careful not to disturb the papers on his desk.

Seeing their rooms had told her more of the Davis family than anything Kiku had told her, and Hana felt now that she knew each of them fairly well. It took her all morning to clean the second floor, with only two interruptions to tend to Mary. At noon, Mrs. Davis called Hana to have lunch with her.

Hana had expected to eat alone in the kitchen, but a place had been set for her in the dining room opposite Mrs. Davis. She was served a bowl of hot tomato soup, a cheese sandwich, a cup of coffee and some cookies. A cloth napkin rolled inside a silver ring engraved with the letter "C" was at Hana's place.

"That belonged to my son, Charles," Mrs. Davis

explained as Hana lifted the ring to look at it. "He died of diphtheria when he was two."

"Then we have both lost a son," Hana said softly, and although Mrs. Davis talked to her of many things as they ate their meal, the memory of the past suddenly came back and for several minutes Hana did not hear a word that was spoken to her.

By the time Hana finished cleaning the entire house, she was ravenous, for she was used to having more than soup and a sandwich for lunch. Furthermore, she was so exhausted, not even the one dollar and twenty-five cents she earned aroused the elation she had anticipated on receiving her first day's pay. And she felt somehow degraded when Mrs. Davis, opening her purse, simply handed her the cash rather than placing it discreetly in a white envelope to spare them both the vulgar sight of money.

When Taro came home, he found the baby screaming, the rice uncooked, the breakfast dishes unwashed, and Hana on the verge of tears. She was trying to shell some peas, but could scarcely move her fingers.

"How was your first day of work?" Taro asked.

"I never knew housework could be so hard," Hana answered dismally. "It was harder than planting rice in the fields all day." Finding it impossible to convey the exhausting details of cleaning the Davis home, she simply said, "I am just so tired."

Taro put a hand on her shoulder. "The first day is always hardest," he said, and pushing the peas away he added, "You go tend to Mary and let me see if I can still remember how to make supper."

"Oh, Taro, would you?"

"Go on, Hana."

While Hana bathed and fed the baby, Taro cooked the rice and heated a can of broiled eel. He filled two large bowls with hot rice and arranged the strips of steaming eel on top. He brewed a fresh pot of green tea and sliced some of Hana's favorite pickled radish.

Hana smiled gratefully when she saw what Taro had done. The taste of Japanese food revived her, and she was finally able to tell Taro more about her first day at work. "It's so hard cleaning a house that isn't your own," Hana explained. "I don't think Mrs. Davis has thrown out a single thing in the last twenty-five years."

Taro waited until Hana's stomach was full, her spirit calmed, and the fatigue of the day began to leave her face. Then he spoke to her of Kenji Nishima, the young seminary student.

"You remember the assistant of the Sunday School?"

"Yes, of course."

"Reverend Okada told me today he has been missing from the dormitory for two days. He is quite concerned about him."

Hana remembered how thin and pale Nishima appeared the last time she saw him. "Is he still upset over what happened?" she asked.

"About that, and about his studies because he is falling behind. But mostly, I think he is just homesick for Japan. I told Reverend Okada we could perhaps invite him to supper some day. When you don't go to work, of course," Taro added.

Hana felt a surge of pity for the young student, knowing he was even more distressed than she about the superintendent's sticky-fingered departure. But tonight she didn't want to think of making supper for him or for anyone else.

"I'll make some *osushi* for him and take it to the dormitory," she offered instead. "Maybe I could do it Saturday."

"That would be nice," Taro said, accepting whatever Hana would offer. "I hope he returns to the dormitory by then."

Hana nodded absently. She simply couldn't summon up further concern for Kenji Nishima now, for her own aching body longed for a hot bath, and she still had another day of work tomorrow, when she must wash and iron. She yawned noisily, lit the burner of the hot water tank for her bath and poured a kettle of hot water into the dishpan.

Taro, who usually spent the time after supper reading the paper, watched Hana stretch and rub the small of her back. He put down the paper and took the washrag from Hana's hand. "I'll wash the dishes tonight," he said.

Hana knew that in Japan a man never did a woman's work in the kitchen, but Taro's years in America had made him more understanding. She wanted to say something warm and loving to him now, but didn't know how. Instead, she went to the cupboard and took down a large bar of sweet bean paste with chestnuts that she had put away for company. She cut several thick slices and put them on a plate.

"We can have dessert first," she said. "After all, I did earn over one dollar today."

Taro smiled and sat down beside her. Although she said nothing more, he understood the meaning of her gesture, and for him that was quite enough.

Chapter 14

Hana didn't make *sushi* very often, for it was a time-consuming and tedious task, even though the result was a tasty satisfaction. On Saturday, however, she remembered her promise to Taro and cooked from early morning. She would make enough for the minister's family as well as Kenji Nishima.

Hana emptied freshly cooked rice into a large bowl, seasoning and fanning it so it would cool before she added the other ingredients. As she flapped the round paper fan back and forth, she sang softly to Mary, who sat in her high chair stuffing a cracker into her mouth.

She thought of Dr. and Mrs. Davis, in their beautiful house, surrounded by all those possessions that bespoke of wealth. Still, they existed on such dull fare as bread and potatoes, meat and cheese. She wondered if they had ever tasted the countless Japanese delicacies that existed outside their own world. There wasn't one bottle of soy sauce or a container of bean paste in Mrs. Davis's sterile white kitchen. What would Mrs. Davis say, Hana wondered, if she could taste a plateful of her *sushi,* heaped like a small mountain and garnished with strips of seaweed, sweetened egg and ginger.

"Poor Mrs. Davis," Hana said. "Shall I make some *osushi* for her someday, Ma Chan?" Mary replied by screaming to be let out and throwing her soggy cracker on the floor.

The most bothersome part of doing a kindness, Hana thought as she put on her coat and hat, was the final effort of getting one's gift and the recipient together. She struggled with Mary in one arm and her *furoshiki* bundle in the other, and climbed with considerable difficulty onto the streetcar. Wrapped inside her silk square was a two-tiered box of red lacquer filled with her handwork, one tier for Mr. Nishima and one for the Okada family. She was pleased her *sushi* had turned out so well today, for she had used only the best canned goods from Taro's shelves.

Hana was tired, but her task today was infinitely more satisfying than doing someone else's wash as she had the day before. Until she had done the Davis family wash, she hadn't realized how much larger white people were than most Japanese. Their clothes, when wet and heavy, had seemed enormous, and her back still ached from washing all morning and ironing most of the afternoon. More than once during the day, she had thought of giving up and never going back to work, but when she thought of the other women at church who labored in similar ways to help pay the rent and support their children, she knew she could not confess her own weakness so soon.

Even Mrs. Okada, the minister's wife, spent one day a week doing housework. Hana sometimes wondered how she must feel being the wife of an impoverished minister barely able to feed his family. She wondered if the woman ever regretted coming to America and why she had made such a choice in the first place. Could theirs have been a true love match? It hardly seemed possible. And yet, whenever Hana saw her on Sundays, playing the organ or greeting church members after the service, she seemed always serene and content, ready with a comforting word for any who needed it. Seeing the strength of Mrs. Okada's faith, Hana felt ashamed of the tenuous hold on her own.

Today Hana felt faintly sanctimonious as she

walked to church with her bundle of good works, thinking how much pleasure it was going to bring. She stopped first at the parsonage and presented the top tier of *sushi* to Mrs. Okada, who received it with a profusion of thanks.

"It is really nothing. I hope you will find it edible," Hana demurred in typical Japanese fashion, even though she had spent hours making it and knew it to be extremely good.

"It will provide us with a fine supper," Mrs. Okada said gratefully, offering to go with Hana to the dormitory to find Mr. Nishima. "Leave little Ma Chan with my daughter," she suggested. "She will watch her while we go."

"He has returned by now, hasn't he? Mr. Nishima?" Hana asked as they walked toward the shabby wooden building behind the church.

"I'm not sure. My husband said his bed didn't look as though it had been slept in last night either." Mrs. Okada shivered as she went on. "We just don't know what to make of it. I hope he . . ." Her voice trailed off.

Hana's spirits sank as she realized Kenji Nishima might not be there to enjoy her bounty.

They climbed the sagging wooden steps of the dormitory that housed eight or nine Japanese bachelors. Some were day workers, some university or seminary students, and some stayed only when there was no work harvesting fruits or vegetables in the valley. The building was filled with a Saturday stillness.

"Is anybody home?" Mrs. Okada called.

There was no sound except for the creaking floor as the two women stepped inside. The smell of cooking oil lingered in the air, and there was a mustiness from inadequate cleaning. As Mrs. Okada struggled to open a window, flakes of old paint fluttered to the floor.

Hana felt like an intruder as they glanced over the row of metal cots in the sleeping quarters. Most of them were in varying degrees of disarray. "That is Mr. Nishima's," Mrs. Okada said, pointing to a cot by the window. Its gray wool blankets were tucked neatly under the mattress, and its pillow was smooth and unrumpled.

They went to the kitchen and viewed it with dismay. A pan of half-eaten rice stood on the stove, while dirty dishes and rice bowls were stacked in the sink, still encrusted with bits of food. On the oilcloth-covered table were an assortment of coffee cups, spoons, a pot of coffee and a piece of burnt toast.

Hana shrank back, revolted by what she saw. "It's little wonder Mr. Nishima was homesick," she observed. And she recalled that both Taro and Kiyoshi Yamaka had once lived in this building, leading the same dreary existence now endured by Kenji Nishima and the other men.

"Well," she sighed. "I'll just leave my *osushi* on the table for whoever wants it."

As she spoke, however, they both heard the sound of footsteps in the attic.

"That's strange," Mrs. Okada murmured. "The attic is used only for storage."

Hana held her breath as they both listened. It was definitely the sound of someone walking slowly and carefully. Then it stopped. The two women looked at each other.

"I think someone is up there," Mrs. Okada whispered.

Hana wanted to run from the building, but was unable to move.

Mrs. Okada hesitated a moment, then said, "I think we must go see who is up there."

"Shall I call Taro first?" Hana asked.

"I don't think we should wait. Will you go upstairs with me?"

Hana nodded and found herself leading the way.

They moved quietly up the dark narrow stairway in the front hall, and Hana swallowed hard, thinking of Mary playing in blissful innocence in the parsonage. She wondered if she would ever see her again.

At the top of the staircase was a small landing, then two doors that led to separate sections of the attic. Mrs. Okada pointed to the first door and Hana flung it open. In the dim light they could see only the dark shapes of trunks, boxes and cartons that once held the belongings of men who had crossed the Pacific. Mrs. Okada looked to Hana for courage, took a deep breath and threw open the second door. As she did, they both saw a shadow dart behind a large steamer trunk.

Hana uttered a cry, and Mrs. Okada stepped back in terror. Then summoning all her strength, she called out, "Who . . . who's there? Come out, or we shall call the police." Her last words were trembling and weak.

There was a long silence, then a movement in the shadows. From the darkness of the attic shapes emerged a thin, bearded man, barely able to walk.

"Mr. Nishima!" Hana shouted.

"What has happened to you?" Mrs. Okada cried out.

But Mr. Nishima shook even more than the two women and was in no condition to speak of his terrible needs. He followed them docilely downstairs and crept gratefully into his cot. Meanwhile, Mrs. Okada phoned Dr. Kaneda and Hana made him some hot tea.

It was a week before Kenji Nishima could speak of his strange withdrawal, and it was to Dr. Kaneda that he confided his agony.

"It was as though I were being sucked into a whirlpool," he explained bleakly. "I was so far behind in my studies, I couldn't begin to catch up. There were exams and papers due, and then there was the extra money I was trying to earn for the Sunday School. I had to get away to be alone . . . to think . . . I hid in the attic and went downstairs only when no one was there."

Sojiro Kaneda listened quietly. He had seen other young students who came from Japan eager to study at the university or the seminary, but their eagerness did not compensate for their inadequate knowledge of English. Bright and intelligent though they were, they soon fell behind. Overwhelmed by homesickness and the need to work at unfamiliar tasks to earn money, some of them eventually collapsed from the strain.

He had been especially concerned about young Nishima since the miserable business of the Sunday School funds. Kenji Nishima was one of the brightest students to help their church. His commitment was intense and he had the gift of conveying it to others with rare enthusiasm. The Sunday School had grown since he became assistant to the superintendent, and the children adored him. Had he not been so conscientious and sensitive, Dr. Kaneda knew he would not have been as traumatized by the superintendent's disgraceful flight. It pained Kaneda now to see Nishima broken in body and spirit.

After the service on Sunday, Dr. Kaneda, Reverend Okada and Taro discussed what they might do to help Kenji Nishima.

Hana came to see if she could pry Taro away before Mary began to fuss. "Why do you all look so solemn?" she asked.

"We were speaking of Kenji Nishima," Taro explained.

Hana remembered how she had watched him one morning as he led the Sunday School worship service. He stood in front of a scattering of children in the dim sanctuary, urging them to sing the hymn printed on a large sheet of paper suspended with clothespins from a metal stand.

"Come now, you can do better than that," he urged. And singing in a loud clear tenor himself, he extracted a swelling sound from the thin childish voices.

"That's it! That's better!" he encouraged, keeping time with this hands, until the children's voices rang out through the chapel.

Hana had watched as he helped the children count their birthday offerings into a jar, one penny for each year of their lives, giving them small gifts—a bookmark bearing a Bible verse or a button with the picture of Jesus. As he presented the gifts, he made each child feel important and totally loved. After the service, they clustered around him, telling him the special secrets they had kept safely until Sunday to share only with him. Hana could tell the children loved him. Please stay in America until Mary is old enough to come to Sunday School, she had thought then. Please wait for her.

She suddenly became aware that Reverend Okada was speaking. "Perhaps the best thing for him now would be to return to Japan. He could rest and restore his mind and his body at home."

"Ah, that would be a pity," Dr. Kaneda said sadly. "He has such promise. Surely there must be another way."

As though God had put the thought in her mind and given her the words, Hana spoke out. "There is," she said brightly. "He can come stay with us for the summer. I'll move Mary into our room, and he can have hers. I will feed him good nourishing food, and Taro and I will help him restore himself."

She looked at Taro now, realizing this was something she should have discussed with him before blurting it out in front of the others. But the impulse had been so strong, she had said the words almost before she realized what she was doing.

If Taro was annoyed with her, he did not show it. "Are you sure you could manage, Hana?" he asked.

"I'm sure I could. And it would be good for him to be with Mary." She was too young to understand his torment, but enough of an individual to demand his affection and love. More important, she had no need or ability to ask questions of him.

"If you are sure, then of course, I am willing," Taro answered, for at the moment no other reply was possible.

Reverend Okada shook their hands, saying, "God bless you both. It is a fine thing you are doing."

Dr. Kaneda couldn't wait to tell Nishima. "You must tell him yourselves," he urged, leading Taro and Hana to the dormitory. This was, he felt, an answer to his prayers.

As they approached the building, Hana remembered again the confused, bearded figure cringing in the dimness of the attic. For a moment, a shaft of doubt leaped through her, but Nishima now was clean-shaven and rested. When Hana saw the happiness that swept over his face at their invitation, she knew she was doing the right thing.

"It will be all right, won't it?" she asked Taro as they drove home.

"I hope so," Taro answered, and Hana did not miss the anxiety in his voice.

She wasn't sure just what concerned Taro. Was it her inability to cope with someone in Nishima's condition, or Kenji Nishima as a man?

Hana wanted to reassure Taro that he had nothing to fear, but she didn't know how to tell him. She was convinced in her own heart that it was the right thing to do. It was a chance to offer help and support to a human being in need and to bring some purpose and meaning into her own life. More and more she knew she didn't want her life to be simply a succession of days spent in doing another woman's housework.

Yet deep in the back of her mind, where she dared not seek it, was the fleeting thought that perhaps she was really doing this for herself. Was she giving this young student a chance to fulfill his hopes and dreams because she wanted to give him the life that Kiyoshi Yamaka had been denied? Was she doing this in an ultimate effort to seek, even now, God's forgiveness? Hana did not know. She just knew it was something she had to try, and she was determined to succeed.

Chapter 15

The day Kenji Nishima was to move into their home, Hana spent the entire morning going over each room, making each one as cheerful as possible, as she anticipated his needs. They had borrowed a cot from the church to set up in Mary's room, and Hana had removed Mary's things from all the dresser drawers. She looked at the Mother Goose pictures on the wall and considered taking them down. They seemed so inappropriate, but having nothing better with which to replace them, she left them where they were, hoping their bright innocence might be diverting.

That evening Kenji Nishima came home with Taro. There was no color in his face and dark shadows circled his eyes. "You are very kind to let me come," he said with a slight bow. "I don't know how to thank you."

"No thanks are needed, Nishima San. We're happy to have you," Hana answered, and she was speaking the truth.

For several days Nishima continued to be listless and withdrawn. He spent long hours in his room or sat in the living room gazing out the window. Sometimes Hana would awaken in the middle of the night to hear him pacing up and down in his room. It disturbed her to see his hand tremble as he lifted his tea cup and to watch the constant nervous movement of his knee as he sat with them after dinner.

"Perhaps he needs more help than we can give him," Taro suggested.

But Hana wasn't ready to admit defeat yet. "I'm going to talk to Mrs. Davis," she said. "Maybe she'll have some ideas."

Ellen Davis watched as Hana did her ironing, working the tip of the iron carefully around the embroidered initials on the pillow cases. She admired the skill and speed with which Hana worked, and thought again how lucky she was to have her.

Hana wasn't Kiku. She was more reserved and reticent. But lately she had begun to speak more freely about her own life and that pleased Mrs. Davis. She grew increasingly fond of Hana, wishing she could penetrate the polite outer veil beyond which she herself was rarely admitted. If only Hana would permit it, she wanted to know her as a person, not simply as a day worker. She listened carefully now, as Hana told her about Kenji Nishima.

Hana glanced at the laundry basket still filled with damp clothes waiting to be ironed. "I don't know why he is still so despondent," she said, without looking up from her work. "He takes no more classes, and he needn't worry now about the Sunday School money. Each family at church is contributing two dollars a month until the money is paid back."

Ellen Davis was touched by the sacrifices of Hana's people. She knew how each family struggled simply to exist, and yet they seemed always ready to help one another when the need arose. Even Kiku, who rarely went to church, had worked an extra day each week for an entire year, to pledge money for the building of a new chapel. Mrs. Davis had wondered how they could raise enough money from their pitiful earnings. And yet, in three years' time, they had not only built their church, they had become independent of the Mission Board.

They were proud, hardworking people, and Ellen

Davis was outraged at the discrimination heaped on them with the sanction of law. There was little she could do about that, but she did what she could for those whose lives touched her own. When Hana told her they had taken in a young seminary student for the summer, she immediately increased Hana's pay.

"I don't deserve so much," Hana had objected.

"Yes, you do, and more," Mrs. Davis insisted, and she found extra clothing from Victor's closet for Kenji Nishima.

Mrs. Davis carefully considered Hana's situation now. Her first thought was to suggest that Kenji Nishima be given professional care, perhaps at some institution. But she knew the concerned care provided in Hana's home far outweighed the advantages of professional scrutiny in a cold institution.

"Perhaps if you could find some way for him to help you," she suggested now. "I'm sure that would be helpful therapy for him. It would be good for him to feel useful."

Hana knew Mrs. Davis was right, but what could she ask Mr. Nishima to do? Surely, she couldn't ask him to clean or wash or mend or cook. There was only one thing, but Hana wasn't ready to let him do that yet. She didn't quite trust him to watch Mary while she went out on an errand, and surely not while she went to work.

Then one afternoon, Kenji Nishima unexpectedly put her to the test. Hana was baking a cake when he came into the kitchen to ask, "Do you think I might take Mary out to the park in her buggy? It's such a beautiful day."

Hana saw the eagerness in his face. She knew he often talked to Mary as she played in her play pen, and had heard him answer Mary's inquiring sounds with tender affection.

She faltered, and yet she knew how much her trust

would mean to him. She also knew the fresh air would be good for them both.

Seeing her hesitate, he added, "I'll be very careful with her, Mrs. Takeda. I won't let anything happen to her."

"All right then," she agreed at last. "But be back in an hour, won't you?"

Nishima promised he would, and Hana watched him wheel the buggy toward the park three blocks away. She finished her cake, put it in the oven and sat in the living room to mend some socks.

The afternoon was warm and without a breeze. Hana opened the window and heard the voices of children shouting and laughing. She darned two socks, but found herself glancing at the clock every five minutes. Finally, she put away the darning and read again the letter that had come from Kiku that morning.

"You should see me now," Kiku wrote in a large sloping hand, the Japanese characters tumbling down the page like scrambling black spiders. "I'm as brown as the field hands and have gained fifteen pounds since you last saw me. It's partly from all the food I eat, but also because, at last, I'm about to give Henry the child he's been longing for. Isn't that a surprise? Henry is elated and wants me to have five more. I'm still working in the packing shed, but will have to stop working in the fields soon."

Hana smiled as she read the letter. So Kiku was going to become a mother at last. It was hard to picture her nursing a child, but it was equally hard to think of her rising at dawn to work in the fields. She had said her hands were now like tree bark, but Hana thought the same of her own, red and roughened from washing, ironing and cleaning for two families.

Hana rarely wrote letters now, even to Japan, for there was so little time. When there was, she was too weary. Today, however, she felt impelled to write Kiku, knowing this would occupy her pleasantly until the cake was done and Mr. Nishima returned with Mary.

She filled six blue-lined pages of her tablet telling Kiku about recent happenings and of her great joy at Kiku's good news. Before she ended the letter, she wrote of Taro's shop.

"Since I no longer help him, I'm not sure how things are going," she confessed. "Taro doesn't talk to me about his business, and lately, I have wondered whether all is well. He doesn't bring home as many cans of bamboo shoot and eel as he once did, and some days he has such an air of defeat about him."

Hana put down the pen and thought about what she had just written. She must talk to Taro soon and ask about the shop. She had been so preoccupied with caring for Mary, going to work, and now looking after Kenji Nishima as well, that often Taro was relegated to the fringes of her life. Even if all was not well, however, Taro probably would not tell her, for he still seemed to think of her as a child and often treated her as one.

Hana put the letter in an envelope, addressed it, and went to the kitchen to take her cake from the oven. She glanced at the clock again. It was time they were back. She went to the front porch and shading her eyes, watched for the sight of Nishima wheeling the buggy back. But he did not come. When a half hour passed and still they had not returned, she knew she had to go to the park.

Not even bothering to lock the front door, she ran all the way, her heart pounding, her mouth dry with anxiety. Perhaps she had been foolish to trust him so soon. Taro would never forgive her if she let anything happen to their Mary.

She reached the park and hurried toward a cluster

of trees that sheltered a circle of benches. There, she saw Nishima sitting on a bench, leaning over Mary, who sat placidly in her buggy holding an enormous ice cream cone in her tiny hand. Not knowing what to make of this unfamiliar largesse, she sat grinning and cooing as the ice cream slowly dripped all over her clothes. Nishima seemed to be urging her to lick it, puzzled that she didn't know how.

Limp with relief, Hana stopped, smiling at the sight of her child. Instinctively, she felt for the handkerchief in her pocket. But as she did, she saw Nishima take his own handkerchief and carefully wipe her child's face. He finally threw the cone in the trash bin, wet his handkerchief at the water fountain and did his best to get Mary clean.

Watching his tender attentions to Mary, who obviously was having a fine time, Hana struggled to overcome her impulse to help him. She knew he would be distressed to know she felt it necessary to come fetch them, and he would probably be embarrassed at the mess he was making of Mary.

Hana decided to leave them alone, and hurried home before he saw her. She had time only to mend another of Taro's socks when she heard the sound of the buggy being pushed up on the porch. Nishima came inside carrying Mary in his arms, both of them beaming, flushed from the sun, and covered with drippings of chocolate ice cream.

"We had a fine time in the park, Mary and I," he said enthusiastically. And for the first time since he had come to their home, Hana glimpsed again the Kenji Nishima she had seen when he taught the Sunday School children to sing.

That night, Hana couldn't wait to tell Taro of all that had taken place.

"I think we've turned the corner," she said beaming. "I think he's finally getting better. It was just the right thing to let him take Mary out this afternoon, don't you think?"

Hana looked at Taro, waiting for him to share her pleasure at the afternoon's outcome and to commend her for her success. But Taro seemed preoccupied and scarcely seemed to hear her.

"I'm glad, Hana," he said absently.

"But don't you think it's wonderful?"

"I said I was glad, Hana," he said, and tossing the newspaper aside, he rose abruptly and went to bed.

Chapter 16

Hana spread some old newspapers on the floor and sat on her haunches to clean her vegetables. Even now the habit of living and working on the floor had not left her, for in Japan the floor was the ever-accommodating area that supported most of their activities, and she still felt most at home working close to it.

As she scraped burdock root and carrots for their supper, she could hear the sounds of Mary and Nishima conversing in their own special language. After the first day in the park, Nishima began to take Mary out every afternoon, at first for only a half-hour and then for longer periods. It was a fine arrangement, for they came back happy, relaxed and brown from the sun, and Hana had some time to herself. But more important, Mary seemed to be giving Kenji Nishima new life and energy and hope.

As Nishima improved, however, Hana had a new concern, for now it was Taro who seemed to be slipping into morose sullenness.

Each evening she would ask, "Is everything going well at the shop?"

Taro would nod and answer, "Yes, it is the same as always."

One day, however, Hana could no longer be satisfied with his bland replies. "I know something is troubling you, Taro," she said flatly, "and if something is wrong, I want to know what it is. After all, I am your wife."

Taro looked at Hana with a sad half-smile. "Yes, you

are, Hana. You are my wife." With a long sigh, he sat down heavily and drew out his words with reluctance. "As a matter of fact, nothing is going well. The new owner has raised my rent, my sales are dwindling, I'm three months behind on my water and light bill, and I owe money to at least five of my suppliers."

Hana couldn't believe what she had heard. Taro had not once spoken to her of being in debt, nor had he bothered to tell her that the building had been sold to a new owner.

"Why didn't you tell me?" she asked, astounded.

Instead of answering her, Taro simply said, "What's the use of it all, Hana? I think I'll just give up the shop and go find a job where I can earn some money. I'm tired of trying to run a shop that brings me nothing but misery and debt."

"Give up the shop!" Hana cried out. "What are you saying? The shop is your life. You can't give it up. I won't have you going back to sweeping floors and washing windows."

Taro looked down at his hands. "What would you have me do then? I must have four hundred dollars before the end of the month or I can't go on."

Where would they ever find four hundred dollars by the end of the month? They didn't even have fifty in their savings account, and Hana, innocently ignorant of Taro's difficulties, had not kept close track of her daily household expenses. Since Nishima had come, she couldn't help but spend more on food, even though the church helped when it could with money from the dormitory fund. How could Taro have gone on for so long concealing such troubles, she wondered.

"Why didn't you tell me?" she asked again. "Why did you keep it from me for so long?"

"Because you've been too busy with your work, with Mary . . . with Nishima."

So that was it. It had never occurred to her that

Taro would resent her efforts on behalf of Nishima, or think that her feelings for him were anything more than purely maternal. Hana was stunned to realize now that the early doubts of their marriage had come back to haunt him. Poor Taro. She had given too little thought to him as a man and thought of him only as Mary's father.

"Oh, Taro," she said limply, "I might have helped."

"How?"

How indeed. With the pittance she earned each week? Hana had no easy reply and said only, "I could at least have shared your anxiety, as any good wife would."

Taro ignored her remark.

"Have you talked to Dr. Kaneda?"

"Yes."

Long before he had even thought of telling Hana, Taro had gone to Kaneda to seek his advice. The two men had sat together at the table in Kaneda's flat and Taro had spread his books before him to show how things stood at his shop.

Kaneda suggested one of the Japanese cooperative credit clubs. "Have you tried the *tanomoshi*?"

"I've already borrowed from them, and can't pay back my loan or even the interest on it."

Dr. Kaneda knew the American banks would consider Taro and his shop a poor risk, scarcely worth an investment on their part. He decided not to mention them.

"There is your hometown association," Kaneda suggested, but even as he did, he knew the *kenjinkai* was no solution. Taro didn't like to join groups. Even in the early days, when the Japanese clustered together for mutual support, the only group Taro joined was the church. Taro was independent and he was a loner. Kaneda knew, too, that beneath his affable exterior, he was a proud and sometimes stubborn man.

"You must find someone willing to lend you the money," Kaneda said urgently. "You must never think of giving up your shop." But the two men had parted that night with no solution in sight.

Now there seemed only one way. Taro felt too overwhelmed by his circumstances even to fight for his shop.

"But what are we to do?" Hana persisted. In her desperate eagerness to solve his dilemma, she said, "I could ask Mrs. Davis. I know she would lend you the money."

Hana was startled by the vehemence of Taro's response. He grabbed her by the shoulders with such force that her head spun, and looking firmly in her eyes said, "Don't you *ever* do that, Hana. Never."

Hana didn't understand. "But why?" she asked. "You would pay it back."

"I have some pride," Taro shot back at her, anger flashing from his eyes.

"I know that."

"You . . . you know nothing!" Taro shouted and stormed out of the room.

Hana had seldom seen Taro so angry. She knew it was his anxiety that made him lash out at her, but still she did not totally understand. Was it because Mrs. Davis was an outsider, a *gaijin*? Was it because Taro couldn't bear to have his wife obtain a loan for him, because he would then be less of a man? Or had his anger been simmering unspoken all these weeks because of Nishima's presence in their home, and only now had boiled over?

"I just wanted to help," she murmured to herself, and a feeling of anger edged into the frustration and bewilderment that flooded over her.

When she went to their bedroom to look in on Mary, she saw that the door to Nishima's room was ajar. He has heard, she thought dismally. He has heard us quarreling, and she was ashamed to have revealed that ugly side of their life to him, not only because she felt his life was geared to a higher plane, but because she didn't want to disappoint him.

Of all the people at church, she felt that Kenji Nishima was the one person who treated her with respect. Perhaps it was because they were both "outsiders," who had not been there at the beginning when the others had worked and sacrificed together to build their church. Or perhaps it was because he had not known Kiyoshi Yamaka or of her love for him. Hana was never sure who at church knew, but she still felt diminished whenever she was in the presence of those who had known Yamaka.

Kenji Nishima made her feel like a lady, and did not treat her as a child. Once when he was reading the Bible, he had asked what she thought of a passage in the book of John.

"I'm not sure," Hana had replied, surprised that he should ask her. "You are much more learned about such things. Now if you asked me how to wash or cook a meal or clean a house, I could tell you all about that."

Hana never forgot what Kenji Nishima had answered. "You must not think less of yourself because you do housework, Mrs. Takeda. God has given you a good mind. You should treasure it and use it."

Hana hadn't given much thought to her mind. It was there. It was filled these days with useless anxieties. She had no time any more even to read a book.

The next morning, after Taro had gone to work, Hana decided to forget her shame and tell Nishima everything. He listened thoughtfully and was silent for so long, Hana was afraid she had pushed him back into his depression.

At last he said, "If you think Mrs. Davis would be willing to give him a loan, then we must find a way to enable Mr. Takeda to accept her help."

Nishima knew how it was with Taro Takeda. It wasn't easy for a Japanese man to keep his pride in this land where he was so often treated as something inferior and unworthy. He could understand why Taro would not want his wife to humble herself before Mrs. Davis by requesting a loan for him. A man wanted to be strong, especially in the eyes of the outside world.

Together, Nishima and Hana pondered Taro's problem. Then somehow, suddenly, it all came clear.

"Mrs. Davis was telling me she wanted her house painted," Hana began. "It would be a big job, but if Taro could do it, he could earn sixty dollars cash."

"I could help him," Nishima volunteered.

"And I could watch the shop for him," Hana said with growing excitement.

"Perhaps that is your answer then."

That was the solution. Hana would change places with Taro for a while. She would become the keeper of the shop, and Taro would work outside where he could earn more cash than she.

"That's the perfect solution," Nishima agreed. "It's the answer for me too, for I know I've been a burden. This would enable me to repay my great debt to you both."

Hana was elated as she made her plans. She spoke first to Mrs. Davis, who was perfectly agreeable and asked only that Hana find someone to come in her place for the housework. The minister's wife, who could use the extra money, said she would be happy to help Mrs. Davis for a while.

"Please don't mention this to anyone yet, Mrs. Okada," Hana whispered. "I haven't told Taro yet. I must think carefully before I speak of it to him."

"Of course," Mrs. Okada nodded. "There are things I have done, too, without the knowledge of my husband."

Hana was surprised. "You have kept things from Reverend Okada?"

"It is not easy to feed three children on a minister's salary," Mrs. Okada confided. "I had rings and hair ornaments and brocade sashes I knew I would never use again. I sold them to put food on our table more than once, but I hadn't the heart to tell my husband."

"And if ever he finds out?"

Mrs. Okada looked pensive. "I have never told him with words," she said, "but it is possible he already knows and hasn't spoken of it to me. As long as we each think the other doesn't know, we can keep a brave face." She smiled then, saying, "Isn't it foolish what we do to each other? But I suppose respect and love makes it possible."

Hana wondered if Taro had enough love or respect for her to understand what she was doing.

Carefully, choosing just the right moment of the day, using words that would not anger him, Hana edged Taro into her plan. First she suggested the possibility of working in the shop while he looked outside for work that would bring in some immediate cash. When he agreed to that, she told him that Mrs. Davis was looking for someone to paint her house. Nishima then asked if he might help, explaining his need to do something physical and to be useful.

Working together like a pair of conspirators, Nishima and Hana persuaded Taro to accept their plan. He seemed unaware of their complicity, but if he did know, he did not speak of it.

Perhaps, Hana thought, he was too desperate to struggle any longer or to have any more pride, but if that was it, she did not want to hear him say those words.

Chapter 17

Under the new arrangement, Taro and Nishima went off each morning in their work clothes to paint, while Hana took Mary on the streetcar to Taro's shop. It had been a long time since she spent her days there and seeing it now, with fresh eyes, she could see why sales were dropping.

"I think we ought to do away with those bolts of cloth and sewing things that nobody buys," she suggested, "and put in more foodstuff that people use every day."

"All right," Taro said wearily, "go ahead and try." Spattered with paint, his back and neck aching from unfamiliar work, Taro agreed to anything Hana proposed at the end of the day.

The sight of Hana working in the shop with little Mary at her side softened the hearts of Taro's suppliers. They extended their credit, and Hana promptly ordered a wider variety of Japanese food and canned goods. She also stocked pieces of barbecued pork, whose tempting aroma no one could resist. She opened a new section of toys and candy to attract new clientele with growing families, and she also added the latest Japanese magazines and periodicals. Soon her feminine touch and presence began to attract housewives other than the loyal church women, and customers came in a steady, increasing stream.

Hana now looked forward to each day as she had not done in many years. She was consumed with ideas, exhilarated as sales increased and new life emerged in Taro's once drab shop. Bending over the abacus, she learned how to keep Taro's books and saw with joy the beginning of some profits.

When Taro and Nishima finished painting the Davis house, they found another job down the street.

"We make a good pair," Nishima observed. "Maybe we should go into permanent partnership as Takeda and Nishima, Painters."

"Good," Hana added, "and I'll become permanent manager of Takeda's Dry Goods and Grocers."

She looked up with laughter still in her eyes. Nishima was laughing with her, but Taro looked alarmed.

"I was only joking, Taro," she said quickly. "You know I could never manage the shop as you've done." And she went to the victrola to put on the record of Mme. Schumann-Heink that Mrs. Davis had given her. Hana always found it comforting to listen to that rich full voice embracing them in song.

Summer was almost over, and Kenji would soon return to the seminary, healthy and confident that he could resume his studies. Hana was pleased. She felt as though she had saved a life; as though she had repaid a great debt that had weighed her down for so long with the burden of guilt. Perhaps, she thought, God would now forgive her. But she wasn't sure if Taro ever could. Although he shared her joy at Nishima's recovery, Hana couldn't forget the doubts and resentment he had revealed in those moments of anger. Taro had never forgotten her one transgression, and perhaps he would never forgive her. With Taro she might never know. That was the pity of it all.

Some days, after Mary was put to bed and the house settled down to an evening quiet, there was time for lemonade and cookies. Often Sojiro Kaneda would stop by, bringing a carton of ice cream or a bag of jelly doughnuts. Then, if the warmth of the day lingered, they would go outside, sit on grass mats, and look up at the night sky.

Seeing the array of stars parading across the darkness, Hana would slip back in memory to summer evenings in Oka Village, remembering how, after a steaming bath, she would put on her cotton kimono and slip into her wooden clogs. She and her sisters would walk along the dark paths by the rice paddies, thick with the small croakings of frogs. They would chase the lightning flashes of fireflies, trapping them with nets and cages until they flickered away their tiny lives.

What was it about summer that made one long for the past? She could almost feel its sounds and smells: the smoke of evening fires drifting to them across open fields; the sound of the breeze filtering through the wind chimes; the incessant buzzing of cicadas sounding like demented musicians who couldn't stop playing.

The men, too, seemed to yearn for their childhood summers, and Hana listened as they recalled their youthful adventures. There was longing in their voices for a peace and contentment long gone.

Even as she thought of the past, however, the present pressed close.

"Are things going well at the shop now?" she heard Dr. Kaneda ask Taro.

"Yes," he answered, "with Nishima's help I've earned enough to begin paying my debts, and Hana has done a fine job of improving the shop. Perhaps . . ." he began, looking at her, "perhaps in the fall, we can work together at the shop and make it successful again."

"You mean I could work for you instead of Mrs. Davis?" Hana asked eagerly.

"Work *with* me, Hana, not *for* me," Taro corrected. "But you will be the assistant, not the manager." He grinned at her.

Hana smiled back. "I'd like that," she said. Maybe it was going to be all right with her and Taro after all.

Kaneda seemed relieved. "Then all is well," he said with a long sigh. "And Nishima, it will go well for you, too. You are going to be a fine minister someday, I know."

"I hope so," Nishima answered, and then, like a benediction to the day and to the summer as well, he said softly, "God bless this home."

It was as though he were already living in a time yet to come and knew that Taro and Hana would need this blessing.

Chapter 18

1930–1940

A week of cold spring rain had nourished the growing things in Hana's garden and left the new green of the maple tree quivering with a thousand glistening drops. She saw with delight that everything seemed ready to burst into bloom at the first sign of warmth. The buds on the roses were swelling with life and the azaleas were already blooming recklessly beneath the generous foliage of the rhododendron bush.

It seemed a time of renewal and growth, and watching her daughter, Hana felt a special tenderness as she realized that Mary's childhood was slipping away. Only yesterday, it seemed she was an infant and now already she was ten.

Mary Yukari was a pale, thin child, with dark uneven bangs in a dutch bob that her father trimmed every two weeks. She had a delicate face with wide double-lidded eyes like Hana's, a thin nose and Taro's full mouth. Her knobby knees were usually scarred from falling while roller skating or scraped from climbing the trees in the backyard.

Taro had wanted another child. "An only child is not good," he protested, but Hana was incapable of giving him another. She had had two miscarriages and now at last, Taro was resigned.

"She is only one, but she is a good one," he said, and he no longer spoke of the son who died at birth or of the others he could not have.

"Next week is Easter vacation, Mama," Mary announced noisily as she came home from school. "Are we ever, ever going any place for a vacation?"

During all the years of their marriage, Hana and Taro had never taken a vacation because of the shop. Dr. Kaneda offered to look after it for them, but Taro always found one reason or another for not going away.

"Everybody goes some place in the summer," Mary pouted each year. "I hate saying 'nothing' when the teacher asks what we did during the summer."

"You could say that you helped your father in his shop," Hana informed her. "After all," she added, "there is nothing shameful about being a dutiful child and working instead of playing all summer."

Someday, when Taro had accumulated enough money, he hoped to put a down payment on the shop and buy it in Mary's name. Because she was an American citizen, she could own property, even though her Asian parents could not.

From the time she was seven, Mary had learned to help at her father's shop. And in the summer, she could be quite useful, especially on the days her mother went to work for Mrs. Davis who had begged Hana to come back. By now housework came easily to Hana and she wanted to earn extra money to put toward Mary's college fund. Besides, going to Mrs. Davis's was a change, and sometimes Hana even looked forward to the days she spent with Mary's "white person godmother."

What Mary most looked forward to were the

Sunday afternoon picnics at Lake Merritt. She would help her mother pack the hamper early Sunday morning, putting in a thermos of tea, some small lacquer dishes, chopsticks, napkins and a box filled with rice balls and *teriyaki* chicken.

The hardest part of the day for Mary came after Sunday School when she had to amuse herself until the adult service ended. Sometimes there were friends with whom she played jacks or marbles, but often she sat in the back of her papa's car and read by herself. As soon as she heard the notes of the Doxology, she ran inside to hurry her mother along. The weekly exchange of greetings seemed interminable, and if her mother were immersed in conversation, Mary went to her father.

"Come on, Papa," she would urge. And Taro usually responded to the persistent tugging of his sleeve.

"Always in a hurry, aren't you, Ma Chan?" Dr. Kaneda would say, and Mary would confide, "We're going on a picnic today. Want to come?"

"Of course. Don't I always come?"

"Well then, let's go," and she would tug at his sleeve as well.

At the park, Mary would turn her back to the adult chatter, watch the boats on the lake and munch silently on Mama's chicken.

Sometimes her father and Dr. Kaneda would rent a row boat and take Mary out to the middle of the lake. She loved looking back at the land, seeing the grass and the bending trees and the bright colors of running children. When she spotted her mother, Mary would shout and wave until Taro told her to sit still, and Hana, seeing her about to upset the boat, would wave back, frantically motioning for her to sit down. As she watched her daughter, Hana wondered, as she often did, what her son would have been like had he lived.

Now, as Mary spoke of Easter vacation, Hana was able to give her more than a Sunday picnic to look forward to. "How would you like to go to Livingston this summer to visit Mr. and Mrs. Toda?"

"You mean a real, honest-to-goodness vacation?"

"Maybe for a whole week. Your papa said he had saved enough to consider closing the shop this summer so we could all drive down."

Kiku and Henry now had two sons and had bought a small farm in their boys' names. As soon as they were settled, Kiku had written to Hana inviting them to come visit. "The country air would do you all good," she wrote. "I'll fatten you up with some country cooking, and my boys would enjoy getting to know Mary. It's time they were introduced to a little civilized female company."

Mary wrinkled her nose at the mention of Kiku's boys. They were only eight and nine and would surely make life a misery for her. Still, she couldn't resist the idea of a real vacation on a farm, for she knew Kiku had two mules, a dog, a cat and some chickens.

Mary didn't have to give the matter much thought. "Let's go, Mama. Let's go," she urged, and she talked of nothing else for days.

The prospect of going on a week's vacation excited Hana and Taro as well. They hadn't seen the Todas since they moved, but still they remained two of their closest friends, for they were the parents of their own days of beginning.

As summer approached, Mary asked each day, "When will we go, Papa? When will we go to Livingston?"

Pressed by Mary on one hand and by Hana on the other, Taro finally decided to go during the first week of July to take advantage of the July Fourth holiday. Hana wrote immediately to Kiku, and now for her too, the thought of the trip was a constant delight.

Early on the morning of the first, they set out for Livingston, their car laden with luggage and gifts of Japanese delicacies from Taro's shop. Hana repeatedly checked every window of their house before they left, fearing that burglars would ransack their home the moment they took off. She hammered nails into the window sashes and tied a string around the back door key so it couldn't be dislodged from its hole.

Taro, too, was uneasy about leaving his shop unattended, even though Dr. Kaneda had promised to stop by each day. He insisted on driving by Seventh Street for one final look before they headed for the highway.

Sitting in the back seat with the bundles and luggage, Mary was brimming with excitement. "Has our vacation started now?" she asked as they drove away from the shop. "Are we really going now?" She stared eagerly as familiar streets faded behind her, and before long, wide fields of lettuce, celery, asparagus and spinach stretched out beside the road.

"Look Mama! Look at the horses. What's that, Papa? What's all that stuff growing out there? Oh, look, there're some cows."

She couldn't wait for an answer, immediately seeing something else that required her attention. She read aloud all the Burma Shave signs that dotted the roadside, and kept up a constant stream of chatter that exasperated Hana. As Mary began to clamor for food, they finally came to the gas station where they were to turn left toward the vineyards of Livingston.

"Thank goodness," Hana murmured wearily.

Now they followed a rough dirt road, bumping along between rows of grapevines heavy with fruit. The dust of the road streamed into the car and clung to their faces. Mary coughed noisily, and Hana held a handkerchief to her nose.

As they came to a cluster of tin mailboxes signaling

the road to the Toda farm, Mary shouted, "Papa, Papa! Something's on fire! Something's burning!"

"I smell it too," Hana said, sniffing. "It smells like burning rubber."

Taro was too close to his destination to stop. "We'll be there in a minute," he said, pressing on down the road. When he saw the small farmhouse standing beneath the water tower he honked the horn.

As Kiku and her boys ran from the house, Kiku took off her small apron and waved it like a flag, signaling them on.

"There's Kiku," Hana cried eagerly.

"Papa, we're on fire. The car's burning!" Mary shouted.

Taro smelled the burning rubber too, and turned to locate its source.

"Watch out for the dog house," Hana called.

But it was too late. With a resounding crash that brought Henry running from the fields, Taro smashed into the dog house, coming to a halt at the clearing in front of the house, his car engulfed in billowing black smoke.

Disturbed in their peaceful scratching, the chickens screeched in alarm, fluttering in every direction. The dog barked furiously at the intruders who had demolished his house, and Kiku's boys charged toward them like two wild animals.

Kiku was right behind them, laughing and crying, calling, "Welcome, welcome! But you didn't have to set yourselves on fire to attract our attention."

"It's the brakes," Taro shouted at Henry, throwing sand at the flames that spurted from his tires. "I guess the garage tightened them too much."

The two boys were eager to help, throwing fistfuls of dirt and sand, first at the smoldering fire and then at each other. "We're putting out the fire, Pa," they shouted. Seeing them, Mary knew at once that they were going to be more of a nuisance than she had ever imagined.

In the hot, lazy afternoon, the adults gathered around the table in the sitting room. Above it hung a roll of fly paper studded with innumerable black corpses.

"Oh, Kiku, it's so good to be here," Hana said, and Kiku demonstrated her own joy at seeing Hana and Taro by bringing from the kitchen an unending stream of food. They had just finished lunch, but she appeared now with a fresh pot of tea and plates of sweet bean paste cakes and rice crackers.

"Don't tell me you're bringing out more food," Taro protested.

"You've already gone to so much trouble for us," Hana added.

Kiku waved aside their objections. "This is just talking food now, while we get caught up."

Henry was the first to begin reminiscing, recalling the day Hana arrived from Japan. "You were just about the prettiest young thing I ever saw from back home," he teased, making Hana blush as he always did.

The boys had long since left the house. Now Mary, too, slipped away, unnoticed by the adults who drifted eagerly into the evanescent past. She was quite accustomed to amusing herself, and she set out to inspect the farm alone. She looked at the vegetable garden beside the house where Kiku grew corn and beans and tomatoes. She peered into the chicken house where some gray hens were making small conversation, and she cautiously fed weeds to the mules as she poked about the barn with its smell of animals and hay. She found Rick, the old sheep dog, lying in the shade of the walnut tree. He thumped his tail as she felt his cold wet nose and scratched his throat, and Mary felt such a longing for a dog of her own that she knew she'd ask for one at Christmas time.

Mary stood in the hot summer sun, looking out at the vineyards that seemed to stretch for miles on end. Maybe they went on forever, she thought. She listened to the stillness all around, and suddenly shouted at the top of her voice. "Kenny! Jimmy! Where are you?"

But there was no answer. They had vanished into the summer afternoon, and the sun beat down on her head like a silent throbbing drum.

"I don't want to see you anyway," Mary muttered, as she left to look for the cat.

The boys didn't appear until supper time, when they came home covered with sweat and dust, grinning happily at their afternoon's adventures.

"We went swimming in the ditch," they announced.

"Look at you!" Kiku admonished. "Not even inviting Mary to go with you, and filthy as two tramps. Go wash yourselves at the pump."

Mary was startled to see them rush to the pump, shake off their swimming trunks and douse each other with buckets of cold water, not caring if all the world saw their nakedness.

Kiku soon forgot them and turned her attention to supper, which they were having outside on mats laid beneath the walnut tree. Hana carried out the dishes and silverware, and Henry barbecued some chicken over hot charcoals. Soon the mouth-watering smell of chicken and soy sauce drifted across the yard, and stray hens came clucking to peck at the broiling meat, unaware it was one of their own they tried to eat.

"Hey, you dumb chickens. Watch out," Kenny shouted. "That might be your brother you're eating."

"Or your cousin," Jimmy shouted. And shrieking with laughter, they stamped to shoo the chickens away.

Kiku emerged from the kitchen bearing platters of

steaming corn glistening with butter, thick slices of ham and an enormous salad of greens and tomatoes from her garden. For dessert, there was apple pie with ice cream that Henry had just cranked up.

It was as though she were trying in this one meal to make up for all the years they hadn't seen one another, and for Hana, it was like a homecoming. Kiku and Henry were her only extended family in America, and she savored fully every moment of her time with them. Watching Kiku, she was suddenly engulfed with thoughts of her mother and sisters, and tears of longing and memory filled her eyes. Even Taro forgot about his shop and allowed himself to relax in the easy comfort of the day.

With their stomachs filled, the boys quieted down, and as the dusky evening settled into night, they stretched out on the mat, contemplating their toes.

Henry lit the kerosene lamp and leaned back on an old crate. "The sight of a moon rising over the fields can bring out a song in a man," he remarked. Then, closing his eyes like a dog baying at the moon, he sang in a high nasal voice.

> *"Kiso no Nakanori San,*
> *Kiso no Ontake San wa nanjara hoi,*
> *Natsu demo samui, yoi yoi yoi*
> *Yoi yoi yoi no yoi yoi yoi . . ."*

Taro soon joined in, as the women and children clapped to the beat of the music.

"Yoi yoi yoi no yoi yoi yoi," the boys shouted.

Hana closed her eyes to hold onto the feeling of utter contentment, but she was soon aware that Kiku was speaking to her.

"I work like an old army horse," she was saying with her quick easy laugh, "but when I go to sleep it's with a weariness in my bones and not in my head."

"That's good, Kiku," Hana said. "There's room for one's soul to stretch out in this kind of peace."

As she looked at the lemon-wedge moon climbing into the dark sky, she heard the eager young voice of her daughter saying, "No, you're wrong, Kenny. There're a million, zillion stars up there." And glancing over, she was pleased to see Mary stretched out head to head beside the Toda boys as they looked up at the glorious night sky.

Chapter 19

Looking back on her vacation, Mary couldn't say which day she liked best, for each seemed better than the one before. Every morning, when the crowing of the rooster brushed away her sleep, she stretched on the cot in the corner of the attic and pinched herself to see if she were truly having a vacation on a farm.

It was impossible to linger in bed. Hurrying into her shirt and overalls, she ran out to the pump to wash her face with cold spring water. She then made a quick tour of the farm, talking softly to each of the animals, but lingering longest with the dog, Rick, whom she liked best. She rolled him over and searched for fleas as the boys had taught her to do, squeezing those she caught with her fingernails, hearing the tiny pop and finding a bit of blood left on her thumbnail. She wondered whose blood it was. Probably hers, for small red welts from flea bites ringed her ankles above her socks.

If she got up early enough, Mary would find Mr. Toda feeding the animals in the quiet of the country morning. Sometimes he would let her pitch hay down to the mules with an enormous fork bigger than she was.

"That's-a-girl," he would encourage her. "You'll make a fine farmer someday."

"Maybe that's what I'll do," she told Henry. "Maybe I'll marry a farmer and live the rest of my life on a farm, like you and Aunt Kiku."

Henry looked at her, wiping his forehead with a rumpled handkerchief. "Say," he said, "shall I save one of my boys for you then? Would you like to marry Kenny or Jimmy and live here raising grapes and peaches?"

That possibility had never crossed Mary's mind. "Golly, no!" she said, horrified. Then, in an attempt to be polite, she added, "I mean, no, thank you." And she fled to the house, as Henry Toda's laughter rang in the air behind her.

One day, Henry explained to her how they planted, irrigated, weeded and finally harvested and packed the grapes. Another day, he told her about the Tree of Paradise that grew near the barn.

"No matter how many times I cut down that darn tree, it comes right back up again. You know, trees are a lot like some people."

Mary didn't understand. "How?"

"The bad ones are the strongest and the good ones die young. Now take that Tree of Paradise. Those trees were planted years ago by the early Japanese pioneers who settled here when no one else would, because of the terrible dust and wind. But those people never gave up. If the wind tore up their seedlings or the dust buried them, they'd go right out and plant them again. They were patient and determined, and made the land fertile by their toil and sweat. They planted those trees for shade, not realizing they'd become a nuisance, but now I can't get rid of them."

"That's okay, Uncle Henry," Mary reassured him. "It's good to have lots of shade when it gets hot." And having given him that comforting thought, she ran off to help Kiku in the kitchen.

Thinking of their week in Livingston, pulling each day from her bundle of remembered thoughts, Mary guessed she liked the last evening best, even more than the Fourth of July picnic by the river.

That last night, there had been a full moon as big as

a beach ball suspended in a carnival sky.

"Say, let's hitch up the mules and go for a ride through the vineyards," Henry suggested.

"Keen!" Jimmy shouted.

"Swell!" Kenny agreed, as Kiku found some old blankets to spread out on the flat wagon.

"Is there room for the grownups too?" Hana asked, filled with a childish longing to be included.

"Of course," Kiku answered. "We can't let the children have all the fun. Come on."

They had all climbed on the wagon then, bouncing slowly over the dirt roads, singing every song they knew.

The boys sang "Old MacDonald had a Farm" at the top of their voices, and Mary sang thirteen verses with them until she had to stop for a sour lemon ball. Then, forgetting her usual shyness, she sang her favorite song.

"John Jacob Jingleheimer Schmidt,
That is my name, too.
Whenever we go out, the people always shout,
John Jacob Jingleheimer Schmidt, da da da
da da da da . . ."

It was a song that could be repeated endlessly, and Kenny and Jimmy learned it soon enough. Mary wanted to see how many times she could sing it without stopping, but Taro finally held up his hand saying, "Enough, enough. Give up, Mary." Then he surprised them all by singing, "In the Good Ol' Summer Time."

"Papa!" Mary said, amazed. It was the first time she'd ever heard him sing anything other than a hymn. And Hana, too, was pleasantly surprised to see Taro abandon his usual reserve.

Henry let Mary take the reins for a while, for the

old mules knew exactly where to go. They plodded along, their heads nodding, even though they had been taken out at an hour when they should have been dreaming in their hay-scented stalls.

By the time they jogged back to the farm, Kenny and Jimmy had fallen asleep. Mary lay stretched out on her back, listening to the quiet murmur of the adult voices, and as she watched the stars spin their lacy patterns in the night, she wished the ride would never end.

As soon as they were back at the farm, Kiku hurried from the wagon and filled the square tin tub with water, while Henry built a fire under it, banking it properly. An old bedspread was suspended between the fig tree and the clothesline pole, and the outdoor bath was ready. Making sure the wood float was in the tub, Kiku called to Mary, "All right, young lady, you're first."

"Mama, make sure nobody can see me," Mary called, washing and rinsing herself on the platform beside the tub in proper Japanese fashion. Climbing into the tub, she felt the rush of warm water as it gurgled and engulfed her. She sank down until the hot water touched her chin, then turned away from the house and the bedspread curtain, so she could see the vineyards stretching out in the quiet darkness.

Hana left her to soak and contemplate the country night in peace, and Mary, in watery grandeur, held her breath, listening to the insects of the fields uttering their small night cries. A cricket sang somewhere nearby, while a frog croaked in friendly conversation. Mary could have sat there all night, but Hana soon appeared to see that she got out so the others could have their turn.

Even after they returned to Oakland, there were nights when Mary would lie awake, remembering the night ride through the dusty fields, still warm with the daytime sun, and the hot bath in the moonlight afterwards. She would think about the picnics, and the farm animals, and the smell of bacon and eggs that drifted to her as she made her early morning tour of the farm. Then she would tell herself, "That was the best vacation I ever had in my whole, entire life."

"I'm going to have a zillion things to tell my teacher this time," Mary told her mother, looking forward to school mainly because of that simple pleasure.

For both Taro and Hana, the week in the country renewed their spirits and gave them strength. It was not only the country air, it was the exposure to the boisterous good spirits of the Toda family. Kiku and Henry were sunburned, healthy and vigorous, and there was no more *sake* on their table. They had gained weight, but not flaccid flesh and muscle. They seemed, somehow, totally at peace from having come to terms with the earth and the elements.

"You can't argue with the sun or the wind or the rain," Henry had said. "You must learn to bow your head and accept gratefully the fruits of the soil."

Hana wondered if she could have adjusted to such a life as easily as Kiku. She wondered if Kiku was ever as lonely as she sometimes was; as many Japanese, never more than unwelcome intruders in this land, were. Hana now spoke to a few of her neighbors, but none were close friends. She never went to a store without wondering if the clerks would ignore or humiliate her because she was Asian. She never spoke to a white person, unless she was first spoken to, for fear of being rebuffed. She could never be completely herself. It was as though she were going through life pressed down, apologetic, making herself small and inconspicuous, never able to reach out or to feel completely fulfilled. What kind of woman would she have been in her native land, she wondered. Would she have been different? More the self she really was? Suppose she had become the teacher in Tokyo she had once longed to be. Would her life have been more rewarding than this spinning out of her days in a land whose language she still struggled to conquer? Or might she have been stifled in another way?

For those few days in Livingston, she had felt completely removed from the restrictions of her city life. There were no white neighbors whom she might offend with some ingenuous act or remark. There were only the friendly vineyards that caused no apprehension. The Toda farm seemed a small world of its own, although she knew that beyond its confines there were still unfriendly white men who resented the Japanese presence in their community.

The free, easy life of the farm was mirrored in the manner of the two Toda children. They were growing up with complete abandon, unhampered by anxiety, with reservoirs of ready energy stored in their lithe brown bodies. Next to them, Mary appeared pale, fragile and suppressed. There was more to it than the fact that she was a girl and a child of the city.

Mary, like many young Nisei, was being reared to be a well-mannered and reserved child; to apply herself at school with diligence so she would be among the outstanding pupils. Hana and Taro, perhaps almost unconsciously, felt it important for Mary to excel, because of pride in their race, because they must dispel the notion that they were inferior people. Always they encouraged her to be good, obedient and docile. Always they told her to study hard so she would become a law-abiding citizen, who would one day be accepted and integrated into the fabric of white American society.

Kiku and Henry, on the other hand, didn't seem encumbered by such complex insecurities. Perhaps it was because of their life in the country. Perhaps it was just because they were Henry and Kiku.

Hana wondered if she might be doing Mary an

injustice, and came home determined to emulate Kiku's easy going ways and relaxed attitudes. But the moment she returned to her old surroundings, she felt again the same restrictions and tensions. Only in her own small circle of Japanese friends did she feel safe and at ease.

"Do you have many friends outside the Japanese community?" Mrs. Davis asked her one day. Seeing Hana's embarrassment, she quickly added, "I was thinking about your daughter. She'll soon be in her teens and she is totally American. The more you know of her country and her language, Hana, the more you will know your daughter."

Hana knew she was absolutely right. It was a thought that had entered her mind more than once. "I know," she murmured. "Yes, I know." And yet she avoided facing that irrevocable fact.

Hana tried to have longer conversations in English with Mrs. Davis, who encouraged her efforts. Still, Hana would never dream of discussing the secret yearnings of her heart with her, for she could not even express such thoughts in Japanese to Taro.

Already she didn't understand many things Mary said to her in English, and had to have them explained in Japanese. As her daughter grew older, however, Hana knew Mary would be inclined to discard her Japanese. Then how would they communicate?

"I must study English so I can talk more with Mary," Hana confessed to Taro, and she sought his help, trying to learn from his old high school English books.

But most evenings, Hana was too tired, or Taro was busy with his bookkeeping. So she slipped into the habit of reading only Japanese books and magazines, getting the day's news from Japanese language dailies, while her text books remained unopened.

"I do talk more with Mrs. Davis," she said to Taro one evening. "Don't you think that's enough practice each week?"

Taro knew Hana wanted him to agree with her. Not wanting to begin an argument, he said simply, "You do have much work to do, Hana. I don't think you need tax yourself further with studying English."

Hana felt as though she had been excused like a good child. She put away Taro's English text books, promised herself that one day she would get back to them, and felt no further proddings of guilt.

Chapter 20

Mary often wished her father were not quite so conscientious about his duties at church. They were often the first to arrive on Sundays so Taro could stoke the furnace in winter, open the windows in summer, and see that a hymnal and Bible were at each seat. They also participated in every activity of the church, most of which Mary could have done without.

The cause of Mary's distress on the Sunday before Armistice Day was the plan of the church members to visit the cemetery immediately after the services.

"Why do I have to go?" Mary complained.

"Because there isn't time for Papa to take you home first. Just come along, Ma Chan. You can wait in the car," Hana told her. "The service at the cemetery will be very short. All right?"

It wasn't all right. Mary knew about Reverend Okada's "short" services. She prepared herself by taking along a new mystery book from the library, but when they got to the cemetery, she slipped quickly from the car because there was one grave she wanted to visit. She carried the bouquet of red button chrysanthemums her mother had asked her to pick for her baby brother.

More than a dozen church members had come, and they made their way slowly toward the graves of those they knew. The men led the way, carrying the hymnals and Bibles, while the women followed with bouquets of homegrown flowers wrapped in newspaper.

Mary was the only child among them and she rushed ahead, wanting to be the first to find her brother's grave. Each time they came, it was more difficult to find, for there were always new headstones that made old landmarks appear different.

The wide lawn stretched off in a gentle slope, dotted with small American flags and flowers, the attempts of the living to cheer the dead in their long lonely sleep.

Mary paused occasionally to inspect a particularly attractive stone bearing a carved lamb or an angel, wishing her little brother could have had such a fine stone. She watched carefully so she would not miss the plain gray stone that marked his resting place. He must take up only a very tiny space on this lawn, she thought, for he had been so small when he died.

"Here he is, Mama. I found him," she shouted, kneeling and reading the words on the stone as though she were seeing them for the first time.

Baby Ichiro Takeda. Died at birth.
November 27, 1918.

She ran to the faucet to fill the metal container with water, and by the time her parents reached the grave, she had already put her bouquet in place. The others clustered about them, bowing and offering their own silent prayers.

"How old would he have been, Mrs. Takeda?"

"Twelve years this month."

"*Mah,* such a pity."

"Yes. Thank you."

Mary watched her mother kneel to brush away the dead leaves and pull out the weeds at the base of the stone. Hana touched the headstone with her hand, as though caressing her infant son. Mary did the same, patting the stone as she would a puppy's head. Then she took her mother's hand to comfort her. Her father simply bowed his head, prayed silently, and moved on to another grave, not daring to reveal the emotions that crowded his heart each time he came to visit his son's grave.

Mary stayed with her mother while she stopped at another nearby grave. It had a simple black head-stone, and Hana left some white chrysanthemums at its base.

Mary read the inscription aloud. "Kiyoshi Yamaka. Native of Japan. Born January 3, 1890. Died November 4, 1918."

"He died the same month as our baby," she remarked. "Was he a nice man, Mama?"

"Yes. He was very nice."

"Was he a good friend?"

"A very good friend," Hana answered, "of both your Papa's and mine."

Then Hana rose. She did not place her hand on this stone, however, and hurried to join the others who were performing similar gestures of devotion and remembrance at other graves. The group slowly gathered at a spot central to all the graves and formed a semi-circle, standing with heads bowed, hands folded.

Mary knew what was going to happen next and hurried back toward the car. She stepped carefully so she would not tread on anyone's bones. With the stones so close together, it was hard, she thought, not to step on someone's stomach or head. She took giant steps, zig-zagging across the grass, moving further and further away from the voices that were now straining toward the high notes of "Nearer My God to Thee."

Mary climbed into the back seat of their car and looked back at the somber gathering. The chill of winter was already in the air, and the men and women looked cold in their thin black coats, like a cluster of drab birds in a field that offered no nourishment or joy. Mary did not relate their being here to either life or death. It just seemed another function of the church, as though these few had come to sing hymns and read the Bible to old friends who could no longer come to church on Sundays.

When the adults returned to the cars, they were smiling and talking to one another, for they had left their mantles of solemnity covering the dead. This, after all, was not a new mourning, but simply a brief fellowship with departed friends on whose peaceful rest they did not want to intrude too long.

Their change in mood now was no more awkward than the serving of food and refreshments immediately following a funeral as an expression of appreciation to those who had come. Death, after all, was a part of life. It was accepted not with terror, but with a proper sense of respect, and because a continuing kinship with the dead was so real to the living, the transition from one aspect of life to the next was not seen as something grim.

Most of them still observed the Japanese custom of gathering on the anniversary of a family member's death. For many years, Hana and Taro held such gatherings for both their son and Kiyoshi Yamaka on special anniversaries of their death. The women of the church helped Hana prepare an elaborate array of food on such occasions.

"Is it a party?" Mary had asked the first time she was old enough to understand what it was about.

"Well, not exactly a party," Hana answered.

"But it seems like one," Mary observed.

The dining room table was extended to its full length with extra leaves and covered with Hana's best crocheted cloth. Taro borrowed folding chairs from the church and fresh flowers were placed in front of a faded snapshot of Mr. Yamaka. Since there was no photograph of the baby, Mary had drawn one with crayon so her mother could place flowers beside that portrait instead.

"We just want to remember Yamaka San and Baby Ichiro and cheer their spirits in Heaven," her mother had explained. "The food is to thank everyone for coming to help us remember them. Do you understand?"

"I think so," Mary answered, but she hadn't been quite sure. It was as though two people from the cemetery were coming to tea, but there was to be no sadness because they were all together, and because, for that brief span of time, they were all one.

Now as Mary waited for the graveside service to end, she popped a piece of chewing gum into her mouth. She was too hungry to sit quietly and read her book, so she sat on the running board of the car, chewing noisily.

She tried to will the minister to stop talking. She stared at him until tears came to her eyes. "Stop talking, Reverend Okada. Stop right now. Stop! Stop!" she pleaded.

A slight breeze swept over the grassy slope and a flurry of dried leaves scattered over the graves like a benediction. As the service finally ended, Mary watched Dr. Kaneda and her father gather the hymnals and Bibles. They walked quickly toward the cars, and Mary was glad that even adults, pious and devoted though they might be, still seemed to get hungry when it was past noon.

Her father smiled as he approached her. "You've had a long wait, Mary," he said gently. "Would you like to go eat some Chinese food?" He felt she deserved this bit of luxury today.

"Oh boy! I'm starving."

Seeing her mother approach with Dr. Kaneda and

Reverend and Mrs. Okada, Mary knew they would be coming with them. It was going to be a long lunch.

Mary ate quickly, anxious to leave when she had finished. But Reverend Okada was pouring himself another cup of tea and looked as though he were ready to sally forth with another sermon. Mary groaned silently. Was he filled from the top of his head to his big toe with words that poured constantly from his mouth, she wondered. She wriggled in her chair and pushed it back noisily.

"Are you ready to go, Ma Chan?" Dr. Kaneda asked sympathetically.

Mary nodded. But Reverend Okada had turned to her father and said, "Perhaps this is as good a time as any to tell all of you. Mrs. Okada and I have reached a decision we have been considering for some time."

Hana and Taro instinctively offered him the attention he always commanded at the pulpit, and Dr. Kaneda turned away from Mary.

"We have decided the time has come to return to Japan," the minister announced, "so our children might be educated in the ways of our home country. Our eldest son is already twelve and if we wait too much longer, he will forget how to speak Japanese."

Hana gasped at the unexpected news. Already she felt abandoned and could think of no proper words to say.

It was Dr. Kaneda who assured Reverend Okada that he understood their feelings, while Taro and Hana both nodded in agreement. Everyone at church knew, after all, that the minister had come not to settle in America, but as a temporary evangelist to sustain his people during their early years in a foreign land.

"We're all going to miss you," Taro said, to which Hana quickly added, "Oh, we will. We will indeed."

"We shall miss you too," Mrs. Okada said quietly, but Hana saw the joy in her face and knew that life for her would probably be happier. Although she would still be the wife of an impoverished minister, in Japan she would at least be free to go anywhere without shame of being what she was.

"I'm happy for you," Hana said to her, "even though we shall be the poorer."

As she spoke the words, however, she felt a twinge of envy stir inside. She looked at her daughter and wondered what would happen if they went back to Japan now. Would it be too late to make a Japanese woman of Mary? She pictured her kneeling gracefully in a silk kimono, preparing ceremonial tea or arranging flowers. She saw her dressed in the finery of a Japanese bride, her face made up with thick white paste. But even in her imagining, Mary slithered quickly out of the stiff strictures of Japanese clothing, and Hana knew that her daughter was already too free and self-willed to become a submissive Japanese wife. She already possessed the same independent spirit that had caused Hana herself to leave her home so many years ago.

When they dropped the Okadas off at church, Hana spoke of the wonderful idea that had suddenly danced into her head.

"I know exactly the right person to invite as our new minister," she said eagerly.

Taro seemed surprised. "Oh?"

But Dr. Kaneda seemed to know. "I think I had the same thought, Hana," he said. "Weren't you thinking of Kenji Nishima?"

"Exactly! I know he wants to come back to Oakland after being in Marysville for eight years."

"Is he nice, Mama? Is he a good minister?" Mary wanted to know.

Dr. Kaneda and Hana answered together, "He's one of the best," they agreed.

"Is he, Papa?" Mary persisted.

Only then did Taro speak. "Your mama is right, as usual. He would make a fine minister for us."

Although he had agreed with her, Taro's words were almost a rebuke, and Hana knew she should have allowed Taro to speak to Dr. Kaneda of such an important decision for the church. She should have waited until Taro reached the same conclusion and let him be the first to speak of it.

Will I never learn, she thought wearily, and leaning back to rest her head, she felt the first sparkling pleasure of her thought fade away.

Chapter 21

Mary studied her face in the mirror. "Sweet sixteen and never been kissed," she mocked herself. Not only had she not been kissed, she hadn't even been out on a date. In fact, the very thought of spending an entire evening with a boy made her knees weak, and her vague feminine urge to make herself attractive had little relation yet to the opposite sex.

Her father told her she was pretty, but Mary knew she had only an ordinary Asian face. Her hair, slightly curled, hung to her shoulders and was swept up in a pompador at the crown. Her eyes, like her mother's, were her best feature. She fluttered them now, turning her head from one side to the other. She tried a new orange red lipstick from the Five and Ten, but the effect was not startling. She had begun to wear lipstick this semester because the other girls did, but still felt uneasy about the crimson streak on her face.

Mary was aware of her own changing body as it moved toward womanhood, and although there were things she wanted to ask, she could not speak of them to her mother. Mary had no close girl friends, for she had long ago learned to amuse herself, confiding only in those imaginary beings that peopled her lonely world.

At Oakland High School where Mary was now a junior, there were only two other Nisei girls. The few Nisei boys were too shy to say more than hello to her, and when she saw them approaching, she usually busied herself at her locker or pretended to be reading something on the bulletin board. She could not imagine herself going out with them, and not in her wildest dreams did she even think of dating a white boy. None, in fact, would have asked her.

Mary had a few white girl friends at school, and knew that among themselves they spoke of skating or swimming parties or the spring prom, but she was never included in such discussions and accepted her exclusion as the normal course of events.

For some years now, Mary had known that her Japanese face denied her certain privileges. White people had their own special world, and the Japanese Americans were not a part of it, except perhaps as servants, day workers, gardeners or cooks. When she went to the City Plunge with her friends one day, she was told, "We don't think you'll enjoy swimming here." When she made her first appointment for a haircut at Corley's Beauty Parlor, she called first to ask whether they would cut Japanese hair. Mary knew that's how life was. She neither questioned it nor resented it, trying only to be unobtrusive, emulating the white American world, hoping desperately to be absorbed into it. She submerged her Japaneseness whenever she could, trying to be less different, shielding herself from hurt by keeping to her own private world.

The one after-school activity Mary enjoyed was the International Club, where she was sometimes forced to acknowledge her heritage on such occasions as the special International Day assembly. Miss Nelson, who advised the club, persuaded Mary and the two other Nisei girls to wear kimonos for their part in the program.

"Do you think your mother could come help you girls get dressed in your kimonos?" Miss Nelson asked Mary.

"Sure, if it's not one of her days to . . . I mean if

she's free." Mary did not want to admit that her mother did housework and could not come on the days she worked.

When Mary spoke of it to her mother, Hana was delighted. "Why, of course, I'll be glad to help," she said, circling the date on the Takeda Dry Goods and Grocers calendar that hung on their kitchen wall.

On the morning of the assembly, Mary instructed her mother to be at school by two o'clock sharp. "Don't be late now," she begged. "You know how to get to my school?"

"Yes, I know. I won't be late." Hana had already determined the time necessary to get there on the streetcar. She had pressed Mary's blue-flowered kimono and hung the brocade *obi* out to air, so it would not smell of moth balls. Both had lain in a trunk since Mary's grandmother sent them from Japan, and when Hana removed them, she had taken out her best silk *furoshiki* in which to wrap and carry the kimonos.

"Mama," Mary said just before she left for school.

"Yes?"

"What will you wear when you come?"

"I thought my navy blue suit and hat. Is that all right?"

"Uh-huh, I guess so."

Hana felt the uneasy disapproval in her daughter's voice. "It's my Sunday suit," she explained. "It's the best I can do."

Mary chose not to discuss the matter further. "I'll meet you at the main entrance at two," she said, and with a whirl of her pleated serge skirt, she was gone.

"Papa, do you know I've never been to Mary's school before?" Hana asked, turning to Taro to complete a conversation she felt had been prematurely ended by Mary's abrupt departure.

"You've been to PTA meetings," Taro reminded her.

"And we've been to some programs."

"But that was in grammar school and junior high," Hana said, recalling how she had tried to attend every PTA meeting she could, even though she didn't always understand what was going on. She and Taro had also made the effort to attend every school play or program Mary mentioned. They had worked hard to be good parents.

Hana thought of all the costumes she had sewn for Mary for may pole dances or Halloween or Christmas. She had saved from her own earnings to buy her the sweaters and dresses Mary needed for school. Even though they had gone without some things for themselves, she and Taro had given Mary everything she ever wanted, from dolls and roller skates to a swing and a sandbox that Taro built for her. They had even bought her the puppy she begged for after their trip to Livingston.

In those days, Mary was still willing to go anywhere with her parents. They took her with them when they went to shop or visit, to church activities, or to the Japanese movies shown at the Buddhist temple hall. But now, she was growing increasingly distant, rejecting them and what they were.

"I mean I've never been to her high school," Hana continued. "I've never met any of her teachers there."

Taro put down the morning paper, giving his full attention to Hana, for he knew she would continue to interrupt his reading until she had said what was on her mind.

"Then you'll have a fine opportunity today."

"But I'm so nervous. What shall I say to her teachers?"

"Just say you enjoyed the assembly and thank them for teaching our daughter. And Mama," he added, "don't bow too much."

That was the last thing Hana told herself as she left

the house. She must remember not to bow too much or to call her daughter "Ma Chan" in front of her friends. She didn't want Mary to feel ashamed of her today. If Mary was with her when she met a Japanese friend on the street, she would poke Hana after the third bow, saying, "Mama, please don't make a spectacle of yourself." And she would hurry Hana off, embarrassed because her mother spoke in a foreign tongue.

Hana took a deep breath as she approached the high school, carrying her best blue leather handbag and Mary's Japanese outfit carefully wrapped in her silk *furoshiki*. Mary was waiting at the door to meet her.

"Mama, you came on the streetcar carrying that thing?"

"What, my *furoshiki*?" Hana was startled. "It's my best one."

"But you look like you just came off the boat from Japan."

Hana had scarcely set foot in Mary's school and already she had embarrassed her. "I'm sorry," she said, and she held the bundle close to her chest, trying to be as inconspicuous as possible. Mary led the way down the polished hall as Hana looked about, impressed.

"It's a fine school, Mary," she said.

"It's okay."

Mary led her into a room full of girls in colorful foreign dress. Rouged and powdered for their performance, they giggled and spoke in shrill nervous voices, excited not only because of the program, but because they had been excused from their regular classes.

"This is my mother," Mary said to Miss Nelson.

"So nice of you to come help us." She offered Hana a hand that clamored with gold bangles and scarlet nail polish.

Hana bowed before she could stop herself. "I'm very happy to meet you, and I'm glad to help," she said carefully.

Mary slipped quickly into her kimono and put the white *tabi* and the *zori* on her feet. Hana unrolled the long brocade sash, winding it skillfully around her daughter's waist, pulling and tugging it into a great knot that burdened Mary like a gilded knapsack. She then did the same for the other two Nisei girls.

The girls gasped for breath as Hana tightened the *obi* around their chests and tried to ease the pressure with their fingers. They stumbled clumsily about the room as the thongs of the *zori* dug at the flesh between their toes. Hana smiled at their awkwardness. Although wrapped in silken grace, their unaccustomed bodies resisted, and at least in Hana's eyes, they did not look like anything other than foreigners in Japanese dress.

Miss Nelson fluttered about, admiring the kimonos and the brilliant red and gold *obis*. She dabbed powder and rouge on the girls' faces and told them they looked exquisite. As the bell signaled the end of the period, squeals and shrieks circled the room. It was time for the girls to go to the auditorium, and Hana was anxious to see what they were going to do.

"All right, everyone. Let's go, quickly now." Miss Nelson gathered a cluster of girls around her and rushed from the room, neglecting to invite Hana to join her or even to attend the assembly.

Mary tugged nervously at her *obi* as she prepared to follow Miss Nelson. "Thanks for coming, Mama," she said briefly. "We can get out of this stuff by ourselves and I'll bring everything home."

"Thank you, Mrs. Takeda. Goodbye," the two other kimono-clad girls called, hurrying after Mary.

Hana sat down in the empty room, surveying the clutter of discarded blouses and skirts and the oxfords stuffed with bobby socks. The desks and chairs were askew from the hurried scramble, and Miss Nelson's makeup kit lay in complete disarray on one of the desks. Hana fought back an instinctive urge to straighten up the mess, to push the desks where they belonged and pair up the shoes. She sat there for several minutes, too disappointed to move.

She told herself that Miss Nelson had, in her excitement, simply forgotten to invite her to the assembly. As for Mary, well, perhaps she felt she could not invite her mother when none of the other parents had been asked.

Hana waited in the empty room until the sounds in the hallway died down and the swarms of young people had shuffled into the auditorium. When the building settled back to an ordered quiet, Hana got up, carefully folded the *furoshiki* square and left it on top of Mary's clothes. Even if she didn't like it, she'd have to wrap her kimono in something to bring it home.

Hana opened the door quietly, looked down the hall to see if anyone was coming, then quickly left the building by the side door.

This is how it is going to be from now on, she told herself. Mary would become increasingly engrossed in her own affairs and friends and have less and less need of her mother. In the end she would marry and leave her entirely. That was how life was supposed to be. Hana told herself she would be ready to free her child when the time came, just as her own mother had done. Still, she mused, there must be a kinder way than the abrupt dismissal she had just received.

Hana knew very well why she and Mary were becoming strangers. They were gradually losing the means of communicating with one another. Hana had never insisted that Mary go to Japanese Language School as some of the Nisei children had done, and she herself had not progressed far in studying English. Now Mary spoke as an adult, while Hana was still a child in the English language. If only she had listened to Mrs. Davis, Hana thought, but there had always been too many other demands that closed in on her. Now it was too late.

Hana could not face the thought of going back to her empty house. Instead, she took the streetcar toward town, shivering in the air that had suddenly turned cold. There was a bleakness to the day that matched her own spirit, as though winter were blowing into the crevices of her heart.

Hana walked briskly toward Taro's shop and found him opening cartons at the back of the shop. His old black sweater was covered with sawdust and a piece of yarn looped out from his sleeve where he had caught it on a nail.

"Why Mama," he called, wiping his forehead with the back of his hand. "Is the assembly over already? How was Mary?"

Hana could not utter the words of explanation Taro was waiting to hear. She simply sat down on one of the crates, took off her hat and said in a tired voice, "It's too late, Papa. It's too late."

Chapter 22

When Mary became a freshman at the university, she discovered boys and the world of science.

"I think I'm going to become a doctor, Papa," she announced at the end of her first year. Her best grades were in zoology and biology, and the thought of a career in medicine appealed to her. Dr. Kaneda, too, had encouraged her.

Taro was pleased. "That's good, Mary. It is an honorable profession and there aren't many women willing even to try."

He leaned back in his chair, watching his daughter as she tossed the contents of a large box into the fireplace. They were her year's notes, and he was surprised that she didn't want to save them as evidence of her accomplishment as he would have done. Somewhere in the closet, he still had his notes from classes he'd attended when he first came to America. But perhaps it was better to be unencumbered like Mary, he thought, for he had never looked at his notes again, and they simply cluttered up his closet.

He gazed lovingly at Mary now. She seemed to be at the peak of her beauty, her long black hair hanging softly against her throat. She was even more fair-skinned than Hana, a true mark of beauty in a Japanese woman. Taro felt a surge of pride. In fact, both he and Hana were enormously proud of her. She had graduated high school with an almost straight-A record, and her teachers had nothing but praise for her work. He felt she would fulfill every dream they held for her and would surely be completely accepted in the white American world. That was how it should be, Taro thought. That was what he and Hana had worked and sacrificed for all these years.

"Becoming a doctor will mean long years of study, Mary," he said to her now. "Have you thought about that?"

Still too young to contemplate the brief span each life is given, Mary was completely unconcerned about the additional years of schooling. "I don't mind," she said absently.

"Our people need more doctors who understand them. I'm glad you're considering such a calling," Taro continued. "It will require dedication and a sense of mission."

"Oh, Papa, I don't have a sense of mission, for heaven's sake," Mary objected. "I just like medicine. That's all."

"Well, that will come in time," he said to himself rather than to Mary. She had now found some old high school notes and was tossing masses of paper into the fireplace, sending a flurry of sparks up the chimney.

"Do be careful, Mary," Hana warned as she entered the room. "You'll set us on fire."

"Everything's under control, Mama," Mary answered briefly and having emptied the last scraps from her box, she got up, drew the fire screen and went to her room.

Taro tried to draw Hana into what remained of the pleasant conversation he'd had with Mary. He saw with increasing frequency the brief moments of friction between Hana and Mary, and he tried in his own way to placate them.

"Mary wants to become a doctor," he said. "Isn't that a fine thing?"

Hana sat opposite him in a rocker and pulled out a sock from her darning basket. She threaded a needle, making a knot at the end of the thread before she spoke. "Yes, it sounds fine, if she can do it."

Hana knew that Mary sustained her projects only while her enthusiasm sailed high. After a month or two, her interest would lag and the project would be forgotten, like the sweater, half-completed, that now lay crumpled in a paper bag in her closet, or the dresses half-sewn, the water colors begun and discarded. Even the dog she had wheedled from her father was cared for by Hana because Mary was too busy.

Hana didn't view Mary's present ambitions with Taro's idealistic hopes, for the Mary she knew was not the same person revealed to Taro. His facility with English enabled them to discuss many things. With Hana, however, Mary was often silent because it was too much trouble to explain something in Japanese. Hana wondered if it was because Mary did not reach out to her with words that she could see a side of Mary that Taro never saw. He was blinded not only by his love for her, but also by the clutter of words she showered on him. It was strange, Hana thought, how human beings revealed themselves to each other in such different ways.

Taro was eager to nourish Mary's dream. "I think she can do it, Mama. At any rate, we must have faith in her."

"Yes, of course," Hana answered, for she did want to have faith in Mary. She would be so proud if her daughter truly became a doctor, with a career of her own, helping the sick, spending her days doing something more than washing and cleaning. Hana loved her daughter and wanted to reach out to her. But somehow, she had the terrible feeling that one day Mary would fail them both.

Mary was popular with the Japanese American boys on campus and went out often. She went to all the dances of the Japanese Students' Club and to parties at the homes of her friends. Young Nisei boys, their hair slicked, suits pressed and shoes shined, appeared stiff and proper, carrying sweet scented gardenia corsages in florist boxes. They came inside and knew enough Japanese to converse briefly with Hana and Taro, speaking of the weather, of their studies and of their parents.

When Mary thought they had been properly polite, she would say, "Shall we go now?" and the boys would leap to their feet, give Mary a look of gratitude and relief, and hurry her from the house.

One day toward the end of her sophomore year, Mary came home, her cheeks flushed, her entire being vibrating with happiness.

"Mama, I'm going out for dinner tonight."

"That's nice, Ma Chan. Who are you going with?"

"Mother, please stop calling me that. I'm going with a friend—a *tomodachi*."

"He's been here before?"

"No."

"But he is a friend from school?"

"He's an assistant in my biology lab."

"A what, Ma Chan?"

"An assistant. He helps the professor."

"Ah, he is a teacher? You are going out with a teacher?"

"Something like that."

"A young man who is a teacher at the university must be a fine person," Hana observed. "I hope he is a good boy."

"Oh, Mother!"

When the young man arrived to call for Mary, she was still in her room fussing with her face.

"Mama, I'm not ready," she shouted. "Will you let him in?"

"Of course. I wasn't going to leave him standing on the porch."

Hana approached the front door with a receptive smile. When she opened it, however, she was startled not to find a Japanese American face smiling at her as she had expected, but a brown-haired, blue-eyed young man in a neat, navy blue, double-breasted suit. He was about two heads taller than Mary and seemed sturdy and strong, as though he could lift a hundred-pound sack of rice with no trouble at all.

"Yes?" she inquired, thinking he must have come to sell her something. "Are you from the Watkins Company?"

Just last week a man had come to sell her some products, and Hana had tried to tell him that she could find most things she needed at her husband's shop. But the man had not understood. Hana thought he had now sent this young man instead, but she did not send him away immediately. She understood there were people who made their living by selling things door to door, and she was never impolite to them.

The young man fingered his tie and shifted his feet uncomfortably. "No, I'm Joseph Cantelli," he answered. "Is Mary at home?"

Hana could not conceal her confusion. "Yes . . . Oh . . ." Was this Mary's young teacher? It was not possible. Mary had never before gone out with a boy who was not a Japanese American.

"You come for Mary Takeda?" she asked, her English disintegrating in embarrassment.

Joseph Cantelli nodded. "We're going out to dinner together, Mrs. Takeda."

He was polished and self-assured, while Hana was rendered completely inept. She finally recovered and asked him inside. She pointed to the sofa. "*Dozo.* Please sit."

She could think of nothing to say to this fine-looking young man who sat across from her and finally asked, "Your parents, they live here?"

"No, they live in Los Angeles."

"Ah."

Unable to bear another moment, Hana rose and went to call Mary. It had been an altogether miserable performance on her part, and she disliked Joseph Cantelli because, through no fault of his own, he had made her feel like a complete idiot.

"But why didn't you tell me he was a *hakujin*, this friend of yours?" Hana asked Mary the next morning. "Why didn't you warn me he was a white person?"

"I didn't think it was necessary, Mama," she snapped, with an impatient look. "After all, what difference does it make if I go out with somebody who isn't a Nisei?"

"It just doesn't seem . . ." Hana groped for the right word. "It just doesn't seem comfortable," she said at last. There was no other way to describe it.

How could she put into words the thoughts that had crossed her mind after Mary and Joe had gone out. She wanted a son-in-law with whom she could speak Japanese, with whom she might share some rice and pickled radish. Most of all, she wanted a grandchild with black hair and a Japanese face, to whom she could teach some Japanese words.

How could a white person possibly understand the subtleties of the Japanese way of life? As Hana spread out her thoughts and unravelled her fears one by one, however, she realized that Mary was more American than Japanese. Having spent so much of her time alone, she was more independent than some Japanese American girls Hana knew, and these days she was drawing away from her Nisei friends at the university. She had long ago stopped coming to their Japanese church.

"I do wish Mary would come to our church," Hana confided to Kenji Nishima, "especially now that you have become our minister."

But Kenji Nishima understood Mary's independence. "She needs to find her own way, Mrs. Takeda," he explained gently. "You must let her seek out her own life. You must trust God to help Mary and to help you too."

Taro agreed and did not seem to share Hana's feeling that Mary needed more watchful guidance.

"She's young and foolish," Hana pointed out.

"We've had eighteen years to guide her, Mama. We can't intrude too much now."

"You're not going to speak to her, then, about seeing so much of Joe Cantelli?"

"If he's a good young man and Mary likes him, what's the harm?"

Sometimes Taro confounded Hana. He was the conservative traditionalist, who expected her to be a submissive Japanese wife. And yet he wasn't concerned that his only daughter, the one being he cherished above all others, might possibly break every tradition he held dear.

"Suppose she wants to marry him?"

"Mama, you worry too much. Mary is too young to think about marriage, and by the time she is ready for it, she will have forgotten all about Joe Cantelli."

Hana wasn't so sure. She wasn't sure at all.

Chapter

It was a long, cold winter, with mornings of brittle frost and nights of brilliant, crystalline stars.

Hana awoke one morning to a dark world and hurried to the kitchen. Lighting the oven for heat, she dressed quickly in front of its feeble warmth. She could hear Taro stirring in their room as she put on the kettle and cooked the oatmeal, but she heard no sound from Mary's room.

Hana looked out the window and could scarcely see the house next door. A thick white fog separated them as though each house were wrapped in tissue and placed in its own box. She shivered as she measured out the coffee. She hated winter fog. It was so impenetrable and all-encompassing. Cars crashed into each other and men became blind. Fog made Hana feel unutterably despondent, and today it brought a premonition of disaster.

"Papa San, will you call Mary? She'll be late for her first class."

Taro grunted. Hana heard him knock on Mary's door and call, "Mary, are you up?"

There was no answer. Then Hana heard Taro cry out. He rushed to the kitchen, thrusting a sheet of pink paper toward her. He looked as though he had been struck a blow to the head. His face was ashen and his voice trembled as he spoke.

"Mama," he said hoarsely. "Mary has left us! How could she have done such a thing?"

He sat down heavily and, covering his face with his

hands, wept only as he had when their son died.

Hana took the note, her hands shaking so, she could scarcely read it. She sat down, but the words danced before her eyes, and she felt as though the fog had come inside to suffocate her in its icy grasp.

"Dear Mother and Dad," Mary wrote. "By the time you read this, Joe Cantelli and I will be in Reno, and I will be Joe's wife. Forgive me, but we had to do it this way. His parents would have objected and so would you. We are very much in love, and I know this is right for me. Joe has a job teaching biology at the university in Reno, and everything is wonderful. Don't worry. I'll write. Love, Mary."

Her handwriting was still uneven and unsure, like a child's. But she had made a woman's decision, and she had now placed Joe Cantelli before her mother and father.

Hana felt numb. She went to Mary's room to see if she really was gone and saw that her bed had not been slept in. She had slipped out late at night, taking some clothing and nothing more. She had no attachment to things as Hana did. She had left behind the souvenirs of her college days, her books and papers, her collection of miniatures and everything that remained of her childhood. With only a year left at the university, knowing how much it meant to her parents that she graduate, Mary had seen fit to drop out of school and their lives, leaving behind only a brief note on a sheet of pink paper.

"Oh, Mary, how could you do such a thing to us?" Hana murmured.

When she returned to the kitchen she saw that Taro had composed himself and was sipping his coffee, staring blankly at the table.

Hana could find no words to console him, and when she spoke, she found herself spilling out the bitterness inside her.

"All our hopes and plans gone in one day," she said blankly. "Kenji Nishima was wrong. We shouldn't have left Mary to find her own way. Look what she's done with her life, with only a year left before she would have graduated. Now we have lost her to an outsider who cannot even speak our tongue. What have we left, Papa?"

In her frustration, she pulled Taro and Kenji Nishima and God into her anger and bewilderment. But when all the words were said, she reached out and put her hand over Taro's.

"I wonder what we should have done? How did we come to lose our only child in such a way?" Hana hadn't the heart to remind Taro that she had warned him this might happen, but he spoke of it himself. "You were right, Hana," he said dully. "I should have listened to you." But it was small comfort to hear Taro admit that he was wrong.

"There is nothing left, but to forgive her," he said. He was surprised how easily he could forgive his daughter, when it had been so hard to forgive Hana.

As for Hana, she could not find forgiveness in her heart, although she searched its darkness well. When she went to church on Sunday, she wore her bitterness and shame on her face.

"You must not blame yourselves," Dr. Kaneda consoled them. "Mary is shaping her own life now."

"We trusted too much and look what has happened to Taro, a good man and a devoted father," Hana said. "Why has he been given such a bitter reward?"

Reverend Nishima could not answer her. "We cannot know the ways of God, Mrs. Takeda," he said. "But we must have faith. Your husband has forgiven your daughter, hasn't he?"

"Yes."

"And you?"

Hana lowered her head, because she could not answer, and walked away in silence.

Mary sat close to Joe as they drove through the darkness along the highway that would take them to Reno and their new life together. Brief moments of guilt edged into her happiness like short stabs of pain as she wondered who would find her note first, and what her parents would say. She knew she had hurt them badly, especially her father, who had such high hopes for her future. And yet she could not afford to risk losing Joe because of compassion for her parents. She had to grasp this chance at love, for she knew it might not come again.

Joe had come into her life when she was confounded by its frustrations. She had gone to him for help in carrying out one of her class projects, and their conversations had moved rather quickly beyond biology.

Joe was the son of immigrants too, and he knew what it meant to be treated as something less than other white Americans. He understood Mary's guilt at being ashamed of her heritage and the Japanese ways of her parents. He understood Mary's lack of self-esteem and was touched by her vulnerability. At first he simply took her out for sodas, then for lunch, and finally, he began to date her seriously. She blossomed under his attentions, revealing a delightful, childlike charm.

Mary discovered she no longer cared about the next Nisei students' Spring Hop or Fall Semi-Formal. When Joe spoke to her as a woman and told her he wanted her, she cared about nothing else. She learned from him what a man was all about, and she knew she wanted nothing more than the chance to make him happy. She no longer cared about becoming a doctor, or about her grades, or anything else in her life.

Now she was Mary Cantelli, Mrs. Joseph Cantelli. She had discarded her old life and everything she detested about it. Now she need never again be humiliated because her name was Takeda. Only the thought of her parents flickered in her mind like a bothersome insect that would not leave.

Joe put a hand on her thigh. "Are you all right?"

Mary nodded in the darkness. "Joe, we did the right thing, didn't we?"

He picked up her small cold hand and pressed it to his lips. "Sure we did, sweetheart. Don't worry. Your parents will understand someday. So will mine."

"In the meantime we have each other, don't we?"

"That's all that matters."

Reassured, Mary leaned her head on Joe's shoulder, feeling the roughness of his tweed coat against her cheek. Soon she stopped worrying about her parents, and her great happiness overwhelmed her small guilt. When, that night, Joe took her in his arms and taught her how to make love, Mary was eager and giving, not wanting him ever to stop.

"I'll love you until the day I die, Joe Cantelli," she whispered into the warmth of his mouth.

In two months Mary was pregnant, and with the approach of motherhood, she thought increasingly of her mother. Her letters home became longer, as she wrote of their neighbors and of Joe's colleagues who invited them to dinner.

"Joe is getting along fine," she wrote, "and my doctor is a good friend of his." At the end of the letter she wrote, "I haven't seen a single Japanese American face since we got here and must confess I haven't missed them. Except for you, of course," she added as a polite afterthought.

Actually, Mary missed nothing at all of her life in California. She loved keeping house for Joe, washing his shirts and socks, shopping for his food, cooking his meals, cleaning his house and being responsible to no one else. It was like playing house with a real man who drank her coffee in the morning, came home tired and smelling of pipe tobacco, ate her simple meals without complaint and made love to her at night.

Joe had known a few other women before Mary, but none brought him her guileless devotion. She knew nothing, was eager to learn and ready to do anything to please him.

"You're like a child, do you know that?" Joe would say. And as Mary came to him, he would caress her smooth small body and add, "but a very feminine child, and you please me very much."

When Hana learned that Mary was expecting a child, the knot of resentment she harbored against her daughter showed its first signs of softening.

"Imagine, Papa," she said. "We are going to be grandparents."

Taro shook his head. "How could it be? It does not seem possible."

It did not seem so many years ago that Hana had come to him from Japan, young and beautiful. He looked at her now and saw traces of bitterness on her face. The lines around her mouth had deepened, like parentheses to her life, and fine wrinkles were gathering at the corners of her eyes. There was even some gray hair at her temples. Still, she surely was not yet an old woman.

Taro remembered that his grandparents had always seemed old to him, but perhaps they had felt exactly as he did now. The thought of becoming a grandfather pleased him enormously. Yet, the fact seemed to deprive him of his middle age, thrusting him prematurely into old age.

He still thought of Mary as a child and felt a vague

resentment toward Joe that he should have burdened her with motherhood so soon. She scarcely seemed ready for marriage, and now, already, she was to become a mother. Had anyone told her what to expect in marriage, he wondered.

"Will you go to help her when the baby comes?" he asked now.

"I've been thinking about that," Hana said slowly. "Shall I offer to go or wait until she asks me? They may not want me to come."

"Nonsense. She is still your daughter," Taro answered. "Offer to go. I know she will want your help."

Still, Hana did not write until Mary was in her sixth month. Then she asked Taro to write for her, because she did not want Joe to see her poor handwriting or to laugh at her spelling. She still confused her l's and r's, and even now could not be sure if it was "cerely" or "celery."

Taro took pains to write the letter in such a way that they would understand Hana would go only if they wanted her. Almost from the day he mailed the letter, Hana waited for Mary's reply. Sometimes she would meet the mailman on the porch and take the letters from him before he put them in their box.

As the days passed, Hana began to think of the ways in which she could help Mary. She would wash the diapers, cook and clean house and do all the heavy work that Mary would not be able to do for a while. She spoke to Mrs. Davis, who encouraged Hana to take the time off. Hana even brought out the old suitcase that had come with her from Japan, filling it with the things she wanted to take. Perhaps she would stay as long as a month if Mary needed her.

When the letter finally came, it was short and written in great haste.

"Sweet of you to offer to come, Mother," Mary

wrote, "but I've already made arrangements with a neighbor who's coming to help me. She's a retired nurse with time on her hands. Besides, I don't want you coming all the way out here just to do more housework. I'm as big as a house, but feeling fine. Love, Mary."

She had enclosed a white linen lace-trimmed handkerchief, as a consolation prize perhaps, Hana thought, for not coming.

Hana put away her disappointment with her suitcase and decided to do housework four days a week instead of two. If her daughter did not want her help, there were plenty of white women in Oakland who did.

"I'm sorry, Mama," Taro said, but there was nothing more he could say or do.

Chapter 24

1941–1943

It was Sunday, and Hana and Taro had just returned from church. When Taro turned on the radio to listen to the news while Hana got lunch, he thought for a moment that he had not heard correctly.

"Hana," he called. "Come here. Listen."

The voice on the radio was taut with alarm and the words came so rapidly Hana couldn't understand.

"What is he saying, Papa? What is he saying about Japan?"

Taro shook his head. "It can't be true, Hana. It must be a mistake. He is saying that Japanese planes bombed Pearl Harbor. He is talking about sabotage . . . about war between America and Japan."

Hana felt faint. "It's a mistake isn't it, Papa? Isn't it?"

Taro sat close to the radio and listened with his entire being. "Some crazy fanatic has done this," he said at last. "The Japanese government would never do such a thing."

He snapped off the radio in disgust, telling Hana to finish making lunch. As they were having a bowl of hot noodles, the doorbell rang.

"I'll go," Hana said. "You finish your lunch."

She opened the door to find Ellen Davis looking distraught and anxious.

"My dear Hana," she said taking her hand. "We just heard the shocking news. I had to come right down to see you."

"But Taro says it's all a mistake. He says it's not true."

"Oh, Hana, I wish that were so, but I'm afraid our two countries are at war. We're all so very sorry. Hana, I want you to know I still love you and want you to continue coming to work for me as you've always done." Her words came awkwardly.

Hana didn't know what to say. Why shouldn't she still love me, she wondered. What have I done? I'm still the same person I have always been.

Mrs. Davis lowered her voice now and asked, "You and Taro . . . you had no idea your country was going to do this?"

Hana was stunned. "No, no! Of course not," she said vehemently. "How could we know such a thing?"

Seeing the astonishment on Hana's face, Ellen Davis immediately wished she had not asked. "Of course you didn't," she said lamely. "I just thought perhaps . . ." She left quickly then, reassuring Hana once more that nothing would be changed between them.

"Papa," Hana said in anguish. "Mrs. Davis says our countries are at war. That means our families in Japan are enemies of America, and Americans will think of us as the enemy too."

"No, Mama, no," Taro reassured her. "If indeed this is war, Americans will know it is the militarists in Japan who are the enemy of all of us who want peace. Americans are fair-minded. They will understand."

Taro wanted to assure himself that the words he spoke were true. He went quickly to Dr. Kaneda's flat, but as he approached, Kaneda emerged, escorted on either side by two well-dressed men. Kaneda tried to smile, but it was a feeble attempt.

"These gentlemen are from the FBI," he explained. "They want me to go with them for a short while."

"But why? What have you done?" Taro asked urgently.

"We just want to ask him a few questions," the men answered, and they maneuvered Dr. Kaneda into the back seat of a waiting car, leaving Taro standing alone, shaken and apprehensive.

Kenji Nishima came to tell Taro and Hana what he had learned. "It seems the FBI had a list of men—executives of Japanese firms, leaders of the community, those who headed certain Japanese associations—they apprehended them all."

"And Dr. Kaneda? Why Dr. Kaneda?"

"No one knows. Perhaps because he organized our Japanese Language School, perhaps because he was president of the Japanese Association . . ."

"Oh, Reverend Nishima," Hana sighed. "What will we do without him?"

"We must be strong. We must help each other."

But it was hard to be strong. Dr. Kaneda never returned to his flat. He was sent to a prisoner of war camp in Montana with hundreds of other interned men. He was not allowed to come home to put his affairs in order or to notify his patients that he would be gone. He was, in fact, a prisoner of war, and Hana listened with horror to rumors that these men were now hostages who might be killed in reprisal for the atrocities of the Japanese in the Pacific.

On a cold night in January, Hana awoke to the sound of distant explosions. Had the war come so close? She turned for the comfort of Taro's arms, but found the bed empty.

"Papa?" she called, her voice hollow in the quiet room.

Hana put on her bathrobe and went to the kitchen where she found Taro hunched over the ledgers, notes and papers from his shop. They were spread out on the kitchen table in complete disarray.

"What in the world are you doing?" Hana asked. "It's three o'clock in the morning."

Taro removed his glasses, blinking wearily. His eyes were red-rimmed and shadowed with dark circles. "I know, Mama. I couldn't sleep. I've been thinking of what I must do with the shop if we are to be evacuated."

For several weeks now their lives had been laced with disturbing rumors that all the Japanese on the West Coast would be uprooted from their homes and incarcerated in government camps. It was referred to as "the evacuation." But Taro refused to believe such talk.

"The United States government would never do such a thing," he explained to Hana, recalling the Constitution he had studied long ago. "After all, there is such a thing as due process of law, and our children are citizens."

Still, false stories of sabotage continued to circulate, and anti-Japanese forces exerted political and economic pressure to rid the West Coast of all the Japanese Americans, citizen and non-citizen alike. Hatred and fear of the enemy were increasingly focused on the Japanese American presence along the West Coast, and rumors of an evacuation grew stronger each day.

Night after night, Taro lay in bed contemplating the enormity of such an uprooting. What would happen to all the Japanese Americans if it should actually come to pass? What was to become of their businesses, nurtured so carefully over a lifetime? What of the small cleaners and shoe repair shops, the laundries, the cafes, the grocery stores, the homes, the farms? What of Dr. Kaneda's medical equipment and the office he'd been forced to abandon in such haste. And what of his own shop? After thirty long years, at last he'd been able to buy it in Mary's name and begun to earn a decent living from it, no longer having to depend on Hana's help. At last, the shop's success was his own triumph, and only last month, he had told Hana she could stop her day work and enjoy some years of leisure.

"I can support you now," he had said, "and give you some good years."

It had given him tremendous satisfaction to be able to say that, and Hana was elated.

"I shall go to school," she'd said eagerly. "I'll learn English so my grandchild won't be ashamed of me."

But now, those dreams were devastated. Each night Taro pondered his dilemma in silence. Should he sell his shop? If he did, there would be nothing to return to after the war. Should he rent it then? But who would want to rent such a shop but another Japanese, and they would all be gone too. If he rented to a non-Japanese, how could he collect the rent, and what would happen to their bank accounts if they were incarcerated? Dr. and Mrs. Davis had offered to help in any way, should the evacuation come to pass, but Taro could not burden the busy surgeon and his good wife with caretaker duties of his small shop on Seventh Street. It was a world too remote and different from their own. Taro asked himself the same questions over and over, only to find that each answer spawned a new array of questions and problems.

Overcome by wakeful thoughts, Taro had come to the kitchen in the middle of the night, carefully blacked out the windows, and spread his jumbled papers on the table. The process of putting them in order, he hoped, might somehow produce similar results in his head.

Without looking up, he acknowledged Hana's presence by voicing the thought that pressed most strongly. "Perhaps I should just sell the shop," he said dully.

Hana sat opposite Taro and was filled with compassion for him. "Has it come to that?" she asked. She had helped save the shop once, but it had been creditors who threatened its existence then. This time it was the United States government itself.

Hana shivered. The cold seeped into her very soul, and she knew there would be no warmth for them in the days ahead. Hana made some hot tea and buttered toast. When they had eaten, the sky was already growing light, and the sparrows were making their early morning sounds.

On the nineteenth of February 1942, the weeks of speculation and uncertainty came to an end. The President of the United States authorized the Secretary of War and his military commanders to prescribe areas from which any or all persons could be excluded. The newspapers carried ominous headlines about the President's Executive Order 9066.

"What does it mean?" Hana asked anxiously. "What will happen to us now?"

"It means we are all going to be evacuated one day soon," Taro explained sadly. "It means we are all going to be uprooted from our homes and interned without even a trial or hearing."

Evacuated. Hana hated the word. She looked it up again in the dictionary to be sure she understood. "To remove; to send away," it said. Hana understood. There were those who had always wanted to be rid of all the Japanese Americans in California. Now, at last, they'd gotten their way, and the President himself had made it seem a respectable act.

"We must pack up our belongings now, Hana,"

Taro instructed. "We must clear everything out of this house, and I must quickly dispose of my shop."

Hana nodded absently, scarcely able to comprehend what must be done in the weeks ahead.

"Nevada is outside the Exclusion Zone," Mrs. Davis said to Hana. "Why don't you go to stay with Mary and Joe? I can't bear to think of you and Taro being herded into one of those government camps."

"I never thought of it," Hana admitted to Mrs. Davis. "I'll ask Taro." But the thought didn't comfort her as much as Mrs. Davis thought it might. That night Hana spoke of the possibility to Taro.

"I'd like to spare you the discomfort of a government camp," he admitted. "Shall I write Mary to ask if we might come?"

Hana pondered the idea carefully. She did not want to be spurned now when they were in need of help.

Before Hana could make up her mind, however, a letter came from Mary herself. "What is all this dreadful talk about an evacuation?" she asked. "I think the government has a lot of nerve talking about 'voluntary relocation' when they're kicking you out of your home. But if you want to, you could come to Nevada. Joe says you're welcome to stay with us until you find a place of your own. It seems safe enough now, but of course one never knows about next week, or even tomorrow. Joe and I are citizens, but you will be looked upon as enemy aliens. There are no other Japanese Americans here, and you may be lonely. At least in the camps you would be with your friends. Think about it and let us know." In a P.S. she added, "We might be moving to Salt Lake City if Joe gets the job he's applied for."

Hana read the letter carefully. She read it many times. Although Mary had opened a way for them, it also seemed she was telling them it would be wiser not to come. And perhaps she was right. They would be isolated out there, and they would miss their friends.

Finally Hana said, "Our place is not in Nevada, Papa. Let us be content to go to camp with our friends."

"That was my thought too, Mama," Taro answered. And the matter was closed.

Chapter 25

Hana started at the sound of the bell. She was so nervous these days, she even disliked answering the telephone.

"Hello?" Her voice was hesitant.

"Is that you, Hana? It's Kiku."

"You're calling from Livingston?" Hana had never before had a long-distance phone call. "Are you all right, Kiku?"

"Yes, yes, we're all right. I just wanted to talk to you one last time before we're all scattered to God knows where. Are you all right? Have you finished clearing out your house? Are you ready to leave?"

Kiku was full of questions, but Hana rushed her answers, fearful of talking too long and causing Kiku to have a terrible phone bill.

"What about your farm, Kiku? What will you and Henry do with your farm?"

"I don't know, Henry's not sure yet. I suppose we'll either sell or lease it. Whatever there's time for." Kiku seemed distracted and unsure.

Hana found herself crying. She had a feeling she might never see Kiku again. "Don't lose touch, whatever happens," she urged. "You can always write to me through Mrs. Davis. Don't forget."

"All right, Hana, I'll remember. Now take care of yourselves. We'll meet again when this blasted war is over. Goodbye, Hana."

Hana could not answer. She clung to the phone as though it were Kiku's hand. She wished she could ask

Taro to drive her to Livingston once more to see Kiku, but Japanese Americans could no longer travel more than five miles from their home. There was also an eight o'clock curfew imposed on them as well. Gradually, in bits and pieces, their freedom was vanishing. Soon they were required to register and obtain identification cards, and next, to turn in short wave radios, cameras and binoculars to the local police. Hana couldn't understand why the young Japanese Americans who were born in the United States lost their freedom along with their alien parents.

"But Papa," she asked, "aren't they American citizens? How can their own country do this to them? What about that Constitution you told me about?"

Hana's questions were endless. But Taro had no answers for her.

Each time a new edict was issued, Taro simply complied because he somehow felt that prompt compliance was one way to show their loyalty, even though it tightened further the circle of restriction placed upon their lives.

The orders to evacuate would come next, but no one knew when. In mid-April, the orders for their area came suddenly from the Western Defense Command, and the departure date was in exactly ten days. On that day, every person of Japanese ancestry in the Bay Area, citizen and non-citizen, was to be uprooted, and in the government's words "evacuated" to the Tanforan Race Track, hastily converted by the army into what it called an "Assembly Center."

Hana was immobilized with anxiety. "But Papa San, I simply cannot be ready in just ten days," she said frantically. "We have only begun to pack."

Taro still had to find a buyer for his shop, and he was spending much time clearing out Dr. Kaneda's flat. "Do the best you can, Hana," he said. There was nothing else to do.

Hana worked erratically, making decisions that made no sense. One day she sold her stove for ten dollars and the next, she carefully packed for storage old letters from her family and friends that should have been discarded years ago. She packed pans she still needed for cooking, keeping muffin tins and jello molds she rarely used. She cleaned out drawers and closet shelves in the bedroom until she was overcome by the welter of possessions. Then she moved to the kitchen, only to be faced with even more belongings.

Hana's frugal upbringing made it impossible for her to throw out anything. She had kept old wrapping paper and bags, balls of old string, rubber bands, clips, old jars, empty boxes, old magazines, wads of tinfoil, stacks of recipes and newspaper clippings she hoped one day to read. If she had been able to live out her life in this house, she thought, everything would someday have found its use. But now, being plucked from her home in ten days, everything became an encumbrance throttling her at the wrong moment.

When Hana read the instructions stating the evacuees must bring their own bedding and eating utensils, she called Reverend Nishima and exploded. "But how can we do this when they also tell us to bring only what we can carry? With a suitcase in each hand, how are we to carry our bedding and dishes? How do I know what to pack when I don't even know how long we will be gone or where we will be living?"

Hana, who had made so many major decisions in her life, now felt incapable even of deciding what to eat for supper. She felt herself disintegrating.

Kenji Nishima sensed the desperation in her voice. "Hold on, Mrs. Takeda. I'll be right over. Put on a kettle and make some tea for me, will you?"

Hana hung up the phone and mechanically made some tea. By the time Reverend Nishima arrived, she had made space on her kitchen table for her tea tray and a plate of cookies.

"Ah, exactly what I needed," he said, taking a noisy gulp of tea, while surveying Hana's predicament.

"I think you should take a hot plate, a kettle, your tea pot and some cups," he began.

"You think there will be electricity?"

"Of course, and you'll be longing for a cup of tea now and then. I'd take a bucket, too, and some clothespins."

"Ah," Hana had not thought of the chores that would follow her into camp.

"Take an umbrella, Taro's boots and your galoshes. And don't forget a flashlight and some batteries."

He helped Hana make a list, telling her he would get a large rucksack for their bedding and bulky items.

"And how do we carry this with us to camp?" Hana asked.

"Don't worry, Mrs. Takeda. Just get everything to the departure area. They'll have to provide a way to get them to camp."

Hana relaxed for the first time that day. "What would I do without you?" she said. "Thank you for coming, Kenji San."

"No thanks needed, Mrs. Takeda," Kenji said, glad to see the tautness leaving her face. "I'm only doing for you what you once did for me." Then rolling up his sleeves, he stayed to help her with further decisions about what to pack, discard and store. By the time he left, Hana had the strength to get through the rest of the day.

Some days Taro would come home to find Hana mending a shirt she was giving to the Salvation Army, instead of preparing supper. But he didn't mind. He had no appetite these days anyway, and often felt as distracted as Hana herself.

One evening as Hana cleaned out a cupboard,

letting the rice boil over on the stove, she heard Taro come in without calling to her as he usually did. "Papa, are you home?"

Hana went to the living room to find him looking around the half-empty room. The carpet was rolled up in one corner and cartons of books lay scattered on the floor. He looked old and tired and there was no color in his face.

"What's wrong, Papa? Are you sick?"

"I sold the shop today." His misery was changing the shape of his face.

"Oh, Papa San. Who bought it from you?"

"A white man. He said there were many Chinese who would rent it from him."

"Was he a good man?"

"As good as any."

Hana was afraid to ask how much he got for the shop. She knew Taro was in no position to bargain. "Did he give you a decent price?"

"Two hundred dollars."

"For everything?"

"For the shop and everything in it."

"But you spent almost thirty years building up that shop."

Taro shrugged. "What was I to do? His was the best of any offer I got."

Hana could find no words to comfort Taro. She knew how important it had been for him not only to own his shop, but to be its true proprietor. She knew that in saving his shop for him once, she had in truth deprived him of it. She didn't want ever to hurt him again, but this time the government had done it with a final, cruel blow.

Now he seemed to have lost the reserve of strength and faith that had succored him through earlier years. He looked down at his hands, as though searching for some answer to his distress. Then, dropping them helplessly, he said, "It's a sad end, Hana."

And Hana knew that for him, life would never be the same again.

With the shop gone, Taro stayed home to help Hana with the last of the packing. Toward the end, the Davis family came to pick up the crates and furniture they would store in their basement. "Leave anything you want to with us," Mrs. Davis urged. "When the basement's full, we'll put things in the attic." She also secured storage space in other homes for the people of Hana's church.

Taro went to the Civil Control Station to register and be processed for the evacuation. He was given a family number, then he sold his car at a nearby gas station for twenty dollars and walked home.

"We're family number 13453," he told Hana, putting tags on all their baggage. "Tomorrow we must be ready to leave."

Like ghosts in a hollow house, Hana and Taro crept into borrowed sleeping bags for their final night in their Oakland home. They had not accepted Mrs. Davis's invitation to stay with them, because until the very end, Hana had things to dispose of.

Now in the dark empty house, there were only four suitcases and two bundles left. Everything else was gone. Hana closed her eyes, but could not sleep. After this night, she and Taro would be in a strange bed in a racetrack called Tanforan. She and Taro had never been to a racetrack before, and now they would be living in one. What strange events life brought, she thought, and what more would happen before it was all over?

Hana sought to escape the fears of the future by turning to the past. She remembered all the days she and Taro had lived in this house, and the happy times they had while Mary was a child. She sighed and turned toward Taro.

"Papa," she whispered, "this *has* been a good home, hasn't it?"

Taro reached out and took her hand. "We will have another home of our own again someday, Mama," he said quietly. "Try not to worry, and go to sleep. Tomorrow is going to be a hard day."

Chapter 26

It was long past midnight. Kiku and the boys had gone to bed, but Henry Toda was in no mood to sleep. They had spent the entire evening discussing the future of their farm and he was still not sure they had made the right decision.

The Japanese American farmers had contemplated the various paths open to them, but found none to be a fully satisfactory solution. They could sell their farms at great losses, try to find someone to rent them or contract with Mel Clarkson to operate the land for them. Clarkson had already signed to operate two thousand acres of farms and vineyards in the area, promising the farmers he would send each of them their fair share of the earnings.

"I'm not sure about Mel Clarkson," Henry had said warily. "He is glib and promises too much." Signing with him was like asking a smiling stranger to hold your bag of gold instead of leaving it on the street. Whether that stranger could be trusted any more than someone who might come along and pick it up was something only time would reveal.

"But if you can't find anyone to lease or sell to, what else is there to do?" Kiku asked. "Besides, if we sell, there will be nothing to come home to after this is all over."

The boys, however, were in favor of selling the farm. "At least we'll have the money in hand if we sell," they pointed out, "and it could be earning some interest in a bank."

"How do you know Clarkson will ever send our fair share?" Kenny asked.

They didn't know, but Kiku and Henry remembered the years of hard work they had put into the land. Whatever grew there now existed because they had planted it and nurtured it in the heat and the wind and the dust.

"It would be like selling my own flesh and blood," Henry explained. He knew the boys did not want to return to the farm, but that was all he and Kiku had. That was their life.

Henry could not have been more proud that his sons had wanted to work their way through the university in Berkeley to study engineering and law. More than anything, he and Kiku wanted their sons to have the best education possible and to become good Americans. He could understand why they did not want to become farmers. That was their decision. But now he had to think of Kiku and himself. When he finally came to a decision it was to sign on with Clarkson as many of the other farmers were doing.

The boys accepted his decision. "The farm's in our name, but it's your land, Pa," they said. "It's up to you." And they had offered no further argument.

Henry looked around their living room now, cluttered with old furniture that Kiku had squeezed into it over the years. The brown couch with its pile worn thin, the faded rug, the round table ringed with glass marks, the Book of Knowledge set that Kiku had begged him to buy for the boys, although they could ill-afford it at the time. It wasn't much of a home, Henry thought, but he didn't want to lose it.

Filled with doubts and anxieties, Henry paced about the room, finally sitting down to read again the letter from his friend, Sojiro Kaneda, interned in Montana.

"It is ten below zero here," he wrote, "and from the

window I can see thick icicles reaching from the barrack roof to the ground. Until they issued us some army winter clothing, we feared we would all perish from pneumonia. One eighty-three year old man has already died, and another has gone insane. There are over . . . men here from . . ." The censor had neatly clipped out names and numbers that he did not want revealed. Exasperated, Henry tossed the letter aside.

He sat in the stillness of the country night, remembering how he and Sojiro Kaneda had come to America on a ship so small, they feared it would founder in the Pacific, sending them to a watery grave. Until Kaneda earned enough to continue at medical school, they had worked together picking fruit in the orchards of the Sacramento Valley or washing dishes in greasy cafes. Henry knew that the only reason Kaneda was locked up in that frigid prisoner of war camp and he was still free in Livingston was because Kaneda liked to join organizations; because he wanted to help the Japanese farmers and teach the young Nisei the language of their parents; because he could not help but be a leader of men.

Engulfed for a moment in the pleasant network of the past, Henry longed to do something for his old friend. Deciding that a package of food might bring Kaneda some cheer, he went to the kitchen and took from the shelves a pound of coffee, three cans of condensed milk, a package of peanut brittle, some canned peaches and some tins of sardines in tomato sauce.

"That ought to give you a nice snack, old friend," he said, packing everything into a carton he found under the sink. Just before he wrapped it up, he put in some old Japanese magazines and two packages of cigarettes. He addressed the package, set it on the table to mail the next morning and felt better than he had all day.

The activity not only pleased him, it gave him an appetite as well, and he brewed a pot of coffee to go with the last piece of chocolate cake in the bread box. The rich, strong aroma of coffee filled the small kitchen, and Henry was tempted to waken Kiku, for she loved a good cup of coffee at any hour of the day. When he went to their room, however, he saw her in the uncaring shape of sleep, her mouth open, snoring lightly, her hands thrown over her head on the pillow.

"You are a good wife, Kiku, and a good mother, too," he said softly. And he thought back to the days when Kiku had worked beside him in the fields with Jimmy tied to her back because he was too small to be left alone. She had worked, too, in the packing shed so she could earn a little extra money. How had she found the time to cook and clean and wash for him and the boys as well? She hadn't complained about watching every penny and she had been content to wear second-hand clothes. Now, at last, when life was getting easier and the boys were learning professions, everything they had worked for was slipping away like sand through their fingers.

"I'm sorry, Kiku," Henry whispered, and he did not awaken her.

If only the boys could have remained behind to complete their education, Henry thought, they could have come down on weekends to keep an eye on the farm. But they'd had to drop out of school and return to Livingston to avoid separation from their parents when they were sent to the government camps. It just wasn't right. The boys were American citizens. They had done nothing wrong, except to be born to parents who were of Japanese birth. Henry knew that if he allowed himself to be overcome by bitterness and anger, he would go under from the weight of it. He went back to the kitchen, ate his cake without really tasting it and lingered over his coffee with a cigarette.

Henry put down his cup. Was that a footstep on the gravel walk outside? He listened quietly, but heard only the ticking of the clock. Who could be wandering around their house at two o'clock in the morning? He turned out the living room light and looked out into the frosty darkness. The night was quiet and there was no moon. Old Rick was dead, but somewhere on another farm, a dog was howling into the night. Henry felt a chill go down his back as he listened. This time he was sure of it, there was someone prowling about in his yard. Henry found a flashlight, opened the door quietly and stepped outside. As he did, a dark figure darted into the shadow of the walnut tree.

"Who is it? Who's there?"

The man did not answer.

"What do you want?"

Henry's flashlight caught the shape of a man whose face was shadowed by a wide-brimmed hat. He held a gun in his hand.

"What do you want?" Henry demanded again.

"Filthy stinking Jap!" the man shouted in a quivering voice.

"Put down your gun. You're drunk." Henry waited, watching for a chance to disarm the man. "Put down your gun. You don't know what you're doing."

Henry took a slight step forward, and in that instant a shot rang out. The man uttered a cry of rage and desperation and ran off into the night.

Henry Toda slumped to the ground, as blood rushed from the bullet hole in his chest.

Chapter 27

"The rain has stopped, Mama. It's going to be a nice day," Taro observed, trying to find something positive to say.

"That's good," Hana answered without really caring.

In just an hour Mrs. Davis would be there to take them to the Civil Control Station. From there, they would be sent to Tanforan racetrack. Hana wasn't sure she could get through the day. Already her heart was pounding and her throat felt dry. Finding a broom she had left in the pantry, she proceeded to sweep out the house.

"What are you doing, Hana? We've got to be ready soon."

"I know. I just want to leave the house clean."

Victor Davis came with his mother to help them with their baggage. "I think it's a crime, what they're doing to you people," he said, as he slung the large rucksack on his back.

"Thank you, Victor," Hana said, not knowing whether she was thanking him for being angry on their behalf, or for carrying out their baggage.

By the time they got to the departure point, a large crowd of Japanese Americans had already gathered and were milling about looking bewildered and lost. Victor and Taro unloaded their baggage and were told to take them to waiting trucks. Kenji San had been right, Hana thought. They weren't going to make them carry everything into camp with them. "I didn't have to practice carrying the bags after all," she murmured. But no one knew what she was talking about.

"Hana, my dear, I can't say goodbye." Ellen Davis gathered her tenderly in her arms.

Hana barely managed to thank her and shook Victor's hand silently, leaving Taro to offer the proper words of thanks and parting for them both.

Ellen and Victor Davis watched as Hana and Taro struggled through the crowd, finally reaching the armed guards who stood at the entrance of the building. They waited until Hana and Taro went inside, but neither looked back.

Hana and Taro sat on stiff folding chairs until it was time to board the buses. Although the hall was noisy with the rumble of voices, they remained silent, each wrapped in thoughts that could not be shared. Neither bothered to look for a familiar face, for their church friends had been sent to Tanforan a few days earlier.

Only the children chattered, as the buses, filled with Japanese Americans, began their trip through familiar streets. Hana watched silently from the window as the bus crossed the Bay Bridge, moved down the peninsula and finally approached the grandstand that loomed beside the highway. As the bus turned in toward the racetrack, she saw that a barbed wire fence surrounded the grounds, and when the last of the buses moved in, armed guards swung the gates shut. Hana swallowed hard as the anxiety and dread of the day rose up and lodged like a knot in her throat.

A large crowd of those already uprooted stood along the track railing watching for friends as each busload arrived. Hana searched for their friends, but saw only a blur of Japanese faces.

She felt far more apprehensive than she had on the day she arrived from Japan. Although this time Taro was with her, he seemed equally stunned. It was as though they were walking in a nightmare. Unable to believe this was actually taking place, Hana looked about in complete disbelief. What on earth are we doing here, she wondered, thrown into a racetrack teeming with thousands of uprooted Japanese Americans.

Not until they had a cursory medical check-up and had been assigned their quarters did Kenji Nishima find them. "There you are," he called. "Welcome to Tanforan."

Hana felt like a lost child suddenly finding its father. "Thank goodness you are here, Kenji San," she cried.

He looked at the slip of paper in Taro's hand. "Barrack Sixteen, Apartment Forty," he read. "I'll take you there. Come with me."

The two men walked slightly ahead of Hana, who followed them down the curve of the track. The ground was muddied by rain, and she skirted the puddles carefully, wishing she hadn't worn her Sunday shoes or dressed as though she were going to church. It had never occurred to her to go out dressed otherwise, but she felt foolish now, for it would have been more appropriate to be in her work clothes.

"Are you all right, Mrs. Takeda?" Kenji looked back and waited for her to catch up.

"Yes. Are we almost there?"

He paused to get his bearings, glancing about at the army barracks constructed in every available space around the track. "Not quite. I think you've been assigned to one of the old stables."

"We are to live in stables where the horses were kept?" Taro had not intended to show his dismay, but the words had slipped out before he could stop them.

Twice Kenji had to ask for directions, then, leaving the racetrack, he led them to a long stable labeled

Barrack Sixteen. They went up a ramp and came to a door marked number forty. Kenji pushed open the door and they stepped into a stall so hastily whitewashed that insects still clung to the walls, immortalized in their small acts of survival by man's hasty white spray. There were two small windows on either side of the door, but the rear half of the stall was dark and windowless. It also smelled of its former occupants.

"So this is our 'apartment,'" Taro said bleakly.

"I'll go find a broom," Kenji offered. "And Mr. Takeda, we'd better go pick up some mattresses so you'll have something to sleep on tonight."

He and Taro set up one of the cots for Hana, telling her they would be back soon. Hana blew the dust from the springs and sat down, removing her hat and her gloves. Shivering as the north wind blew in from the crevices around the door and windows, she gathered her coat close around her, wondering if the horses, too, had been so cold. She got up to pace the floor, feeling the grit and dust and wishing she'd had the sense to bring a broom.

There was a pounding at the door. "Mr. and Mrs. Taro Takeda?"

Pleased to think one of their friends had somehow found them already, Hana flung open the door. A young boy with a pimpled face held out a yellow envelope. "Telegram," he said, as he hurried away.

It seemed ludicrous that such amenities could follow them to a horse stall behind barbed wire. Hana was reluctant to open it. Telegrams never brought good news, and her fingers shook as she struggled with the envelope. At first, she could not believe what she read.

TODA SHOT TO DEATH LAST NIGHT STOP FUNERAL SUNDAY KIKU

Hana read the telegram over and over before she

understood what it said. Still, she could not believe it. Why would anyone want to kill such a warm, lovable man? Henry never would have harmed another living creature. Hana continued to read the telegram again and again, as though by reading its terse message something of the awful circumstances might be revealed.

"Kiku, oh Kiku. I cannot even go to comfort you."

Hana shuddered, suddenly depleted and drained of all feeling. She could not really be here, sitting in this miserable horse stall, shivering on a dusty cot, mourning the loss of an old friend. It just was not happening. She could not even cry.

When Taro and Kenji returned with two straw-filled mattresses, their faces streaked with dust and sweat, they found Hana sitting silently on the cot looking stunned. She was still clutching the telegram.

In the Montana prisoner of war camp, a similar telegram reached Sojiro Kaneda as he taught a class in English literature. The men had organized classes in English, American history, music and art, taught by internees, to help the internees pass the long hours of each day.

Dr. Kaneda took the wire hopefully, wondering if by some miracle it was bringing word of an early release for him. He read it silently, then dismissed his class.

"I am sorry, gentlemen," he said gravely. "I have just learned of the death of a dear friend and must ask you to excuse me."

He was glad to be assigned to kitchen duty that day, and he went to the mess hall early. He sat alone in a dark corner, tore open a sack of potatoes, then peeling as fast as his fingers could move, he let the tears come.

When Henry's package reached him almost a month later, Dr. Kaneda invited the men of his barrack to gather around the roaring wood stove that night. He made a pot of coffee and opened the cans, not knowing what they contained, for no paper was permitted in their packages and all the labels had been torn off.

He passed out the cigarettes and the peanut brittle so every man had a share. Then as they sat together, to comfort and be comforted, Sojiro Kaneda spoke quietly.

"We are remembering tonight a good friend of mine, Hisakazu Henry Toda. He died because the two countries we love are at war with one another. He died because of hatred and fear. Let us remember him here tonight with love."

Chapter 28

"There's only one way to get your wash done, missus, and that's to go to the laundry before anyone gets up."

The woman in the stall to their right sat on a box in front of her door and called to Hana as she returned from the laundry barrack with her laundry still unwashed. No matter what time Hana went, there was a long line, and by the time she reached a tub, the hot water was gone.

Today, Hana had not waited. She couldn't bear the thought of standing in line exchanging complaints, rumors and pleasantries and had returned to her stall. She disliked indulging in idle chatter with strangers and felt degraded each time she had to stand in line for something. It had begun the evening of their arrival when they had stood in a long weaving line outside the grandstand for their supper. Clutching their plates and forks, buffeted by a sweeping wind, they had finally reached the serving area only to receive two weiners and a potato. A man had dropped them on their plates from a dishpanful, using his fingers to serve them. Ever since, they had stood in lines for everything—meals, showers, the post office, the canteen and even the latrines during the first few hectic days.

Unlike Hana, the woman in the next stall thrived on any crumb of conversation, cornering anyone who passed by. Fat and slovenly, she wore a spot-splattered black skirt, an unpressed blouse with several missing buttons and sagging stockings held in place below her knees with rubber bands.

"That's what I did," she said now. "I got up at four o'clock and had the whole laundry barrack to myself. Now I can sit here and do nothing until lunch." She grinned in self-approbation.

"Ah yes, I see. I'll try doing that tomorrow." Hana tried to enter her own stall, but the woman was not ready to release her.

"How does your daughter like being married to a white man?" she asked shamelessly.

Hana caught her breath. "You know my daughter?"

The woman threw back her head and laughed, revealing a glittering array of gold fillings. She pushed back her graying hair and fastened the loose ends in an unwieldly bun.

"I heard you and the mister speaking about her last night. Her name is Mary, isn't it? And she lives someplace far off, Nevada, was it?"

"Yes, but they're moving to Salt Lake City soon. Her husband will teach there."

Hana remembered that she and Taro had indeed been speaking of Mary the night before, forgetting that even a sigh or the ticking of a clock could be heard in the neighboring stalls. A wide opening ran the length of the stable between the sloping roof and the dividing walls of the stalls. Any conversation or argument could be heard by many people, the number increasing as one's voice rose. A variety of smells travelled through the space as well—toast being made for an evening snack, coffee being heated on a hot plate or the sweet, smoky scent of moxa being burned on a sore muscle.

Hana deplored the lack of privacy. When she first went to the latrine and discovered there were no doors to the toilet cubicles, she had run back for a bath towel to tack up at the doorway. She hated washing her face in the long tin trough of the community washroom where some women casually emptied their bedpans, and she despised the showers, not only because they also lacked doors, but because she'd never used one before and nearly burned her back with the scalding water that shot out.

Since her neighbor seemed determined to engage her in further conversation now, Hana decided to counter with some questions of her own. "Is that your son living with you?" she asked. "You're lucky to have him with you."

The woman hooted and slapped her thigh. "Lucky! I wish he lived a thousand miles from me. Ever since his father died, he's caused me nothing but misery and heartache. He's been smoking since he was thirteen, and drinking almost as long. Now he spends all his spare time gambling. He hasn't brought me a day's pleasure in the last ten years."

The woman was finally silenced by her own misery.

"We all have our problems, I suppose," Hana ventured. "Our children hurt us in different ways."

The woman shed her sorrow quickly and motioned Hana to come into her stall. "Come see what he got for me yesterday," she said with obvious pleasure. "I don't know where he found it, but it's certainly going to be useful."

Hana couldn't refuse and followed the old woman into her stall. She was amazed to see how different it was from her own, although they had once been identical. The day after their arrival, Kenji had taken Taro to the scrap lumber pile, and in a few days they had constructed a crude table and two benches for their "sitting room" in the front half of the stall. In the rear, where they put their cots, Taro had put up some shelves and even made a small dressing table for Hana. Mrs. Davis had sent her some chintz, and with it Hana made curtains for the windows and covered cushions for their benches.

The woman next door, however, had done nothing to relieve the crude penury of her stall. Her two cots were covered with government-issue army blankets. Two boxes and a crate served for a table and chairs. The object of the woman's pride, however, was a large wooden barrel just inside the door.

"Look," she said, rubbing its sides proudly. "I'm going to roll it down to the shower and fill it with hot water. Then I'm going to climb inside and have myself a nice long soak."

Hana couldn't restrain the laughter that welled up inside her. "What a wonderful idea," she said, admiring the woman's resourcefulness.

"I thought so myself," she agreed. Warmed by Hana's praise, she offered to share her new treasure with Hana. "You can borrow it anytime you like, missus," she said with a broad grin. "My son can roll it down to the showers for you whenever you want."

"Thank you. That's very kind of you." Hana backed away, leaving quickly before the woman could prolong their visit any further.

She was glad her neighbors to the left were as quiet and restrained as this woman was garrulous. They were a widow, Mrs. Mitosa, and her daughter, Sumiko. Hana knew little of them because they always spoke in hushed voices. She did know, however, that Sumiko taught at the elementary school, and the few times she had spoken to her, she had seemed gracious and gentle.

As she was returning to her stall, Hana saw Taro and Kenji coming up the ramp. Kenji had taken Taro's arm and was helping him as though he were an old man. Taro did seem old these days, even to Hana. He had aged with each new shock that had violated the peace of his small secure world, and now he seemed to be slipping into numbing lethargy. Dr. Kaneda's abrupt seizure by the FBI had shaken him badly. The loss of the shop into which he had poured his life's energy eroded his being even further, perhaps beyond salvage. The last blow had been Henry Toda's senseless death. Taro was like a man who had been struck down once too often, and Hana wondered if he could ever rise again.

"Can you help him?" she had asked Kenji.

"I'll do my best, Mrs. Takeda." He had promised, but Kenji was aware that he could not give Taro the kind of friendship or support he longed for. It was as though Taro still thought of him as the floundering young seminary student who had almost lost his grip on life. He was still not sure how much Taro knew of or resented his collusion with Hana to help save his shop.

Kenji Nishima had learned many things during the years he ministered to the Japanese. He understood how it was with men such as Taro whose pride kept them from drawing close to anyone to whom they were obligated. He knew that Taro had kept him at arm's length so they never quite shared the closeness he had with Hana.

Kenji tried to draw Taro into the activities of the camp church, but there was an abundance of leadership and Taro's small voice was heeded only by his own church friends. He suggested a job, but Taro did not want the jobs open to him. "I'm not going to sweep out mess halls or wash any more dishes," he said acridly.

Finally, one day, Kenji took Taro to one of the recreation centers where tools were available for woodcarving and carpentering. Taro showed only mild interest in the clogs and bookends some men were making, but when he saw a hand-carved washboard, he suddenly said, "I'd like to make one of those for Hana. It will help her with the washing."

"She'd like a container for carrying dishes to the mess hall too," Kenji pointed out, and he was pleased when Taro wanted to stop at the scrap lumber pile on the way home. They had not been there since the first days when they had put together the crude pieces of furniture.

Watching them return together now, Hana felt hopeful. She hoped Kenji could help Taro come to life once more.

Hana smiled and waved to them. Her wave included her young neighbor, Sumiko, who was coming up the ramp behind them. Sumiko waved back cheerfully.

In that instant, Hana's matchmaking instincts blossomed like a flower in the sun, and she knew if she did nothing else in camp, she would find a good wife for Kenji Nishima. Until now he had been too involved with studies and his ministry to take time to find a wife. Or perhaps God intended that he wait until just this time and place, so Hana could find the right woman for him. It was a tantalizing thought.

Hana wondered how to proceed as a go-between. Perhaps she should talk to Sumiko's mother first. But as these thoughts danced in her head, Hana saw Taro himself stop to introduce Sumiko to Kenji Nishima. The three of them paused to chat, and Hana caught herself just as she was about to rush down to join them. For once I will let Taro do this thing in his own way, she told herself, and going inside, she waited for them to come to her.

Chapter 29

Taro and Hana sat in their stall waiting for the evening headcount.

"How many?" the headcounter would ask, knocking at their door, and they would obligingly answer, "Two."

It seemed such foolishness, this counting of heads each morning and evening, as though any of them would try to escape. Where could they go if they did manage to climb out of the barbed-wire enclosure? Their Japanese faces would trap them in a matter of minutes.

Sometimes the boy next door would answer "None," or "Twenty-five," provoking the headcounter into a heated exchange of words.

"I'm only doing my job," the headcounter would shout angrily.

And the boy shouted back, "Aw, go soak your head."

Hana would laugh softly. The boy was certainly rude, but she admired his spirit, for the headcounter was arrogant and took himself far too seriously. At least the boy and his mother had maintained their sense of humor, which was more than could be said of many others in the camp. There had even been serious bickering over the election of a camp council, which permitted Hana and Taro to vote for the first time in America, an ironic privilege granted only because of their incarceration. Hana had been surprised at the ill-tempered arguments among the candidates for office.

After the evening headcount, Hana and Taro often went for a walk around the track. It was like a reward, a release from their small cell, after having had to rush back from supper to be in their stall to answer "two." No one minded the morning count, which came at six when everyone was still in bed. But the rush back for the evening count seemed an affront to their dignity. They could scarcely speak of human dignity, however, when the boundaries of their lives had already been forced into the space of a single horse stall.

"Let's go sit in the grandstand," Taro suggested as they started their evening walk.

"Again? I don't like to go near those guards."

"You don't have to look at them. We'll climb up into the stands and look out where we can see the hills."

Taro liked climbing up to the highest seats where they could see the highway with its speeding cars, and beyond that the coast range, turned glorious mauves and blues by the sunset.

Tonight as they looked down on the racetrack from the grandstand, Hana saw Kenji Nishima walking with Sumiko Mitosa.

"Look, Papa," she said, pointing. "Isn't that Sumiko and Kenji San?"

She was pleasantly surprised to hear Taro say, "She's a little young for him, but she is a good person. She would make him a fine wife, and it's time he was married."

"Why, Papa, that is exactly what I was thinking myself," Hana said, delighted that Taro should have spoken of it first. And rummaging about in her pocket, she offered him a lifesaver so they might savor this pleasant thought together over a sweet.

Before they could speak further of it, however, two church friends appeared to join them. They nodded their greetings and spoke of the beauty of the evening sky. Then engaging in the pastime endemic to camp, they traded the latest rumors.

"Have you heard the FBI are coming to camp?"

"Yes. Do you know why?"

"To search for contraband . . . radios, guns, Japanese books, maybe even sugar. Who knows?"

"When?"

"Maybe tomorrow. Maybe the next day."

Taro felt a wave of apprehension as he thought of Dr. Kaneda. "I hope they're not coming to take anyone away," he said gravely.

For several days, the rumor about the FBI search had fluttered through camp. Hana heard it in the showers, in the latrine, in the washroom and in every line in which she stood. The entire camp was growing uneasy, not because anyone had anything to hide, but simply because the whole idea seemed ominous and threatening. Then the official notice was issued, and rumor became fact, as it often did.

The day of the search, no one was to leave his quarters until an inspection was made. Hana and Taro waited all morning in their stall, but at noon, there was still no sign of the inspectors.

"Do you think we can go eat lunch?" Mrs. Mitosa called from her stall.

"I'm sure it's all right if we have lunch," Hana said. "Don't you think so, Papa?"

Taro was carving a handle for the dish container he had made for Hana. "I suppose," he said absently. "It really doesn't matter. I'm not hungry."

"Well, I am," Hana said. "And you've got to eat too."

The mess hall was teeming with new rumors. The FBI were turning the camp upside down. They were confiscating all radios. They had found a gun. They were molesting women. No one knew whether there was a crumb of truth to any of it, but the residents of Tanforan wallowed in a constant morass of half-truths and rumors. They amassed them, hoarded them, sifted through them during sleepless nights, and passed them on during the tedium of waiting in line.

As they whiled away the long afternoon, Hana told Taro of a new rumor she had begun to hear. "They say we'll be sent somewhere to another state, Papa. Do you think we will?"

"I don't know, Mama. But I have heard Idaho and Utah mentioned."

"Ah, so far away."

Taro wanted to be careful about giving Hana any more easy assurances. He had been wrong about the entire uprooting, and he could be sure of nothing any more. He considered for a moment the wisdom of sharing a faint hope he had been mulling alone on nights when sleep eluded him. Then he spoke.

"If we do get sent to Utah . . ."

"Yes? What?"

"It is possible our train might pass through Salt Lake City."

"And we could see Mary?"

"That did cross my mind," Taro admitted. "It's only a vague thought, Mama."

But Hana grasped it eagerly. "That would be so nice," she said thoughtfully. "I would truly like to see our grandchild."

Now that she had become a parent, Mary wrote more often, especially since Hana and Taro had been sent to camp. She sent snapshots of little Laurie, and when Hana saw them, she could no longer deny her love for the small creature.

At some moment, she did not know just when, Hana found that she had forgiven Mary for everything. She no longer remembered many of the things Mary had done to hurt them, and she understood her daughter's need to be free.

Now, the faint possibility of seeing Mary and Laurie eased a little the dread of leaving California and everything that meant home to her.

It was three-thirty and still the inspectors had not arrived at their stable. Everyone was growing jittery and uneasy. People moved in and out of their stalls, unable to leave, wondering, worrying and passing on new rumors. The longer they waited the more threatening the situation seemed.

"Papa, I must go to the latrine," Hana said at last.

"Go then."

"But suppose they come while I'm there."

"Then they come," he said, glancing at her. "If you must go, then you must go."

Taking her soap dish and towel, Hana hurried off. She had the terrible thought that the inspectors would appear the moment she left. When she came out of the washroom, it was exactly as she had feared. Their entire stable was surrounded by soldiers carrying guns mounted with bayonets.

She hurried to one of them and tugged at his sleeve. "I must get through, please. I live in this stable and the inspectors have come."

The young guard looked at her with a hint of compassion, but he would not let her pass. "Sorry, ma'm. We have orders not to let anyone pass until the inspection is over."

"But I live here. I have been waiting all day. Please." Hana was frantic.

But the soldiers were firm. She waited, standing for almost an hour, watching as three men went in and out of every stall. They didn't seem to be taking very long. What were they doing? When at last the inspection was over the soldiers marched off, and Hana ran back to her stall.

"Papa, the soldiers wouldn't let me come back.

What did they do? What happened?"

"I saw that they wouldn't let you through," Taro acknowledged. Then he told her that the men had been in the stall for less than two minutes. "They just looked around, asked if I had any contraband, and when I said no, they left."

"That was all?"

Taro nodded, "That was all."

"We waited all day just for that?" Hana sank onto the bench and held her hands over her face.

"Mama, are you crying? What are you crying for?"

Hana didn't know herself whether she was weeping with rage or relief. "I'm crying for the stupidity of it all," she cried out. And in the silent stable she realized that all her neighbors had heard her anguish. But she didn't care. There was no place to hide. There was no place to cry. They all shared their grief and anger and frustrations together.

Chapter 30

By late August, it became evident that the Tanforan "Assembly Center" was to be phased out and that the internees would be sent to Utah.

"I hate having to pack again," Hana said dismally. "I was finally getting used to this old horse stall."

"The new camp might be better," Taro said, trying to find a cheering thought. "We might have more room."

"But we won't be in California any more."

The thought of leaving California left Taro with an ache of despair too. The state had not always been kind to them, but he had always considered it his home.

When Kenji and Sumiko knocked on the door, they found Hana and Taro looking bleak and discouraged.

"Have we come at a bad time?" Kenji asked. He expressed concern, but he could not conceal his happiness. He was smiling and holding Sumiko's hand. She was dressed in her Sunday clothes, looking self-conscious and a little embarrassed.

"No, no. Please come in," Hana said brightening. She knew immediately why they had come.

"Sit down, sit down," Taro urged, moving so the guests might share the bench opposite him. "Mama, why don't you make some tea?"

Hana had already plugged in the hot plate, and as she put the kettle on, she thought gratefully of the gifts Mrs. Davis had brought when she visited them the day before. Ashamed of what their country was doing to the Japanese Americans, ashamed of her own brief moment of doubt, Ellen Davis had joined a group of concerned citizens who organized to assist the Japanese Americans in any way they could. But knowing it was too late to reverse the damage already inflicted, she did everything possible to ease the pain. She had stood in line waiting in the hot sun for two hours, carrying a large basket filled with cookies, nuts, fruit and candy for Taro and Hana. The visit had exhausted her, but it also helped assuage the terrible guilt she felt as an American.

I will serve a little of everything, Hana thought now, for she knew this was going to be a very special occasion.

"We have some good news," Kenji began.

Hana and Taro smiled, waiting, eager to hear what they hoped he would say.

"Sumiko and I are engaged and hope to be married before we are sent to Utah."

"And we wondered," Sumiko continued, "if you would act as our go-between. Just as a formality, of course."

"What could be nicer than being go-betweens for a match already made?" Taro said, stretching his hands to them both. "We would be happy and proud."

"You've made us happier than we can say," Hana added.

Immediately, there was a pleased murmur from the stall next door. The sound of cards being shuffled stopped, and the woman called out, "Congratulations, Reverend, you've picked yourself a fine bride."

Sumiko's mother, who had been waiting for the proper moment in the conversation, now appeared with a gift wrapped carefully in white paper and red ribbon. Bowing several times to Hana and Taro, she thanked them for bringing Kenji and Sumiko together.

"Yes, it was Mr. Takeda who introduced us right

here on the ramp," Sumiko said brightly. "Remember, Kenji?"

Her eyes were full of love, and Hana felt an ache at the sight. Sumiko was young, but she had the inner strength that would enable her to become a good minister's wife. Hana thought fleetingly of Mary, longing to do for Kenji and Sumiko what she had been unable to do for her daughter and Joe.

"We'll see that you have a wonderful wedding and a fine reception, too," she began.

"Yes, I want a real church wedding," Sumiko interrupted. "I've already ordered a gown. It's going to be as though we weren't in camp at all."

Hana remembered those words as she sat with Mrs. Mitosa in the front row of folding chairs set up in the church barrack. She was glad she had brought one good dress, and she wore her hat and gloves, as she would have done were she in Oakland. She watched Taro as he came down the aisle with Sumiko on his arm, and was pleased to see him looking so proud and happy. At last, you are the father of the bride, she thought.

Sumiko was radiant in a white satin gown, with a froth of a veil. She carried a bouquet of white roses ordered from outside, and a flower girl threw rose petals in her path. It was exactly as Sumiko had wished, as though they were not in a concentration camp at all.

Sumiko's friends had obtained rice from the mess hall to throw at the couple as they left the church. Laughing and ducking, Kenji and Sumiko hurried into one of the official cars borrowed for the occasion. It was hung with streamers and tin cans and "just married" signs. As soon as they climbed in, the driver began to honk the horn and the car pulled away.

The reception tea was held at the mess hall at four

o'clock. When the young couple left, Hana and Taro watched and waved as the car headed toward the racetrack where it drove around a half dozen times, honking and stirring up the dust. People shouted and waved as they passed, caught up for a moment in the joy of the event, and a few children tried to run after the car, shrieking with laughter and excitement. But the car could not go beyond the gate and eventually, it left the track to go to a stable at the southern end of the camp. There it deposited Kenji and Sumiko in front of a horse stall which would be their first home together, and their wedding night was spent in a self-conscious effort to be as quiet as possible in their love-making.

Sumiko and Kenji volunteered to join the first contingent going to the Topaz Relocation Center. Composed of doctors, nurses and administrative personnel, this group would prepare the new camp for the internees.

Two weeks later, when the departure date for their area was set, Taro wrote to Mary and Joe.

"Perhaps you could check with the War Relocation Authority or the railroad and find out when our train will pass through Salt Lake City. If you could possibly come to the station, we would be so happy to have a glimpse of you."

Even as he wrote, however, he said to Hana, "It might not be so easy for them to learn when our train will pass through. It might be in the middle of the night."

"I know," Hana said. "I'm not going to expect them. Then I won't be disappointed if they don't come."

In their last days at Tanforan, Taro converted their furniture into crates for shipping their belongings to Utah. Hana, seeing the disorder of their possessions, was afraid the inspectors might reprimand them for having too much.

But Taro reassured her that they had no more than anyone else. "Besides," he said, "we'll need all these things when we get to Utah."

"You'd better take everything," their neighbor called, leaping into their conversation. "I'm filling up my barrel and I know I'll be glad to have everything at the new camp."

"You're probably right," Hana agreed, and she completed her packing with no further concern.

When it was time to leave Tanforan, Hana was surprised at her reluctance to move from their shabby horse stall, but knew it was only the pain of still another uprooting and parting.

"Are you ready to go?" she called to Sumiko's mother.

Mrs. Mitosa was coughing again. Hana had often heard that rasping cough in the middle of the night and worried about her.

"Yes," she answered hoarsely. "I'm ready."

"Well, I'm not," her other neighbor called. "I've still got to put things in my shopping bag."

"We'll see you in Topaz then," Hana said to her.

The loquacious woman, like the horse stall itself, had become comfortable and familiar, for neither possessed a shred of pretense. They simply were what they were, and nothing more. Hana had learned something from the woman even though she was often a meddlesome fool. "Take care of yourself," she said, "and don't miss the train."

Once again their baggage was inspected at the departure area before they were assigned numbers. Then they waited until they were called to board the train, walking single file between a row of armed guards.

Taro was astonished to see gas light fixtures on their coach. "They must have pulled this car out of storage," he observed. "It must be some kind of relic."

Hana could not keep her eyes from the window. A vast crowd of those who remained behind were jammed against the fence, waving to those who were going ahead. It reminded her of the farewells at the dock in Yokohama when her ship had sailed for America. The train could have been her ship and she could have been leaving Japan again.

Hana could no longer see the church friends who had come to see them off, but she waved to the sea of faces, and the hands waved back like a field of moving grain.

The train gave a heaving lurch and began to move slowly. Hana watched silently as the rows of barracks and stables clustered inside the barbed wire fence slowly slipped from view.

"Goodbye Japan . . . goodbye Tanforan . . ." she whispered.

Chapter 31

Hana was shocked to realize how total their isolation had been during the past four months. What had seemed so ordinary before, now seemed like a strange new world. Everything she saw outside the window intrigued her—the houses, gardens, trees, streets, cars, buses, traffic lights, blond children riding bicycles, adults driving cars, restaurants, people moving about freely and going about their business seemingly unaware of the war in the Pacific. Seeing the free world rush by just beyond her reach, Hana felt more of a prisoner than she had in their horse stall. Yet she could not take her eyes from it. She stared out the window until it grew dark and the car captain ordered all shades drawn until sunrise.

It was a miserable night. No one could sleep on the stiff hard seats, and many, riding a train for the first time, became carsick. The restrooms overflowed with filth, and the coach was soon littered with paper cups, candy wrappers and fruit peelings as restless children ran up and down the aisle.

Hana's head throbbed from the stale air of the coach and every bone in her body ached.

"Will we ever get to Utah?" she asked wearily.

Taro did not answer. He was struggling from one position to another, trying to get comfortable enough to sleep. In the seat behind them, Mrs. Mitosa was coughing again. She continued to cough all night, and hearing her, Hana thought morning would never come.

Another long day passed, with a short stop in the middle of a bleak Nevada desert where a low fence ran parallel to the tracks. As armed guards stationed themselves along the fence, the car captain announced that everyone could detrain. "But only for ten minutes," he warned, "and stay in the area between the train and the guards." It was a brief respite, but the fresh air was a relief. As the train continued its slow lumbering journey, Hana felt she could somehow endure another day.

As evening approached, Taro glanced nervously at his watch. "It looks as though we won't be in Salt Lake City until very late tonight," he said to Hana.

"They might not be there then," Hana answered.

Each tried to prepare the other for the disappointment they feared was waiting for them. As the train neared the city, a current of conversation ran through the coach. The train would stop for supplies and water, and, although they could not get off, a stop in a city was too big an event to sleep through. About ten o'clock the car captain announced that they could all raise their shades to see the Great Salt Lake.

"Ah, it is so large . . . like a sea. . . ."

"It is so beautiful, so peaceful in the moonlight."

Everyone was talking now and sleep was quite out of the question. Mrs. Mitosa leaned over to whisper to Hana. "I hope they will be there, your daughter and son-in-law."

"We really aren't expecting them," Hana answered. "After all, it is so late."

"Yes, but still, perhaps they will come," Mrs. Mitosa said, voicing the thought that Hana hadn't the courage to contemplate.

As midnight approached, Taro and Hana sat rigid and stiff, stifling the turmoil that stirred in their hearts. They could see the lights of the city now as the train slowed down, and at last, it eased into the station. Outside, they could hear the sound of hissing steam, the voices of the conductors, the shouts of the maintenance men as they serviced the train. And inside, the excited voices of the internees trying to get a glimpse of the station. Taro struggled with the window, veins bulging as he strained to open it. Then he leaned out.

"Papa, do you see them?"

"No, not yet."

Hana edged beside him, straining for a glimpse of a familiar face. "I guess they couldn't come," she said at last. "I guess . . ."

Suddenly they saw Mary in a bright red coat. Holding on to Joe's hand, she was rushing from window to window of the car just ahead.

"Mary, Mary! Here we are!"

"Ma Chan! Ma Chan!"

It wasn't until she was almost upon them that Mary finally saw her parents waving to her. She rushed toward them.

"Mama, Papa! Joe, there they are!"

They ran together, holding hands. Taro and Hana leaned out as far as they dared, as Mary hugged them both. "Oh, Mama. Papa." There was so much to say, she had no words.

"Are you all right? Are they treating you all right?"

"You're looking fine, Mr. and Mrs. Takeda," Joe said. "Are they really taking good care of you in the camps?"

"Yes, yes," Taro answered.

Hana nodded. "We're fine. We're fine. Where's Laurie?"

"Oh, Mama, we wanted to bring her, but she's had a bad cold all week and we didn't think we should bring her out so late." Mary and Joe poured out their story together, saying the same thing in different words.

"She eats well?" Taro asked. "She's growing strong?"

"Yes, she's fine. She's fine," Mary repeated. "Tell us if you need anything. Is there anything you want? Send us your address when you get to this camp—this Topaz, will you?"

They talked of small things, repeatedly asking each other if everything was all right. Repeatedly assuring each other that it was. Finally Mary remembered that she had brought some snapshots of Laurie. "I thought this would be next best to seeing her," she said, thrusting the envelope at Hana. "They're for you to keep. And here, this is for you too." It was a box of chocolates and a bag of fresh fruit.

Now the calls and signals for departure were sounding up and down the length of the platform. A hissing stream of steam forced Mary and Joe to step back. Mary just had time to reach out and touch Hana's hand.

"Be careful now. Take care of yourselves."

The train gave a jerk, then moved slowly out of the station.

"Goodbye, Mama, Papa."

"Bye bye, Ma Chan. Bye bye . . ."

Hana felt the hot tears come and sat down to hide her face in her hands. She felt Mrs. Mitosa's hand on her shoulder. "I'm so happy for you that they came," she said softly.

Taro was still leaning from the window, waving his big white handkerchief as long as he could see the red coat, and long after it became a blur on the platform. Then he sat down beside Hana.

"They came, Mama," he said gently. "They came after all."

It made the last night on the train endurable.

Chapter 32

On the third day after leaving Tanforan, the train reached the town of Delta, Utah, bearing its load of exhausted men, women and children. The internees left the train under guard and were counted on to waiting buses.

"Well, we're almost there," Taro said, wearily.

"Maybe it won't be so bad," Hana said with some hope, as they passed homes with lawns and gardens and trees. Soon there were fertile farmlands stretching out on both sides of the highway.

She turned to speak to Mrs. Mitosa. "Maybe we could send for some flower and vegetable seeds and have small gardens."

"Oh, I hope so," Mrs. Mitosa answered eagerly. Before the war, she and her husband had owned a carnation nursery, and she missed working with flowers and growing things. Her main joy in Tanforan had been a small flower garden she had planted in front of her stable. The manure-rich soil had produced an abundance of colorful blossoms, and she wondered now if anyone was watering them.

For a while there was much eager conversation on the bus, for the long journey was almost over and the sight of homes and farms filled everyone with a burst of energy and good spirits. But as the bus travelled on, their hopes began to subside in the face of the reality around them. Gradually, vegetation of any kind disappeared, and they were surrounded on all sides by miles of bleak, arid land. They were moving now into the Sevier Desert, where only clumps of sagebrush stirred in the hot dry wind.

Hana dared not look at Taro, knowing she would see only a reflection of her own dismay in his eyes. She looked silently out the window as the bus continued along a narrow dusty highway that unwound like a black ribbon into the heart of the desert.

Then abruptly, it turned off the highway toward rows and rows of black, tar-papered barracks clustered in a vast pool of chalky white sand. Their bus drove past sentries at the main gate and pulled to a stop, as several more buses followed close behind.

A group of people who had arrived earlier stood in the hot sun, squinting and shading their eyes as they looked up at the bus windows searching for friends. They were covered from head to toe with white dust and looked like a work gang given a brief reprieve from digging ditches.

"There's Sumi Chan," Mrs. Mitosa called out. "And Kenji San."

They looked forlorn and diminished in the midst of this endless enveloping desert. They smiled, however, and waved as they came forward to help with the baggage.

"I know it was a hard trip," Kenji said sympathetically.

"Are you all right?" Sumiko asked as she led them toward the processing barrack.

"Mama, you're going to come live with us," she said. "We have a room big enough for three."

"Oh no, I couldn't do that," Mrs. Mitosa objected. "That wouldn't be right."

"But there's no other place for you to go," Sumiko answered. "That's how it's got to be."

Hana removed herself from their discussion, glad that it was not a decision she had to make. She sat down on a dusty bench while Taro registered for them both.

He came back with a slip of paper. "We're assigned to Block Seven, Barrack Two, Apartment A," he said. "They told me it's an end room, for two people."

"You'll be nearby," Sumiko said, looking pleased. "We're in Block Six, next to yours."

Sumiko and Kenji led the way down the long dusty road toward Block Seven. With each step, they sank almost ankle-deep into the fine powdery sand. The army, in its search for a site to deposit the thousands of Japanese Americans uprooted from California, had located this utterly desolate land that had once been a peaceful lake bed. It had sent in its bulldozers and trucks to disturb the creatures that lived among centuries-old bones and stone; it had uprooted the sagebrush that once held down the sand, and it had churned the desert into a seething mass of dust that floated, suspended, everywhere. It had further defiled the desert by building on this loose bed of sand a wretched barrack camp encircled with barbed wire, with guard towers at its four corners. The camp was then called Topaz.

Hana felt the dust seep into her nostrils and eyes. Both she and Mrs. Mitosa coughed as they plodded slowly through the drifts of glaring white sand. No one spoke as they walked on.

At Block Six, Sumiko and her mother stopped. "We'll leave you here," Sumiko said. "Your block is just ahead."

Kenji tried to encourage Hana. "We'll be there soon," he said. "Just one more firebreak to cross and we'll be in Block Seven. That's the hospital over there to the left, and over in the corner, just beyond the guard tower, are the soldiers' barracks."

Hana turned her head. She did not want to see the guard towers or the barracks where the soldiers lived.

Apartment A was one of the small rooms at the end

of each barrack, not much larger than the horsestalls. The rooms in the center were for families of four or more. The barracks were far from complete, and as they arrived, workmen were still pouring tar on the roofs. Dust sifted into the room from every crevice and from the hole in the roof where the stove chimney was to go. Two army cots lay folded on the dusty floor and a single light bulb dangled from the ceiling.

"So this is Topaz, 'jewel of the desert'," Taro said, recalling the words he had read on the instruction sheet.

Hana had no words to utter. She was so exhausted, she could have stretched out on the dusty floor and gone right to sleep.

"It will be better when the wood stove and the sheetrock walls are installed," Kenji said, offering the only encouragement he could summon. "Anyway, let's set up the cots, and I'll go find a broom in the mess hall."

At that moment, however, Sumiko rushed into the room without stopping to knock.

"Kenji! Come quickly! It's Mama. She couldn't stop coughing. She's collapsed!"

It could have been the heat or the altitude or sheer exhaustion. Hana felt strangely light-headed herself.

"Oh, Papa," she said desperately as she watched Kenji and Sumiko hurry off. "What are we ever going to do in this godforsaken desert?"

They did what they had done in Tanforan. They worked hard to make their room livable. Taro stuffed newspapers in the crevices to keep out the dust. He tacked cardboard over the hole in the roof, and when their crates arrived, he patiently pried them apart, hammering them together again into benches and a table. They were instructed not to put up any shelves until the interior sheetrock wall was installed, so they lived out of their suitcases, waiting as they were told.

It was weeks before they adjusted to the altitude and extremes in temperature. Water froze in the frigid mornings. Yet, by afternoon, the unrelenting desert sun caused people to faint from the heat. Mess hall refrigerators broke down, food spoiled and everyone suffered from diarrhea.

Mrs. Mitosa was in the hospital with a severe attack of asthma and was to stay there until she regained her strength. "They say if she has another bad attack she could . . ." Sumiko couldn't go on.

"She's far better in the hospital where the temperature is controlled and there's less dust," Kenji said quickly.

"Also she can have water whenever she needs it," Taro added. He had already been caught in the shower when the water abruptly stopped flowing, as it often did.

"And there are probably doors there," Hana said, thinking of the toilets that had neither doors nor seats. "I wonder why they couldn't have waited to bring us here until the camp was ready?"

"You'd think they could have," Kenji agreed wearily. He served on the housing committee and was often up until three in the morning listening to complaints that poured in. He listened patiently because he knew the people had every right to complain. Internees were being sent from Tanforan faster than barracks could be completed. Some were housed in laundry barracks and some even in the hospital corridors. It was a wretched situation.

Kenji Nishima worried about the physical hardships his people were enduring, but more than that, he was concerned that this bleak life would destroy their spirit. They were hardworking, patient and capable of withstanding the most cruel hardships, but this barren wasteland might cause them to despair. Already he saw some from his church growing old before their time, and he encouraged those who could find employment and sponsors to apply for early release.

"No one should stay in Topaz too long," he said, "for it will surely erode the spirit." He was still worried about Taro Takeda and confided as much to his wife. "It's as though he has no further goals in life."

But Sumiko could understand what had happened to Taro. "He's been cast adrift from everything he had, Kenji, and he has no safe harbor now except here in Topaz."

Kenji knew she was right. There were some in California who wanted to deport anyone of Japanese ancestry so they could never return again to that state. Beyond the barbed wire, there was still hatred for anyone with a Japanese face.

"The only good thing about Topaz," Hana wrote to Ellen Davis, "is the sunset each evening."

Hana had never seen such an expanse of space as the sky that arched over the desert. As the sun dipped each evening behind the towering mountains that ringed their desert, the entire sky turned a brilliant, flaming red that faded into the lavenders and pinks of dusk. Hana and Taro usually stayed outside long enough to watch the mountains melt into the dark shadows of night. Sometimes they would walk to the hospital to visit Mrs. Mitosa or visit a church friend in another block. By the time they returned home, the first stars would appear, and Hana gazed at the sky until she could see the River of Heaven. It was as though the stars sang out in an explosion of brilliance to console the creatures fenced in beneath them.

She often thought of Kiku as she looked up at the night sky. She and her boys had been sent to Amache Camp in Colorado, and she had written only once to say that she had not received a penny from the man who managed their farm. "It seems no one else has either," she added. "I suppose he is getting rich and laughing at our stupidity."

When Taro received a letter from Sojiro Kaneda, he opened it eagerly, only to find that it contained shattering news.

"I have been moved again," Kaneda wrote, "and who knows how many more times we will be uprooted before this is all over. One morning half the men in our barrack were told to be ready to move in an hour, and now, here we are in North Dakota. It is cold and bleak and lonely here. Even the Bible holds little comfort for me."

Hana shuddered as she listened to Taro. In all the years she had known Dr. Kaneda, he had always found strength in his faith. She had never known him to lose hope.

"I am tired and growing old," Taro read on. "And I am all alone. I have neither wife nor children, and am separated from the friends I hold dear. I have had much time to think and agonize and pray over what I am about to tell you.

"I have asked to be repatriated to Japan whenever it is allowed, for there I still have one brother. There I can be free, and I know now that without freedom, a man can be crushed and defeated. Please understand what I am doing. I hope some day when the war is over, we can meet again. Until then, God bless you and keep you, dear friends."

Taro stopped reading. He remembered how eager and full of hope Sojiro Kaneda had always been. He remembered how hard he had worked to help his countrymen be accepted in their new land; how firmly he believed that one day America would allow them to become citizens and to live as other Americans did. It was Sojiro Kaneda who had reinforced Taro's own hope and belief in America. And now, the country had betrayed them both.

"Oh, Taro, how can we stop him?" Hana asked.

Taro was silent for a long while. Then he folded the letter carefully and put it back in its envelope.

"We cannot stop him," he said slowly. "We have no right."

"The war will end someday. . . ."

"It is already too late for Kaneda," Taro said, and rising abruptly, he went outside to be alone.

Chapter  33

Kiku sat close to the roaring pot-bellied stove, wondering again why she had not inspected more carefully the papers she had signed with Clarkson. What a fool she had been to trust him so completely. But Henry would have done the same, wouldn't he? They had all signed with Clarkson in a panic of haste, not having had the time to labor over the fine print.

As it was, she scarcely remembered how she had cleared out the house. She had sold all her furniture for a few dollars and left the house a vacant shell.

"What does it matter?" she had asked her friends. "What does anything matter any more?"

For a while Kenny and Jimmy were tender and loving, but as they settled into the strange, fragmented life at camp, they soon went their own ways. Now Kiku scarcely saw them. Kenny worked as an orderly at the camp hospital for sixteen dollars a month. Jimmy had a job driving one of the camp trucks and earned fourteen dollars.

"I'm really making good use of my college education, Ma," he said.

Kiku didn't know what to say. "Well, at least you have a little spending money for the canteen."

"Yeah, so we can buy canned carrot juice."

"I heard they were going to get some yardage and yarn soon," Kiku countered.

"Yeah. Big deal."

No matter what Kiku said, it didn't seem to be the right thing. The boys were bored and frustrated, and vented their exasperation on her. They got on each other's nerves in the small twenty-by-twenty room, and Kiku often told them to go out and stop bothering her. The boys were glad to oblige. They disappeared until past midnight, not bothering to return for supper with her, but eating with friends in other mess halls. It was the same with many other families. They seemed to be disintegrating.

In January 1943, President Franklin D. Roosevelt issued a statement declaring that "no loyal citizen should be denied the democratic right to exercise the responsibilities of his citizenship, regardless of his ancestry." The Secretary of War then declared that Nisei men, until then classified IV-C (not acceptable for service because of ancestry), would be recruited for a special All-Nisei Combat Team.

Army recruiters were soon sent out to all the camps where the Japanese Americans were incarcerated. An all-Nisei unit, they maintained, would allow the Nisei to gain special attention rather than being diffused throughout the army as additional manpower. As a separate unit, they said, the Nisei could prove their loyalty in a dramatic, forceful way that might well determine their future in America.

When they arrived in Amache, the recruiters caused a turmoil of anguish, as they had in every camp they visited, for the army not only required registration of all draft-age men, but of all the camp residents as well.

Kiku, like every other Japanese resident, was horrified at question 28, which asked for unqualified allegiance to the United States and the forswearing of allegiance to the Emperor of Japan.

"That is an impossible question to answer," she said indignantly, "when United States law classifies Asians as 'aliens ineligible for citizenship.' If we said yes to that, we would be left without a country! Who can answer a question like that?"

"You're right, Ma," her sons agreed. "That question implies allegiance to the Emperor too. It's a goddamn loaded question!"

But young draft-age men had similar problems with question 27 on their questionnaire, which asked, "Are you willing to serve in the armed forces of the United States in combat duty, wherever ordered?"

Many of Kenny and Jimmy's friends would answer yes to that question only when their civil rights were restored.

"Hell, the government violated the Constitution and imprisoned us without even a hearing or a trial," they said. "We'll answer yes to 27 when the government gets us and our families out of these damn concentration camps. And we don't want segregated units either."

Answering no to 27 and no to 28, which implied a nonexistent allegiance to a foreign power, these young men became known as the "no-no boys."

One night Kiku heard her sons talking about volunteering for the combat team.

"You mean you boys would volunteer, risking your lives for a country that put you—its citizens—behind barbed wire just because you look like the enemy?" She was astounded.

Kenny was thoughtful. "Well, if we don't prove our loyalty now, they might use that as reason to justify these damn camps, Ma," he answered. "It's a chance to prove our loyalty once and for all."

"It's a chance to get killed, too."

Kenny shrugged. "Pa got killed right in his own front yard."

"But you don't have to walk up to a bullet!"

Jimmy supported his brother. "It might be better than wasting our lives sitting around this hell hole. At least we could show them we're as good as any other damn American."

But Kiku was not about to give up her two boys without a fight. "Why can't you say no-no to the stupid army?"

She knew that saying no probably took as much courage as saying yes. Her heart ached for the boys who were being asked to make such a terrible decision while imprisoned in bleak desert concentration camps. She hoped her sons had the strength they would need.

Many of the parents felt as Kiku did. They resented the fact that the army, which once spurned their sons, now wanted them for a segregated unit, possibly to be used as cannon fodder in the most dangerous combat zones.

Kenny and Jimmy spent long hours agonizing, discussing the matter with their friends and with Kiku, trying to determine the right thing to do.

In the end, they decided to volunteer for the combat team.

"We're going to fight those damn Nazis just like any other good American," they told Kiku. "We've got to do what we think is right."

So Kiku gave in.

"They're adults now," she explained to her friends. "I cannot stop them. Besides," she added wistfully, "maybe what they do now will make a better future for the rest of us."

Her boys came home one night looking solemn and serious. "Well, we did it, Ma," they said. "We joined up. We'll be leaving next week."

Kiku held back her tears and finally found it in herself to say, "If that's your decision, I support you. I'm proud of you, and I know your papa would have been proud too."

Kiku helped them pack their bags and went to the gate to see them off. There were twenty-five other young men who had volunteered, and a large crowd gathered to wish them well. The high school band provided music, and the camp director made a speech lauding their action.

Like their father, neither of the boys had displayed much affection, but now each of them kissed Kiku on the cheek, and she hugged them for a brief moment before they broke away.

Kiku looked hard at the faces staring back at her from the bus window. The boys looked so young and vulnerable. Most of them tried to smile, but a few looked as though they wanted to cry.

"Goodbye, Kenny, Jimmy. Be careful."

"Okay, Ma. Take care of yourself. So long."

The bus started with a noisy roar, rumbling down the dusty road toward town. Kiku watched with the others until the bus disappeared. Then she walked slowly back to her block. She went directly to the mess hall to sign up for kitchen help. One of the cooks had been taken ill and they were in need of an extra hand.

"Can you begin today?" they asked.

"I can begin right now," Kiku answered, and was promptly put to work washing rice for two hundred people in an enormous metal pot.

Chapter 34

It was Sunday, and Taro and Hana started out early for church. It took them at least twenty minutes to walk to church in the center of camp, since Taro walked so slowly, head down, watching the ground.

"Papa, must you always walk looking down?" Hana asked, not wanting to be late for church.

"Go on. I'll catch up," Taro answered.

Ever since he and Kenji had found two perfect arrow heads and a fine trilobite one day, Taro had succumbed to collector's fever. He never went out now without keeping a close watch on the ground.

"At least he's taken an interest in something," Kenji confided to Hana, "and that's good for him."

Hana was glad for Taro's new interest in his desert findings, but even more for his deeper friendship with Kenji. Taro talked often with him, and it was Kenji to whom he had taken Kaneda's letter.

"It's hard to know what God has in store for each of us," Kenji had said. "Perhaps there is work for Dr. Kaneda to do in Japan. He may find the fulfillment there that he was denied in this country. Accept his decision in peace, and try now to start a new life for yourself and Mrs. Takeda. Perhaps you could look for work outside. We must all think about going out beyond the barbed wire."

"To what?" Taro asked. "To the kind of hatred that killed Henry Toda?"

"There has always been hatred, Mr. Takeda. You've known it before in California. You survived in spite of it."

"I was younger then."

"And now?"

"I haven't the strength to go to a strange city to seek new roots. I want to wait here until the war ends, and I can go home again to Oakland."

"What will you do there?"

"Begin again. But at least I will be home."

Taro turned more and more to the desert for solace. It fascinated him in a strange way as it gave up its treasures from the past.

"You can be happy here in the desert then?" Hana asked.

"I would not call it happiness."

"What then?"

"Acceptance. There is no other way to find peace."

"Then you don't want to go out and find a job?"

"Picking sugar beets in Idaho or being a houseboy in Chicago?"

"I know you don't want that, Papa."

"Someday we'll go back to California," Taro said patiently. "I'd do any kind of work there. We could both work, and maybe earn enough to buy back my shop. Wouldn't you like that?"

"Yes, I would, Papa."

"Well then. Be patient. Accept what has to be. One day, perhaps this country will redeem itself."

Hana would not push Taro any more. He had had enough of her assertiveness in his life. She would try now, as Taro always had, to accept quietly what life brought.

So Hana tried to accept the desert, but she hated its brittle, dry growth and the creatures it sheltered. She was afraid of the scorpions that she sometimes found in her shoes, and she longed for the sight of something green, and for the sound of the song sparrows. One morning she had seen two seagulls winging their way across the sky, and the sight of them had filled her with such longing for San Francisco Bay, she almost wept.

For several months, they had watched anxiously as trees were brought in and planted throughout camp. But none had survived the heat or the hostile soil. Now they thrust barren limbs into the sky as their roots shrivelled in the sand.

Hana and Taro passed dozens of these skeletal trees as they walked to church. When they arrived, the pianist was already playing the prelude. They quickly found a place on one of the benches, and Hana was pleased to see that Kenji Nishima was preaching that day. She thought he seemed particularly handsome as he stood at the lectern. His face was serene and his hair, now touched with gray at the temples, gave him a look of dignity. Sumiko's love had given him new dimensions and there was no one in camp who could not turn to him for sustenance or comfort. He had become a giving, loving person—a true man of God.

Hana felt proud of him and allowed a moment's pride in herself as well. He is one person I can truly say I have helped, she thought, hoping perhaps God might feel, at last, that she had redeemed herself.

As Kenji spoke, the desert wind began to howl and Hana found it difficult to concentrate on what he said.

"Dear God, please, not another dust storm," she prayed. The dust storms terrified her, and with each storm she feared Sumiko's mother would die of suffocation.

Hana could see the dust swirling outside and soon the screaming wind caused the dust to seep like smoke into the church. The windows rattled, pebbles rained like hail on the glass, and garbage cans, boxes, anything not secured, were hurled against the building like toys. The sound of coughing rippled through the congregation, and people covered their noses and mouths with handkerchiefs.

Hana felt the building quiver, and instinctively clung to Taro's arm. Kenji, sensing the mounting anxiety of the people, stopped in the middle of his sermon.

"I'd like to read to you from the book of Joshua," he said calmly. "Please listen. 'Be strong and of good courage; be not frightened, neither be thou dismayed, for the Lord thy God is with you wherever you go.' He is with us here and now. Do not be afraid."

A woman screamed as the wind suddenly flung open the door and the entire desert seemed to pour into the building. "Mama, Mama!" a child cried out in terror.

Kenji rushed from the pulpit to help secure the door. Then, raising his hand, he hurriedly gave the benediction. The storm might last for hours, but when there was a lull, he knew everyone must try to get home.

"Those needing help to return to their barrack, please come forward. We will try to find people going back to the same block. I will go with anyone who needs me," he offered. And Sumiko gathered the older people who wanted someone to accompany them.

Hana tied her scarf around her head, covering most of her face, ready to leave the moment the wind subsided a little. They would certainly not be any safer in their own barrack, but an instinctive urge to be in her own room surpassed her fear of facing the storm.

"Do you want to go now?" Taro asked.

"Yes, I can't bear to stay here another minute."

They plunged out together in the sea of dust, feeling like two blind people. The powdery dust swept about them like great billowing veils of white and they could not see more than ten feet ahead. Hana felt the sting of pebbles and sand raining against her legs, and she gasped as they stumbled on. Every few yards, Taro would draw her toward a barrack where they would rest for a moment and then plunge on. Sometimes the wind pushed them, almost lifting them from their feet, while the next instant, it flung angry fistfuls of dust in their faces. Hana thought of seeking shelter as they passed a laundry barrack, but she could not open her mouth to suggest it to Taro. They clung to each other and struggled on, passing other huddled figures plodding in the opposite direction.

When at last they reached their room, it was smoky with dust. A layer of white covered everything. Hana tasted the dust in her mouth and tried to shake the dust from her clothing.

"It's lunch time," Taro said looking at his watch.

But Hana could not think about food. She felt as though she had swallowed half the desert. She was dizzy and light-headed. Retching, she crept into her dusty bed and stayed there the rest of the day.

By evening, the wind died down, the stars came out, and it was as though there had never been a dust storm. Sumiko and Kenji came to see if they were all right, and brought news that upset Hana even more than the dust storm.

"The doctors tell me Mama must get out of the desert," Sumiko began. "They say we must take her out to Salt Lake City where the air is clean and clear."

"And you will go with her?"

"I must."

"And Kenji San, you too?"

"Sumiko and her mother will go first. I will stay here and be useful as long as I can."

"But you must apply for permission to join them soon," Taro concluded. "Your place is beside your wife, no matter how much we need you here."

Kenji looked troubled and pained. "I cannot bear to leave all of you behind," he said. "And yet, maybe now my work is on the outside. There I could look for jobs and sponsors to enable you and others to be released from camp. You *will* give serious thought to applying for leave clearance before too long, won't you?" he asked.

Taro nodded, but said nothing. They all knew how he felt, and Hana knew that the two of them would probably remain in camp until the terrible war came to an end.

Chapter 35

Kenji and Taro bent together over the general camp registration form that everyone was required to fill out and sign. Taro had answered every question but one. That one he could not answer. He was glad Kenji was still here to advise him, for Sumiko had already taken her mother to Salt Lake City, and Kenji would join her as soon as a suitable apartment was found.

"Listen," Taro said, reading the question aloud again as he had done so many times. "'Will you swear unqualified allegiance to the United States of America and forswear any form of allegiance or obedience to the Japanese Emperor or any other foreign government power or organization?' If we answer yes, we would be left without a country, wouldn't we?"

"We certainly would," Kenji agreed. "Because this country denies us citizenship, we would, in effect, be left stateless."

"Then how can they ask us to do such a thing?" Hana asked.

"It is completely unreasonable," Kenji said, indignant.

Taro spoke as though he were addressing the unreasonable government itself. "Japan is the land of my birth," he began, "but I decided long ago to make my home in America. I would gladly give up my citizenship in Japan, if only I were allowed to become a citizen of America. I must have one or the other. I cannot give up both."

"That is exactly what I will tell the administration

officials when our committee meets with them this afternoon," Kenji assured him. "I will insist that we cannot answer such an eminently unfair and impossible question."

"Good," Hana said, relieved. "I know you will convince them."

"Well, I'm certainly going to try," Kenji said, rising to leave. "Now don't worry about it any more. We're going to work until we get that question removed from the registration form entirely."

Hana felt better, but the question continued to fester in Taro's mind. What was America trying to do to them now? It had already deprived them of their freedom, their homes and their livelihoods. And now this.

Taro was as much troubled by what the country was doing to itself as by what it had done to him and his fellow Japanese Americans. He had learned well its early history. The principles and ideals on which the founding fathers had established this country were lofty and good. He admired them and had long ago determined to make those beliefs his own.

He believed that what this country had done to the Japanese Americans since the war was the result of fear and hatred and greed among bigoted and misguided men. He believed this was not the real America he knew.

He could understand its hatred for the militarists of Japan, but how much more anger and vengeance was it going to vent upon the innocent Japanese Americans who had chosen to live on its shores? The angry giant would destroy itself and everything it stood for before it crushed those it harassed, for the Japanese Americans, by not becoming embittered, had not yet allowed themselves to be destroyed. Taro longed to talk to Sojiro Kaneda of these things.

"Hana, I'm going out for a walk," he said, still

troubled and unsure.

"Shall I come with you?"

"No, I want to be alone. I want to think."

"All right. Be careful then."

Hana heard Taro's footsteps crunching on the gravel walk. She knew he was turning to the desert for peace. There was still a little light left to the day. Perhaps the desert would be generous and allow him to find another of its treasures.

Hana went to the laundry barrack and filled her kettle with water. She put it on the pot-bellied stove and added a few lumps of coal to stir up the fire. By the time Taro returned, the water would be hot enough to make him a cup of cocoa.

Hana tried to keep her mind on the red wool sweater she was knitting for little Laurie, but she made so many mistakes in the cable stitch pattern, she had to rip out more than an inch. Finally, she put her knitting aside and decided to write to Kiku. It was still Kiku to whom she turned when she was most in need of a friend.

She longed to write to her mother, but the war had cut off those she loved in Japan. She wondered how they were and what tragedies the war had brought them. What would they say if they knew that she and Taro now lived in one small room, behind barbed wire, in the middle of a barren desert. She could almost hear her mother saying, "I knew you should not have gone off to America. If only you had stayed here. If only. . . ."

"Dear Kiku. If only you were here, I could tell you how despondent I am. Did you agonize, too, over the camp registration questionnaire? Have you heard that Sojiro Kaneda is asking to be repatriated to Japan? We may never see him again. And now, Kenji San will be leaving us soon, too. . . ."

Hana tore up the page she had written. She would

not burden Kiku with her troubles, for she knew Kiku must be lonely without her boys. Hana was rewriting the letter on a more pleasant note when she heard footsteps pounding down the path and then a banging on her door.

"Mrs. Taro Takeda?" It was a young messenger. He was breathless, panting from having run so hard.

"Yes."

"Come with me quickly, please."

"What is it? What is wrong?"

The young boy had been instructed not to elaborate. "You're wanted at the hospital," he said urgently. "Please hurry."

Hana did not even put on her coat or scarf. She took the boy's hand and let him lead her along the path to the hospital. It was growing dark now and she had to be careful not to stumble.

They didn't speak as they rushed toward the lights of the hospital barrack, and when they arrived, Hana, with a pain in her side, was breathless. The boy led her to a door where a nurse was waiting for her.

"Mrs. Takeda? Come in."

She ushered her into a small room where a doctor and the camp director stood beside a single cot, their faces serious and grim. And lying on the cot, looking lifeless and ashen, was Taro.

"Papa! Papa San!" Hana called, rushing to his side. She knelt beside the cot asking, "What happened? What has happened to him?" Taro's eyes remained closed. His breathing was harsh and labored. The nurse put an oxygen mask over his face.

"There was an accident, Mrs. Takeda," the director began. "Your husband was shot by one of the guards. He was walking near the barbed wire fence and the soldier thought he was trying to escape."

"Escape? How could he? Where could he go? He was probably only looking for arrowheads!" Hana heard herself shouting at the director.

She looked now at the doctor. "Is he going to be all right?"

"His condition is critical, Mrs. Takeda."

"But you can save him?"

The doctor was young. His eyes filled with tears. "We're doing everything we can," he said.

Hana heard the director whisper to the doctor. "Are there relatives? Should someone be notified? Has the minister been called?"

The director put a hand on her shoulder. "The soldier said he called to him to halt. He said he aimed over his head . . ." His voice drifted off, for Hana showed no sign of hearing him. She was not going to ease the soldier's guilt by saying she understood. "I'm so very sorry, Mrs. Takeda."

Hana was aware of nothing except that Taro lay dying. He was so still, he seemed already to be slipping away. She felt someone raise her gently to a chair and felt a hand touch her shoulder. It was Kenji Nishima.

He knelt beside Taro, and taking his hand, he prayed for him. He also prayed for Hana. Then he told her he would call Mary. "She will want to know and be here," he said gently. Hana simply nodded, allowing the decision to be made for her.

As the director and doctor left the room, the nurse whispered that she would be back shortly.

"Please take that thing off so he can talk to me," Hana begged. The nurse removed the oxygen mask.

At last, Hana was alone with Taro and the waiting presence of death. She prayed to the God whom Taro had taught her to love and trust.

"Taro . . . oh, Papa San. . . ."

Hana held his hand in both of hers and watched his face, searching, waiting for a sign that he knew she was there. It seemed a long time before he finally opened his eyes, and when he looked at her, she understood that he knew everything.

"Hana," he whispered with supreme effort. "I'm sorry . . . I wanted to give you a better life."

Hana shook her head. "We had a fine life together, Papa San," she murmured. "Forgive me for all the times I hurt you."

Taro squeezed her hand slightly and closed his eyes.

Hana didn't know how long she sat there watching him, trying to find words to tell him how much he meant to her. The doctor and nurses came in and out, keeping a watchful eye on the feeble rhythms of Taro's life. And Kenji returned to pray with her, sustaining her with his love and concern.

"Your daughter is coming," he said quietly. "Sumiko is coming, too."

As the gray light of dawn slowly widened across the desert sky, Hana, her head still resting on Taro's hand, awakened with a start from a moment of sleep.

"Taro?" she called. "Papa?"

But at that moment, Taro died quietly and peacefully, without hearing her call to him.

Mary and Joe arrived the day after Taro's death, bringing little Laurie with them. "If only Papa could have seen her," Mary wept. "If only I had taken her to the station that night."

It was Hana who comforted her daughter. "Papa knows you have brought her to him now," she said. "Don't cry, Mary, your papa is at peace."

Hana sent three telegrams. One to Ellen Davis in California, one to Kiku Toda in Colorado and one to Sojiro Kaneda in North Dakota. The answering wire from Kaneda was full of grief and shock. Ellen Davis sent loving words to embrace and console her. But there was no word from Kiku. Perhaps she was too overcome, Hana thought. Or perhaps she was not permitted to send a wire.

Taro Takeda was the first fatality of the Topaz Relocation Center, and the entire camp was infuriated by his senseless death. The maintenance men made a rough pine coffin for him, and the women of the church made lilies and roses and irises with crepe paper from the canteen. They shaped them into wreaths and bouquets on which they hung ribbons bearing Taro's name.

So many people came to the funeral that hundreds stood outside in the hot sun listening by loudspeaker to the words of Reverend Kenji Nishima. Sumiko had come, and sat next to Hana, giving her the support of another daughter.

"We gather here today in memory of Taro Takeda," Kenji began. "We deplore his needless death, but we can rejoice in the peace he finds now, far beyond the barbed wire that imprisoned him in life. He was a good Christian, a devoted husband and a loving father. More than many who were born in this land, he loved America and what he believed it stood for."

Hana nodded as she listened. Taro would have liked what Kenji was saying about him. It was true, all true.

Yes, Taro, Hana thought, you were a good husband—steadfast and dependable—and you were good to me. You understood that I could not accept life in the quiet patient way you did.

"Mrs. Takeda." Sumiko was helping her to her feet. The service had ended. The mourners paid their respects. It was time to bury her husband.

Mary and Joe were horrified to learn that Taro was to be buried in the desert beyond the gate. "Must he be left out there all alone?" Mary asked.

Kenji told them there was no choice. "There is no room for a cemetery inside the gate," he explained, "and there will be others before it is all over."

"Never mind," Hana told her. "It's all right. Your

papa had come to like the peace of the desert. He loved the sunsets and the great wide sky and the old treasures he found in the sand."

"Your mother is right," Kenji added. "Your father had come to terms with life here better than most."

Hana nodded, "Better than most," she repeated.

A small wooden cross marked his grave in the desert, and the church women placed their crepe paper flowers around the cross. Their gaudy colors were vivid in the sun, seeming grotesque in the drabness of the surrounding desert. During the graveside service, the wind tore at the flowers, sending bits and pieces whirling into the desert to adorn the sagebrush and tumbleweed with the ornaments of death.

Mary, Joe and Laurie stayed with Hana for three days. Laurie's innocent cheer touched her deeply, but through the dark days of numbing sorrow, it was Kenji who comforted her most. He had been through the darkest moments of life with her and knew her needs best. He made all the arrangements for the funeral and the memorial meeting that followed. He helped her fill out the papers and forms that were all the government wanted now of Taro's life.

Sumiko was there too, going to the canteen for cookies and crackers, helping serve tea to the callers who came to pay their respects to Hana.

Through it all, Mary seemed dazed, an outsider, not knowing quite how to behave in the closeness of the Japanese American community. She did not know how to cope with death, nor did she feel the close kinship with the dead that the others felt from times past. She felt ill at ease among her mother's friends, and yet she admired their dignity and strength even in so desolate a place. She grieved bitterly, consumed with guilt, because she knew she had not been the daughter Taro hoped she would be. Each day Mary tried to persuade her mother to leave camp and return to Salt Lake City with them.

"They said you could leave if you had a place to go, Mama. And you do. Come home with us," she urged.

"We'd really like to have you," Joe added. "You shouldn't stay in this godforsaken place alone." He had been shocked to see the utter desolation of the concentration camp.

But Hana shook her head. "I can't leave Papa all alone in the desert," she said. "When the war is over, I'm going to take him home to Oakland where he and I both belong."

"I think that is what he would have wanted," Kenji agreed. "He would want to go home and be buried beside his son."

"I know," Hana said. "That is what I'm going to do. And I am going back to work so someday, one day, I can buy back Papa's shop." Hana straightened up, tilting her chin. "And if they ever let me, I'm going to become a citizen of this country just like Papa always wanted. I'm going to live the life he wanted, for both of us."

"Oh, Mama," Mary wept, "I've been such a miserable daughter to you and Papa."

Hana took her hand. "We must learn to forgive and to be forgiven, Mary. I had to learn that too."

Joe saw Hana's strength and respected her resolve. "I understand what you want to do, Mrs. Takeda," he said. "We'll help you in any way we can."

"Thank you, Joe. Help Mary understand."

After they put Mary and Joe and Laurie on the bus returning to town, Kenji and Sumiko went with Hana to visit Taro's grave. A few crepe paper flowers still remained, but the wind had strewn the others across the face of the desert.

Hana knelt at the grave and brushed the wooden cross with her fingertips. "Ma Chan asked me to go home with her," she said softly, "but I'm staying here, Papa, until I can take you home."

They reached the gate to camp just as the incoming bus from Delta was arriving. Hana scarcely looked up, for only a few people were straggling from the bus.

"We'll walk you to your barrack," Kenji said.

Then they all heard the cry. It was shrill, like a child's call.

"Hana! Hana! Hana! I'm here!"

Hana turned, squinting into the sun. "Kiku? Is that you?"

Kiku rushed toward her with a suitcase in each hand. "I've come, Hana," she said, her face breaking into a broad grin. "I got a transfer to come live in Topaz."

"Oh, Kiku!" Hana hugged her friend and they wept together. They wept for joy. They wept for Henry and for Taro.

"It's all right now, Kenji, Sumiko," Hana said brightly. "My friend has come. I'm going to be all right."

Kenji and Sumiko watched the two women go arm in arm toward the administration building where Kiku would register as a new resident.

"It breaks my heart to think of leaving Mrs. Takeda here," Sumiko said slowly.

But Kenji told her not to worry. "They're strong, Sumiko, both of them. They each crossed an ocean alone to come to this country, and they're going to survive the future with the same strength and spirit. I know it."

They turned then, and began the long walk to Block Six. Sumiko looked back once more, shading her eyes. She saw Hana and Kiku deep in conversation as they walked down the dusty road. They did not even seem aware of the murky gathering of clouds in the sky or to feel the ominous gusts of the hot, trembling wind. They did not know that by the time they walked to Hana's barrack at the opposite end of camp, another dust storm would be coursing over the desert sands, enveloping all of Topaz in its white fury.

Related Readings

CONTENTS

from City in the Sun

by Paul Bailey

The following reading summarizes America's relationship with Asian immigrants prior to the bombing of Pearl Harbor. Paul Bailey highlights American laws and policies from the late 19th and early 20th centuries that were sparked by feelings of anti-Asian sentiment. As you read, look for parallels to events in Picture Bride.

"Remember Pearl Harbor!" was the verbal thrust which tumbled the United States into a war for its survival, and remained the rally cry for as long as that vicious struggle persisted. To 127,000 Americans of Japanese descent, caught suddenly like ants in a vise, the slogan was just as shockingly persistent and compelling, but in a peculiar and different way.

"A day of infamy," President Franklin D. Roosevelt dramatically reminded the nation. But to Japanese Americans, who neither asked for nor wanted this sudden war, no more than did any other average American, the "day of infamy" had an ironic and tragic consequence almost unbelievable in retrospect. The roust of 112,000 Japanese people from the Pacific Coast during World War II, their detention in 15 "assembly centers," their transfer and incarceration in 10 immense concentration camps, represents an unsavory page of American history. It is not an affair often mentioned, and this nation, since it cannot point to the record with pride, would just as soon forget about it.

America is still hard put to justify or explain how a crime of such magnitude against a peaceful and law-abiding minority could have occurred in so democratic and easy-going a nation—a nation that claimed to be the melting pot of races and cultures—the hope of the world. Were its resident Japanese as vociferous as other minority groups, a lot more would have been said and written about it; a few "Little Tokyos" might have been burned; and the average American would have been considerably less prone to consign this betrayal of a people into conscienceless oblivion. Quick to forgive, anxious and industrious about retrieving loss and honor, Japanese Americans have never given the nation the castigation it deserves. "*Shikata nai,*" they call it—Which is their way of saying, "What happened, happened. There was nothing we could do about it."

The only logical excuse so far advanced for this most illogical page of history is to blame it on wartime hysteria. Plenty of reasons were voiced at the time it occurred. Not one of these excuses—including sabotage, aid to the enemy, "fifth column," or lack of patriotism—has stood up under the caustic scrutiny of time and justice.

The "big roust" has no parallel in American history, unless one searches back to a little more than 100 years before the "day of infamy." Then a likeness might be drawn—to America's expulsion of the Cherokees, the Chickasaws, the Creeks and the Choctaws. Once before, in America's earliest days, the nation moved another immense minority group. These Indians were forcibly expelled from homes, land, and the roots of family habitation. They were mature Indian nations that had been living in the east and south long before the white man set foot on this hemisphere. When America shoved these Indians far out to the western prairie, it was not wartime hysteria.

White men simply needed and coveted the land. It was greed. A century later, Japanese Americans were to taste a little of this greed. It was mixed with the hysteria. In eviction and evacuation, there was historical precedence.

From the beginning the United States has taken immense pride in its role as a melting pot—the assimilating, catalyzing wonder machine of the world. Here peoples of different nationalities, religions, and races are turned into citizens and patriots. America's door was always open; ever beckoning to the oppressed. But to say that those 100-percent Americans who had already made the grade were not capable of hating, persecuting, and discriminating against those only heading into the racial melt would be to utter a palpable lie. Hate and discrimination, unfortunately, have been with the nation from its beginning.

The African American knows this well; so does the ousted, defrauded, and slaughtered Indian. Mistreatment of Asians, particularly the sad page of California history mentioned here, is something America is anxious to sweep under the rug. The record of discrimination against Asians is long and painful.

Up to the year 1853, when Commodore Matthew Calbraith Perry sailed his American warships into Tokyo Bay, and at gunpoint forced Japan to open its harbors to trade and foreign intercourse, there was no such thing, anywhere in the world, as a Japanese émigré, Japan's Shoguns had shut out the universe. The Japanese people, turned inward, were having nothing whatever to do with the greedy and turbulent outer world. This national isolation lasted for 200 years. The America who forcibly opened Japan's doors, who shoved that nation into the strident 20th century, would, less than a century later, be facing Japan's challenge in war.

Chinese were the first Asians to come to America's shores. They were a part of the mass of peoples from many nations who swarmed into California with the discovery of gold at Sutter's Creek. White Americans, from 1849 onward, flooded California in even greater numbers. As usual, they considered everyone but themselves as foreigners. Even the Mexican-Californians, owners of the land being usurped, and natives of its culture, were termed "greasers," and viewed as interlopers. "Greasers" caught the same contempt handed out to Indians, Chinese, Hindus, and Chileans. Plenty of racism came west with the Argonauts.

In California, the Indian fell first to the guns and greed of the Caucasian superpatriots, who took over the province wrested from Mexico in 1848. The sordid tale of California's Indian extermination has had only fragmentary mention in America's history books. The running battle with the Mexicans took longer—but, in the end, was just as overwhelming and thorough.

What befell the Japanese Americans in 1941 had much of its roots in the anti-Chinese pogroms that began in the 1850s. Asian immigrants who worked their gold claims in groups were slaughtered en masse by greedy miners who coveted or disputed their claims. When Chinese began congregating in California's cities, many Americans vented their fury on these inscrutable heathens from another land. In Los Angeles a white man lost his life in dispute with a Chinese man. The pueblo's Chinese section was quickly overrun by alert citizens. Six Chinese men were killed in the first bursts of gunfire. Fifteen others—men, women and children—were summarily hanged from anything handy enough to support a rope.

In San Francisco, latent anti-Chinese sentiment broke out into violence in 1877; and 15 California communities drove out their Chinese residents at gunpoint. The tumult swept up the Pacific Coast to Washington where, in the same year, Tacoma burned its Chinese quarter.

The racists were well organized. Politicians found the minorities, especially the Chinese, a handy whipping post for economic woes, and a never-failing vote-getter. California's Workingman's Party, dominated by the Irish, whose immigrant fathers had, a generation earlier, come under similar attack in the east, rose to dominant power on its cry of "The Chinese Must Go!" The Chinese, brought in by the thousands to build the railroads, stood as lethal threat to the Irish, who had considered railroad-building their own province.

From the beginning the workingmen and voters fought the Chinese. An incredible number of discriminatory laws against the "yellow peril" were passed, on city, county, and state levels. In 1882, enlisting the help of southern states congressmen, California's representatives succeeded in pushing the Chinese Exclusion Act through the United States Congress. While this put immediate and effective stop to further Chinese immigration, the congressmen, in their eagerness to get the measure adopted, did make one real blunder. They failed to include the Japanese in their new law.

This was understandable because, at that time, the Japanese were scarcely thought to be a menace. Nipponese boys, from age 15 to 30, had only begun to arrive—mostly through the port of San Francisco. They brought with them no wives or children. English was a harsh and complex language, understood by few of them, and spoken by none. Hotel and innkeepers met the bewildered lads at dockside, used them as menials, or acted as employment agents—on commission—and hired them out for any kind of labor the bright and intuitive young men could do.

While the Exclusion Act failed to prevent the immigration of Japanese to America's shores, dozens of other laws were directed against these pollutants to the Anglo-white concept of national purity. Naturalization and citizenship privileges were withheld from the new arrivals. These first Japanese emigrants were the Issei generation. In spite of economic obstacles, language difficulties, exploitation, and discrimination, they made homes for themselves along the Pacific Coast.

But the Japanese men desperately needed wives and homemakers. This want was uniquely filled by the "picture brides." Photos of eligible and willing girls were sent from Japan. For a fee, and after choice from a picture, a *nakadachi*, or go-between was appointed. The bridegroom picked up his picture bride at dock-side in San Francisco or San Pedro. The marriage was quickly consummated. Rate of disappointment over this evanescent courtship could not have been too great, because, by 1910, the Japanese population in the United States, men, women, and children, had risen to 72,157.

The Isseis, of course, were aliens, and became increasingly unwanted in the American body politic. But their children, by birth and Constitutional guarantee, were American citizens. Considering language, culture, and the many problems they were forced to overcome, the Japanese Isseis, up to the time of Pearl Harbor, had made astonishing adaptation to the American way of life. They were most willing and anxious to integrate. Desperately they wanted to be a part of their newly adopted land.

The problem of Chinese incursion had been halted by the 1882 Exclusion Act, but now the Issei invasion was the new threat. Japanese, like the Chinese, were Asians. Americans were never very adept at telling them apart. The mantle of hate, once so virulent against the Chinese, was quickly and securely fastened to the Japanese segment of the "yellow peril." And, in California especially, it stuck.

Public outcry, and political oratory, never wavering through nearly a century, now at last caught up with the Japanese. In 1900 they were considered a threat. By 1930 they had become a sinister menace. Their numbers, according to the scaremongers, were increasing. Startling statements were made—the public was warned that their proliferation, in numbers, were as high as half a million. The danger they posed to labor, industry, and national security held continuous mention in the press—especially the California press. Long before Pearl Harbor, the newspapers—particularly the Hearst newspapers—were vitriolic in their attacks.

Organizations were formed to root out the problem. In 1906 Japanese children were excluded from San Francisco's public schools. Youngsters were forced to take classes in a claptrap schoolhouse bordering Chinatown. More national and state laws were passed. In the Ozawa Case, decided in 1923, the Supreme Court came up with the unique finding that since the Founding Fathers had never contemplated the presence of Japanese in this country, they were therefore ineligible for naturalization.

In 1913 California passed her Alien Land Law, which effectively prevented Isseis from acquiring or owning land. The politicians, however, were unable to plug all the loopholes. The American Constitution guaranteed the right of citizens to own property. Isseis simply purchased their land and fishing boats in the names of their Nisei children, who were citizens.

It was constantly prated that the Japanese, through

their picture brides, were breeding like rabbits; that in a few decades they would outnumber the white population by sheer fecundity. The Japanese Exclusion League was formed. Patriotic societies, veterans' organizations, Native Sons and Native Daughters, took up the cudgel. V. S. McClatchey, wealthy owner of two influential California daily newspapers, retired from newspaper managing to head up the Joint Immigration Committee, to lecture, lobby, and campaign against California's Japanese. Like the Hearst press, his publications carried on a drumfire against the Japanese menace up to and including the war years.

It was inevitable that racial hysteria, so consistently pounded home by press and radio, would move public opinion to action. In 1924 Congress passed its Japanese Exclusion Act. Finally and effectively the doors were slammed shut to further Japanese entry into the United States—as had the Chinese Exclusion Act in 1882. Politicians, property owners, and propagandists could now breathe easier. Tide against the "yellow peril" was turning.

Of the ethnic groups coming to America's shores, only the Asians were affected by these drastic measures. The Japanese naturally reacted with hurt and shock. The nation of Japan, beginning with Commodore Perry's brusque Naval incursion, had, by now, not only awakened to the 20th century, but had blossomed with incredible swiftness into a world power. Already she was challenging America for control of the Pacific. Japan vociferously protested the Exclusion Act as an insult to her citizenry, and a national affront. Unquestionably the Act contributed to the development of strained relations between the two countries which, commencing with Japan's alliance with Germany and Italy, eventually ended in war itself.

By the time of the Exclusion Act, the Issei males and their imported brides were middle-aged and had only begun to rear their families. At the time of Pearl Harbor the Isseis were 50 to 60 years of age. Their children—the new generation, the Niseis—were mostly between the ages of 17 and 23. Here was a real generation gap. The youngsters, for the most part, were guiding the destinies of 40,000 older people, who had been born in Japan.

On the day the bombs fell on Hawaii, two-thirds of the nation's "yellow peril" were American citizens by right of birth.

from # Farewell to Manzanar

by Jeanne Wakatsuki Houston
and James D. Houston

Like the Takedas, author Jeanne Wakatsuki Houston and her family were imprisoned during World War II in a relocation camp. This reading is taken from the memoirs of Wakatsuki Houston, who was seven years old when her family was evacuated to Manzanar.

In December of 1941 Papa's disappearance didn't bother me nearly so much as the world I soon found myself in.

He had been a jack-of-all-trades. When I was born he was farming near Inglewood. Later, when he started fishing, we moved to Ocean Park, near Santa Monica, and until they picked him up, that's where we lived, in a big frame house with a brick fireplace, a block back from the beach. We were the only Japanese family in the neighborhood. Papa liked it that way. He didn't want to be labeled or grouped by anyone. But with him gone and no way of knowing what to expect, my mother moved all of us down to Terminal Island. Woody already lived there, and one of my older sisters had married a Terminal Island boy. Mama's first concern now was to keep the family together; and once the war began, she felt safer there than isolated racially in Ocean Park. But for me, at age seven, the island was a country as foreign as India or Arabia would have been. It was the first time I had lived among other Japanese, or gone to school with them, and I was terrified all the time.

This was partly Papa's fault. One of his threats to keep us younger kids in line was "I'm going to sell you to the Chinaman." When I had entered kindergarten two years earlier, I was the only Oriental in the class. They sat me next to a Caucasian girl who happened to have very slanted eyes. I looked at her and began to scream, certain Papa had sold me out at last. My fear of her ran so deep I could not speak of it, even to Mama, couldn't explain why I was screaming. For two weeks I had nightmares about this girl, until the teachers finally moved me to the other side of the room. And it was still with me, this fear of Oriental faces, when we moved to Terminal Island.

In those days it was a company town, a ghetto owned and controlled by the canneries. The men went after fish, and whenever the boats came back—day or night—the women would be called to process the catch while it was fresh. One in the afternoon or four in the morning, it made no difference. My mother had to go to work right after we moved there. I can still hear the whistle—two toots for French's, three for Van Camp's—and she and Chizu would be out of bed in the middle of the night, heading for the cannery.

The house we lived in was nothing more than a shack, a barracks with single plank walls and rough wooden floors, like the cheapest kind of migrant workers' housing. The people around us were hardworking, boisterous, a little proud of their nickname, *yo-go-re*, which meant literally *uncouth one*, or roughneck, or dead-end kid. They not only spoke Japanese exclusively, they spoke a dialect peculiar to Kyushu, where their families had come from in Japan, a rough, fisherman's language, full of oaths and insults. Instead of saying *ba-ka-ta-re*, a common insult meaning *stupid*, Terminal Islanders would say *ba-ka-ya-ro*, a coarser and exclusively masculine use of the word, which implies gross stupidity. They would swagger and pick on outsiders and persecute anyone who didn't speak as they did. That was what made my own time there so hateful. I had never spoken anything but English, and the other kids in the second grade despised me for it. They were tough and mean, like ghetto kids anywhere. Each day after school I dreaded their ambush. My brother Kiyo, three years older, would wait for me at the door, where we would decide whether to run straight home together, or split up, or try a new and unexpected route.

None of these kids ever actually attacked. It was the threat that frightened us, their fearful looks, and the noises they would make, like miniature Samurai, in a language we couldn't understand.

At the time it seemed we had been living under this reign of fear for years. In fact, we lived there about two months. Late in February the navy decided to clear Terminal Island completely. Even though most of us were American-born, it was dangerous having that many Orientals so close to the Long Beach Naval Station, on the opposite end of the island. We had known something like this was coming. But, like Papa's arrest, not much could be done ahead of time. There were four of us kids still young enough to be living with Mama, plus Granny, her mother, sixty-five then, speaking no English, and nearly blind. Mama didn't know where else she could get work, and we had nowhere else to move *to*. On February 25 the choice was made for us. We were given forty-eight hours to clear out.

The secondhand dealers had been prowling around for weeks, like wolves, offering humiliating prices for goods and furniture they knew many of us would have to sell sooner or later. Mama had left all but her most valuable possessions in Ocean Park, simply because she had nowhere to put them. She had brought along her pottery, her silver, heirlooms like the kimonos Granny had brought from Japan, tea sets, lacquered tables, and one fine old set of china, blue and white porcelain, almost translucent. On the day we were leaving, Woody's car was so crammed with boxes and luggage and kids we had just run out of room. Mama had to sell this china.

One of the dealers offered her fifteen dollars for it. She said it was a full setting for twelve and worth at least two hundred. He said fifteen was his top price. Mama started to quiver. Her eyes blazed up at him. She had been packing all night and trying to calm down Granny, who didn't understand why we were moving again and what all the rush was about. Mama's nerves were shot, and now navy jeeps were patrolling the streets. She didn't say another word. She just glared at this man, all the rage and frustration channeled at him through her eyes.

He watched her for a moment and said he was sure he couldn't pay more than seventeen fifty for that china. She reached into the red velvet case, took out a dinner plate and hurled it at the floor right in front of his feet.

The man leaped back shouting, "Hey! Hey, don't do that! Those are valuable dishes."

Mama took out another dinner plate and hurled it at the floor, then another and another, never moving, never opening her mouth, just quivering and glaring at the retreating dealer, with tears streaming down her cheeks. He finally turned and scuttled out the door, heading for the next house. When he was gone she stood there smashing cups and bowls and platters until the whole set lay in scattered blue and white fragments across the wooden floor.

The American Friends Service helped us find a small house in Boyle Heights, another minority ghetto, in downtown Los Angeles, now inhabited briefly by a few hundred Terminal Island refugees. Executive Order 9066 had been signed by President Roosevelt, giving the War Department authority to define military areas in the western states and to exclude from them anyone who might threaten the war effort. There was a lot of talk about internment, or moving inland, or something like that in store for all Japanese Americans. I remember my brothers sitting around the table talking very intently about what we were going to do, how we would keep the family together. They had seen how quickly Papa was removed, and they knew now that he would not be back for quite a while. Just before leaving Terminal Island Mama had received her first letter, from Bismarck, North Dakota. He had been imprisoned at Fort Lincoln, in an all-male camp for enemy aliens.

Papa had been the patriarch. He had always decided everything in the family. With him gone, my brothers, like councilors in the absence of a chief, worried about what should be done. The ironic thing is, there wasn't much left to decide. These were mainly days of quiet, desperate waiting for what seemed at the time to be inevitable. There is a phrase the Japanese use in such situations, when something difficult must be endured. You would hear the older heads, the Issei, telling others very quietly, *"Shikata ga nai"* (It cannot be helped). *"Shikata ga nai"* (It must be done).

Mama and Woody went to work packing celery for a Japanese produce dealer. Kiyo and my sister May and I enrolled in the local school, and what sticks in my memory from those few weeks is the teacher—not her looks, her remoteness. In Ocean Park my teacher had been a kind, grandmotherly woman who used to sail with us in Papa's boat from time to time and who wept the day we had to leave. In Boyle Heights the teacher felt cold and distant. I was confused by all the moving and was having trouble with the classwork, but she would never help me out. She would have nothing to do with me.

This was the first time I had felt outright hostility from a Caucasian. Looking back, it is easy enough to explain. Public attitudes towards the Japanese in California were shifting rapidly. In the first few months of the Pacific war, America was on the run. Tolerance had turned to distrust and irrational fear. The hundred-year-old tradition of anti-Orientalism on the west coast soon resurfaced, more vicious than ever. Its result became clear about a month later, when we were told to make our third and final move.

The name Manzanar meant nothing to us when we left Boyle Heights. We didn't know where it was or what it was. We went because the government ordered us to. And, in the case of my older brothers and sisters, we went with a certain amount of relief. They had all heard stories of Japanese homes being attacked, of beatings in the streets of California towns. They were as frightened of the Caucasians as Caucasians were of us. Moving, under what appeared to be government protection, to an area less directly threatened by the war seemed not such a bad idea at all. For some it actually sounded like a fine adventure.

Our pickup point was a Buddhist church in Los Angeles. It was very early, and misty, when we got there with our luggage. Mama had bought heavy coats for all of us. She grew up in eastern Washington and knew that anywhere inland in early April would be cold. I was proud of my new coat, and I remember sitting on a duffel bag trying to be friendly with the Greyhound driver. I smiled at him. He didn't smile back. He was befriending no one. Someone tied a numbered tag to my collar and to the duffel bag (each family was given a number, and that became our official designation until the camps were closed), someone else passed out box lunches for the trip, and we climbed aboard.

I had never been outside Los Angeles County, never traveled more than ten miles from the coast, had never even ridden on a bus. I was full of excitement, the way any kid would be, and wanted to look out the window. But for the first few hours the shades were drawn. Around me other people played cards, read magazines, dozed, waiting. I settled back, waiting too, and finally fell asleep. The bus felt very secure to me. Almost half its passengers were immediate relatives. Mama and my older brothers had succeeded in keeping most of us together, on the same bus, headed for the same camp. I didn't realize until much later what a job that was. The strategy had been, first, to have everyone living in the same district when the evacuation began, and then to get all of us included under the same family number, even though names had been changed by marriage. Many families weren't as lucky as ours and suffered months of anguish while trying to arrange transfers from one camp to another.

We rode all day. By the time we reached our destination, the shades were up. It was late afternoon. The first thing I saw was a yellow swirl across a blurred, reddish setting sun. The bus was being pelted by what sounded like splattering rain. It wasn't rain. This was my first look at something I would soon know very well, a billowing flurry of dust and sand churned up by the wind through Owens Valley.

We drove past a barbed-wire fence, through a gate, and into an open space where trunks and sacks and packages had been dumped from the baggage trucks that drove out ahead of us. I could see a few tents set up, the first rows of black barracks, and beyond them, blurred by sand, rows of barracks that seemed to spread for miles across this plain. People were sitting on cartons or milling around, with their backs to the wind, waiting to see which friends or relatives might be on this bus. As we approached, they turned or stood up, and some moved toward us expectantly. But inside the bus no one stirred. No one waved or spoke. They just stared out the windows, ominously silent. I didn't understand this. Hadn't we finally arrived, our whole family intact? I opened a window, leaned out, and yelled happily, "Hey! This whole bus is full of Wakatsukis!"

Outside, the greeters smiled. Inside there was an explosion of laughter, hysterical, tension-breaking laughter that left my brothers choking and whacking each other across the shoulders.

We had pulled up just in time for dinner. The mess halls weren't completed yet. An outdoor chow line snaked around a half-finished building that broke a good part of the wind. They issued us army mess kits, the round metal kind that fold over, and plopped in scoops of canned Vienna sausage, canned string beans, steamed rice that had been cooked too long, and on top of the rice a serving of canned apricots. The Caucasian servers were thinking that the fruit poured over rice would make a good dessert. Among the Japanese, of course, rice is never eaten with sweet foods, only with salty or savory foods. Few of us could eat such a mixture. But at this point no one dared protest. It would have been impolite. I was horrified when I saw the apricot syrup seeping through my little mound of rice. I opened my mouth to complain. My mother jabbed me in the back to keep quiet. We moved on through the line and joined the others squatting in the lee of half-raised walls, dabbing courteously at what was, for almost everyone there, an inedible concoction.

After dinner we were taken to Block 16, a cluster of fifteen barracks that had just been finished a day or so earlier—although finished was hardly the word for it. The shacks were built of one thickness of pine planking covered with tarpaper. They sat on concrete footings, with about two feet of open space between the floorboards and the ground. Gaps showed between the planks, and as the weeks passed and the green wood dried out, the gaps widened. Knotholes gaped in the uncovered floor.

Each barracks was divided into six units, sixteen by twenty feet, about the size of a living room, with one bare bulb hanging from the ceiling and an oil stove for heat. We were assigned two of these for the twelve people in our family group; and our official family "number" was enlarged by three digits—16 plus the number of this barracks. We were issued steel army cots, two brown army blankets each, and some mattress covers, which my brothers stuffed with straw.

The first task was to divide up what space we had for sleeping. Bill and Woody contributed a blanket each and partitioned off the first room: one side for Bill and Tomi, one side for Woody and Chizu and their baby girl. Woody also got the stove, for heating formulas.

The people who had it hardest during the first few months were young couples like these, many of whom had married just before the evacuation began, in order not to be separated and sent to different camps. Our two rooms were crowded, but at least it was all in the family. My oldest sister and her husband were shoved into one of those sixteen-by-twenty-foot compartments with six people they had never seen before—two other couples, one recently married like themselves, the other with two teenage boys. Partitioning off a room like that wasn't easy. It was bitter cold when we arrived, and the wind did not abate. All they had to use for room dividers were those army blankets, two of which were barely enough to keep one person warm. They argued over whose blanket should be sacrificed and later argued about noise at night—the parents wanted their boys asleep by 9:00 p.m.—and they continued arguing over matters like that for six months, until my sister and her husband left to harvest sugar beets in Idaho. It was grueling work up there, and wages were pitiful, but when the call came through camp for workers to alleviate the wartime labor shortage, it sounded better than their life at Manzanar. They knew they'd have, if nothing else, a room, perhaps a cabin of their own.

That first night in Block 16, the rest of us squeezed into the second room—Granny, Lillian, age fourteen, Ray, thirteen, May, eleven, Kiyo, ten, Mama, and me. I didn't mind this at all at the time. Being youngest meant I got to sleep with Mama. And before we went to bed I had a great time jumping up and down on the mattress. The boys had stuffed so much straw into hers, we had to flatten it some so we wouldn't slide off. I slept with her every night after that until Papa came back.

No Speak English

by Sandra Cisneros

How would you feel if you moved to a new country and you couldn't speak the language? Like Hana Omiya, the woman in this story struggles to adjust to life in her new environment.

Mamacita is the big mama of the man across the street, third-floor front. Rachel says her name ought to be *Mamasota*, but I think that's mean.

The man saved his money to bring her here. He saved and saved because she was alone with the baby boy in that country. He worked two jobs. He came home late and he left early. Every day.

Then one day *Mamacita* and the baby boy arrived in a yellow taxi. The taxi door opened like a waiter's arm. Out stepped a tiny pink shoe, a foot soft as a rabbit's ear, then the thick ankle, a flutter of hips, fuchsia roses and green perfume. The man had to pull her, the taxicab driver had to push. Push, pull. Push, pull. Poof!

All at once she bloomed. Huge, enormous, beautiful to look at, from the salmon-pink feather on the tip of her hat down to the little rosebuds of her toes. I couldn't take my eyes off her tiny shoes.

Up, up, up the stairs she went with the baby boy in a blue blanket, the man carrying her suitcases, her lavender hatboxes, a dozen boxes of satin high heels. Then we didn't see her.

Somebody said because she's too fat, somebody because of the three flights of stairs, but I believe she doesn't come out because she is afraid to speak English, and maybe this is so since she only knows eight words. She knows to say: *He not here* for when the landlord comes. *No speak English* if anybody else comes, and *Holy smokes*. I don't know where she learned this, but I heard her say it one time and it surprised me.

My father says when he came to this country he ate hamandeggs for three months. Breakfast, lunch and dinner. Hamandeggs. That was the only word he knew. He doesn't eat hamandeggs anymore.

Whatever her reasons, whether she is fat, or can't climb the stairs, or is afraid of English, she won't come down. She sits all day by the window and plays the Spanish radio show and sings all the homesick songs about her country in a voice that sounds like a seagull.

Home. Home. Home is a house in a photograph, a pink house, pink as hollyhocks with lots of startled light. The man paints the walls of the apartment pink, but it's not the same, you know. She still sighs for her pink house, and then I think she cries. I would.

Sometimes the man gets disgusted. He starts screaming and you can hear it all the way down the street.

Ay, she says, she is sad.

Oh, he says. Not again.

¿Cuándo, cuándo, cuándo? she asks.

¡Ay, caray! We *are* home. This *is* home. Here I am and here I stay. Speak English. Speak English. Christ!

¡Ay! Mamacita, who does not belong, every once in a while lets out a cry, hysterical, high, as if he had torn the only skinny thread that kept her alive, the only road out to that country.

And then to break her heart forever, the baby boy, who has begun to talk, starts to sing the Pepsi commercial he heard on T.V.

No speak English, she says to the child who is singing in the language that sounds like tin. No speak English, no speak English, and bubbles into tears. No, no, no, as if she can't believe her ears.

A Migration Created by Burden of Suspicion

by Dirk Johnson

Though Hana pledges to return to California and reclaim the family business, many Japanese internees did not go home following their release from the camps. Instead, families migrated to other parts of America in search of a new life.

When his fellow Chicagoans find out that Sam Ozaki is a native Californian, they almost always ask: "How in the world did you end up in this cold, windy city?"

The answer, the 70-year-old Mr. Ozaki explains, is rooted in war and racism.

On Feb. 19, 1942, after the outbreak of World War II, President Franklin D. Roosevelt signed an order sending more than 100,000 Japanese-Americans on the West Coast into internment camps scattered amid mountains and desert. They endured squalid living conditions behind barbed wire and the humiliation of being deemed suspect because of their ancestry. The nation was at war with Germany and Italy, as well as with Japan, of course, but there were no moves to lock up any European-Americans.

The internment did more than temporarily deprive Japanese-Americans of their freedom. It subtly changed the face of America, setting off an eastward migration of Japanese to places where few had lived before, like Chicago, Salt Lake City and Denver, because people released from the camps before the end of the war were not allowed to stay on the West Coast, and many chose not to return there.

In Chicago, there were churches offering help, and factories, short of labor during the war, offering jobs. Mr. Ozaki eventually became the first Asian-American principal in Chicago public schools, and he is now living a quiet retirement on the North Side. But 50 years after the end of the war, he recalls the burden of suspicion and the limited ways internees were able to escape the camps early. Many signed loyalty oaths and found sponsors inland, as required by the Government.

But Mr. Ozaki and thousands of other second-generation Japanese, or Nisei, chose another escape route from the camps: they volunteered to fight in the United States Army.

"There was a feeling that it was the only way we could prove our loyalty as Americans," said Mr. Ozaki, who served as an intelligence officer in a unit made up of Japanese-Americans, the 442d Regimental Combat Team. He worked as an interpreter—after a four-month crash course in Japanese at Camp Savage, Minnesota.

The 442d became one of the most highly decorated regiments in American military history. The 442d suffered huge casualties; Capt. Daniel K. Inouye, now a United States Senator from Hawaii, lost his right arm in battle. The team became famous for its rescue of the Texan "Lost Battalion," saving more than 200 men who had been surrounded by German troops.

By war's end, about 600 of the approximately 5,000 Nisei soldiers had lost their lives.

Less well known is the role played by Japanese-Americans who worked on the Pacific front as interpreters, interviewing prisoners of war, translating Imperial battle plans and deciphering secret codes.

One hero of the intelligence effort was Art Morimitsu, now 83, who interviewed wounded Japanese soldiers. "As they came to," he recalled, "they would look up and see this Japanese face, and there would be great relief and happiness." Then they would get a look at Mr. Morimitsu's American uniform, and the relief would vanish.

Mr. Morimitsu is a bedrock American patriot who has served as a commander of an American Legion post. He was among the veterans who protested the original Smithsonian exhibit on the Enola Gay, the plane that dropped the atomic bomb on Hiroshima. "These revisionists make it look like the U.S. was the aggressor and Japan was the victim," said Mr. Morimitsu, who went into the carpet-cleaning business in Chicago after the war.

Yet he still runs into people who take him for a member of the enemy forces from 50 years ago, even though he was born and reared in Sacramento, California.

For Japanese-Americans, memories of the triumph in World War II is inextricably twined with memories of the camps and of being made to feel like traitors.

"For decades, there was silence in the Japanese-American community about the camps," said Prof. Ronald Takaki, who teaches history at the University of California at Berkeley and is the author of "Strangers From a Different Shore" (Little, Brown and Company, 1989). "It was seen as a shameful time."

It was not until the 1980's, when many Japanese-Americans who had been imprisoned began seeking reparations from the Federal Government, that more of them began to speak out. In 1988, President Reagan signed a law that apologized to Japanese-

Americans for the internment and awarded each survivor $20,000 in damages. No case of espionage or sabotage by Japanese-Americans during the war has ever been documented.

For years before World War II, prejudice against Asian-Americans had been building. In 1882, Chinese were excluded from immigrating. In 1924, the Japanese were excluded from immigrating. They were also forbidden to own land or marry a white person in some states.

Mr. Morimitsu's wife, Virginia, recalled that on Dec. 7, 1941, she and her sister were attending a Christmas concert of Handel's "Messiah," at Santa Monica College. "Before we stood for the 'Hallelujah' chorus, it was announced that Japan had bombed Pearl Harbor," she said. "And it felt like all the eyes in the auditorium were placed on us."

In the weeks after the outbreak of war, Japanese-Americans anticipated a backlash. A headline in *The San Francisco Examiner* blared: "Ouster of All Japs in California Near!"

By February, signs were posted on telephone poles instructing all people with Japanese ancestry to prepare for evacuation.

The Morimitsus' daughter, Kathryn, a writer and computer consultant in Portland, said that her parents had never talked much about the internment camps but that she knew the experience had been 'incredibly traumatic.'

"My father's life," she said, "has been devoted to validating his part on the American scene as a patriot."

Being sent to the camps meant a loss of honor for people like her parents, who knew they were being tagged as second-class citizens, Ms. Morimitsu said. "And it's something that's subtly transmitted to my generation," she said. "So that while there is pride in our heritage, there is also a certain ambivalence."

In those frightening times, said Mrs. Morimitsu, who spent about a year at the Manzanar Camp in California, her mother destroyed all of her mementos from Japan, fearful that the authorities would see them as evidence of treason.

"Now I have nothing from my family's past," Mrs. Morimitsu said. "The Swedish ladies at my church will show me things handed down from their grandmothers, and I have nothing to show—nothing."

Breaking Silence

by Janice Mirikitani

*What kind of relationship do you think Mary
had with Hana after the war? This poem speaks
of the admiration a daughter has for her mother
as she testifies before a commission examining
the wartime relocation and internment of
Japanese-American civilians.*

There are miracles that happen
she said.
From the silences
in the glass caves of our ears,
5 from the crippled tongue,
from the mute, wet eyelash,
testimonies waiting like winter.
     We were told
that silence was better
10 golden like our skin,
     useful like
go quietly,
     easier like
don't make waves,
15   expedient like
horsestalls and deserts.

     "Mr. Commissioner . . .
     . . . the U.S. Army Signal Corps
      confiscated
     our property . . . it was
      subjected to
20   vandalism and ravage. All
      improvements

we had made before our
incarceration
was stolen or destroyed . . .
I was coerced into signing
documents
giving you authority to take . . ."
25   to take
to take.

My mother,
soft as tallow,
words peeling from her
30   like slivers of yellow flame.
Her testimony,
a vat of boiling water
surging through the coldest
bluest vein.
35   She had come to her land
as shovel, hoe and sickle searing
reed and rock and dead brush,
labored to sinew the ground
to soften gardens pregnant with seed
40   awaiting each silent morning
birthing
fields of flowers,
mustard greens and tomatoes
throbbing like the sea.
45   And then
All was hushed for announcements:
          "Take only what you can carry . . ."
We were made to believe our faces
betrayed us.
50   Our bodies were loud
with yellow screaming flesh
needing to be silenced
behind barbed wire.

"Mr. Commissioner . . .

55 . . . it seems we were singled out
from others who were under
        suspicion.
Our neighbors were of German
        and
Italian descent, some of whom
        were
not citizens . . . It seems we were
60 singled out . . ."

She had worn her work
like lemon leaves,
shining in her sweat,
driven by her dreams that honed
65 the blade of her plow.
The land she built
like hope
grew quietly
irises, roses, sweet peas
70 opening, opening.
        And then
all was hushed for announcements:
        ". . . to be incarcerated for your own
                good"
The sounds of her work
75 bolted in barracks . . .
silenced.

Mr. Commissioner . . .
So when you tell me I must limit
testimony,
80 when you tell me my time is up,
I tell you this:
Pride has kept my lips
pinned by nails
my rage coffined.

But I exhume my past
to claim this time.
My youth is buried in Rohwer,
Obachan's ghost visits Amache
    Gate.
My niece haunts Tule Lake.
Words are better than tears,
so I spill them.
I kill this,
the silence . . .

There are miracles that happen
she said,
and everything is made visible.
        We see the cracks and fissures in our soil:
We speak of suicides and intimacies,
of longings lush like wet furrows,
of oceans bearing us toward imagined riches,
of burning humiliations and
crimes by the government.
Of self hate and of love that breaks
through silences.
We are lightning and justice.
        Our souls become transparent like glass
revealing tears for war-dead sons
red ashes of Hiroshima
jagged wounds from barbed wire.
We must recognize ourselves at last.
        We are a rainforest of color
and noise.
        We hear everything.
        We are unafraid.

Our language is beautiful.

(*Quoted excerpts from my mother's testimony,
modified with her permission*—J.M.)

For My Father

by Janice Mirikitani

In this poem, a daughter takes another look at the extraordinary strength and perseverance of her father.

He came over the ocean
carrying Mt. Fuji
on his back/Tule Lake on his
chest
5   hacked through the brush
of deserts
and made them grow
strawberries

       we stole berries
10   from the stem
       we could not afford them
       for breakfast

his eyes held
nothing
15   as he whipped us
for stealing.

the desert had dried
his soul.

wordless
20   he sold
the rich,
full berries

to hakujines
whose children
25 pointed at our eyes

    they ate fresh
    strawberries
    with cream.

Father,
30 I wanted to scream
at your silence.
Your strength
was a stranger
I could never touch.

35   iron
    in your eyes
    to shield
    the pain
    to shield desert-like wind
40   from patches
    of strawberries
    grown
    from
    tears.

Clothes

by Chitra Banerjee Divakaruni

Do you think an arranged marriage would succeed in this day and age? Compare Hana and Taro's life together with the marriage of the contemporary couple in this short story.

The water of the women's lake laps against my breasts, cool, calming. I can feel it beginning to wash the hot nervousness away from my body. The little waves tickle my armpits, make my sari float up around me, wet and yellow, like a sunflower after rain. I close my eyes and smell the sweet brown odor of the *ritha* pulp my friends Deepali and Radha are working into my hair so it will glisten with little lights this evening. They scrub with more vigor than usual and wash it out more carefully, because today is a special day. It is the day of my bride-viewing.

"Ei, Sumita! Mita! Are you deaf?" Radha says. "This is the third time I've asked you the same question."

"Look at her, already dreaming about her husband, and she hasn't even seen him yet!" Deepali jokes. Then she adds, the envy in her voice only half hidden, "Who cares about friends from a little Indian village when you're about to go live in America?"

I want to deny it, to say that I will always love them and all the things we did together through my growing-up years—visiting the *charak* fair where we always ate too many sweets, raiding the neighbor's guava tree summer afternoons while the grown-ups slept, telling fairy tales while we braided each other's hair in elaborate patterns we'd invented. *And she married the handsome prince who took her to his kingdom beyond the seven seas.* But already the activities of our girlhood seem to be far in my past, the colors leached out of them, like old sepia photographs.

His name is Somesh Sen, the man who is coming to our house with his parents today and who will be my husband "if I'm lucky enough to be chosen," as my aunt says. He is coming all the way from California. Father showed it to me yesterday, on the metal globe that sits on his desk, a chunky pink wedge on the side of a multicolored slab marked *Untd. Sts. of America*. I touched it and felt the excitement leap all the way up my arm like an electric shock. Then it died away, leaving only a beaten-metal coldness against my fingertips.

For the first time it occurred to me that if things worked out the way everyone was hoping, I'd be going halfway around the world to live with a man I hadn't even met. Would I ever see my parents again? *Don't send me so far away.* I wanted to cry, but of course I didn't. It would be ungrateful. Father had worked so hard to find this match for me. Besides, wasn't it every woman's destiny, as Mother was always telling me, to leave the known for the unknown? She had done it, and her mother before her. *A married woman belongs to her husband, her in-laws.* Hot seeds of tears pricked my eyelids at the unfairness of it.

"Mita Moni, little jewel," Father said, calling me by my childhood name. He put out his hand as though he wanted to touch my face, then let it fall to his side. "He's a good man. Comes from a fine family. He will be kind to you." He was silent for a while. Finally he said, "Come, let me show you the special sari I bought in Calcutta for you to wear at the bride-viewing."

"Are you nervous?" Radha asks as she wraps my hair in a soft cotton towel. Her parents are also trying to arrange a marriage for her. So far three families have come to see her, but no one has chosen her because her skin-color is considered too dark. "Isn't it terrible, not knowing what's going to happen?"

I nod because I don't want to disagree, don't want to make her feel bad by saying that sometimes it's worse when you know what's coming, like I do. I knew it as soon as Father unlocked his mahogany *almirah* and took out the sari.

It was the most expensive sari I had ever seen, and surely the most beautiful. Its body was a pale pink, like the dawn sky over the women's lake. The color of transition. Embroidered all over it were tiny stars made out of real gold *zari* thread.

"Here, hold it," said Father.

The sari was unexpectedly heavy in my hands, silk-slippery, a sari to walk carefully in. A sari that could change one's life. I stood there holding it, wanting to weep. I knew that when I wore it, it would hang in perfect pleats to my feet and shimmer in the light of the evening lamps. It would dazzle Somesh and his parents and they would choose me to be his bride.

When the plane takes off, I try to stay calm, to take deep, slow breaths like Father does when he practices yoga. But my hands clench themselves on to the folds of my sari and when I force them open, after the *fasten seat belt* and *no smoking* signs have blinked off, I see they have left damp blotches on the delicate crushed fabric.

We had some arguments about this sari. I wanted a blue one for the journey, because blue is the color of possibility, the color of the sky through which I would be traveling. But Mother said there must be red in it because red is the color of luck for married women.

Finally, Father found one to satisfy us both: midnight-blue with a thin red border the same color as the marriage mark I'm wearing on my forehead.

It is hard for me to think of myself as a married woman. I whisper my new name to myself, Mrs. Sumita Sen, but the syllables rustle uneasily in my mouth like a stiff satin that's never been worn.

Somesh had to leave for America just a week after the wedding. He had to get back to the store, he explained to me. He had promised his partner. The store. It seems more real to me than Somesh—perhaps because I know more about it. It was what we had mostly talked about the night after the wedding, the first night we were together alone. It stayed open twenty-four hours, yes, all night, every night, not like the Indian stores which closed at dinnertime and sometimes in the hottest part of the afternoon. That's why his partner needed him back.

The store was called *7-Eleven*. I thought it a strange name, exotic, risky. All the stores I knew were piously named after gods and goddesses—*Ganesh Sweet House, Lakshmi Vastralaya for Fine Saris*—to bring the owners luck.

The store sold all kinds of amazing things—apple juice in cardboard cartons that never leaked; American bread that came in cellophane packages, already cut up; canisters of potato chips, each large grainy flake curved exactly like the next. The large refrigerator with see-through glass doors held beer and wine, which Somesh said were the most popular items.

"That's where the money comes from, especially in the neighborhood where our store is," said Somesh, smiling at the shocked look on my face. (The only places I knew of that sold alcohol were the village toddy shops, "dark, stinking dens of vice," Father called them.) "A lot of Americans drink, you know. It's a part of their culture, not considered immoral, like it is here. And really, there's nothing wrong with it." He touched my lips lightly with his finger. "When you come to California, I'll get you some sweet white wine and you'll see how good it makes you feel. . . ." Now his fingers were stroking my cheeks, my throat, moving downward. I closed my eyes and tried not to jerk away because after all it was my wifely duty.

"It helps if you can think about something else," my friend Madhavi had said when she warned me about what most husbands demanded on the very first night. Two years married, she already had one child and was pregnant with a second one.

I tried to think of the women's lake, the dark cloudy green of the *shapla* leaves that float on the water, but his lips were hot against my skin, his fingers fumbling with buttons, pulling at the cotton night-sari I wore. I couldn't breathe.

"Bite hard on your tongue," Madhavi had advised. "The pain will keep your mind off what's going on down there."

But when I bit down, it hurt so much that I cried out. I couldn't help it although I was ashamed. Somesh lifted his head. I don't know what he saw on my face, but he stopped right away. "Shhh," he said, although I had made myself silent already. "It's OK, we'll wait until you feel like it." I tried to apologize but he smiled it away and started telling me some more about the store.

And that's how it was the rest of the week until he left. We would lie side by side on the big white bridal pillow I had embroidered with a pair of doves for married harmony, and Somesh would describe how the store's front windows were decorated with a flashing neon Dewar's sign and a lighted Budweiser waterfall *this big*. I would watch his hands moving excitedly through the dim air of the bedroom and think that Father had been right, he was a good man, my husband, a kind, patient man. And so handsome, too, I would add, stealing a quick look at the strong curve of his jaw, feeling luckier than I had any right to be.

The night before he left, Somesh confessed that the store wasn't making much money yet. "I'm not worried, I'm sure it soon will," he added, his fingers pleating the edge of my sari. "But I just don't want to give you the wrong impression, don't want you to be disappointed."

In the half dark I could see he had turned toward me. His face, with two vertical lines between the brows, looked young, apprehensive, in need of protection. I'd never seen that on a man's face before. Something rose in me like a wave.

"It's all right," I said, as though to a child, and pulled his head down to my breast. His hair smelled faintly of the American cigarettes he smoked. "I won't be disappointed. I'll help you." And a sudden happiness filled me.

That night I dreamed I was at the store. Soft American music floated in the background as I moved between shelves stocked high with brightly colored cans and elegant-necked bottles, turning their labels carefully to the front, polishing them until they shone.

Now, sitting inside this metal shell that is hurtling through emptiness, I try to remember other things about my husband: how gentle his hands had been, and his lips, surprisingly soft, like a woman's. How I've longed for them through those drawn-out nights while I waited for my visa to arrive. He will be standing at the customs gate, and when I reach him, he will lower his face to mine. We will kiss in front of everyone, not caring, like Americans, then pull back, look each other in the eye, and smile.

But suddenly, as I am thinking this, I realize I cannot recall Somesh's face. I try and try until my head hurts, but I can only visualize the black air swirling outside the plane, too thin for breathing. My own breath grows ragged with panic as I think of it and my mouth fills with sour fluid the way it does just before I throw up.

I grope for something to hold on to, something beautiful and talismanic from my old life. And then I remember. Somewhere down under me, low in the belly of the plane, inside my new brown case which is stacked in the dark with a hundred others, are my saris. Thick Kanjeepuram silks in solid purples and golden yellows, the thin hand-woven cottons of the Bengal countryside, green as a young banana plant, gray as the women's lake on a monsoon morning. Already I can feel my shoulders loosening up, my breath steadying. My wedding Benarasi, flame-orange, with a wide *palloo* of gold-embroidered dancing peacocks. Fold upon fold of Dhakais so fine they can be pulled through a ring. Into each fold my mother has tucked a small sachet of sandalwood powder to protect the saris from the unknown insects of America. Little silk sachets, made from *her* old saris—I can smell their calm fragrance as I watch the American air hostess wheeling the dinner cart toward my seat. It is the smell of my mother's hands.

I know then that everything will be all right. And when the air hostess bends her curly golden head to ask me what I would like to eat, I understand every word in spite of her strange accent and answer her without stumbling even once over the unfamiliar English phrases.

Late at night I stand in front of our bedroom mirror trying on the clothes Somesh has bought for me and smuggled in past his parents. I model each one for him, walking back and forth, clasping my hands behind my head, lips pouted, left hip thrust out just like the models on TV, while he whispers applause. I'm breathless with suppressed laughter (Father and Mother Sen must not hear us) and my cheeks are hot with the delicious excitement of conspiracy. We've stuffed a towel at the bottom of the door so no light will shine through.

I'm wearing a pair of jeans now, marveling at the curves of my hips and thighs, which have always been hidden under the flowing lines of my saris. I love the color, the same pale blue as the *nayantara* flowers that grow in my parents' garden. The solid comforting weight. The jeans come with a close-fitting T-shirt which outlines my breasts.

I scold Somesh to hide my embarrassed pleasure. He shouldn't have been so extravagant. We can't afford it. He just smiles.

The T-shirt is sunrise-orange—the color, I decide, of joy, of my new American life. Across its middle, in large black letters, is written *Great America*. I was sure the letters referred to the country, but Somesh told me it is the name of an amusement park, a place where people go to have fun. I think it a wonderful concept, novel. Above the letters is the picture of a train. Only it's not a train, Somesh tells me, it's a roller coaster. He tries to explain how it moves, the insane speed, the dizzy ground falling away, then gives up. "I'll take you there, Mita sweetheart," he says, "as soon as we move into our own place."

That's our dream (mine more than his, I suspect)— moving out of this two-room apartment where it seems to me if we all breathed in at once, there would be no air left. Where I must cover my head with the edge of my Japan nylon sari (my expensive Indian ones are to be saved for special occasions—trips to the temple, Bengali New Year) and serve tea to the old women that come to visit Mother Sen, where like a good Indian wife I must never address my husband by his name. Where even in our bed we kiss guiltily, uneasily, listening for the giveaway creak of springs. Sometimes I laugh to myself, thinking how ironic it is that after all my fears about America, my life has turned out to be no different from Deepali's or Radha's. But at other times I feel caught in a world where everything is frozen in place, like a scene inside a glass paperweight. It is a world so small that if I were to stretch out my arms, I would touch its cold unyielding edges. I stand inside this glass world, watching helplessly as America rushes by, wanting to scream. Then I'm ashamed. Mita, I tell myself, you're growing westernized. Back home you'd never have felt this way.

We must be patient. I know that. Tactful, loving children. That is the Indian way. "I'm their life," Somesh tells me as we lie beside each other, lazy from lovemaking. He's not boasting, merely stating a fact. "They've always been there when I needed them. I could never abandon them at some old people's home." For a moment I feel rage. You're constantly thinking of them, I want to scream. But what about me? Then I remember my own parents, Mother's hands cool on my sweat-drenched body through nights of fever, Father teaching me to read, his finger moving along the crisp black angles of the alphabet, transforming them magically into things I knew, water, dog, mango tree. I beat back my unreasonable desire and nod agreement.

Somesh has bought me a cream blouse with a long brown skirt. They match beautifully, like the inside and outside of an almond. "For when you begin working," he says. But first he wants me to start college. Get a degree, perhaps in teaching. I picture myself in front of a classroom of girls with blond pigtails and blue uniforms, like a scene out of an English movie I saw long ago in Calcutta. They raise their hands respectfully when I ask a question. "Do you really think I can?" I ask. "Of course," he replies.

I am gratified he has such confidence in me. But I have another plan, a secret that I will divulge to him once we move. What I really want is to work in the store. I want to stand behind the counter in the cream-and-brown skirt set (color of earth, color of seeds) and ring up purchases. The register drawer will glide open. Confident, I will count out green dollars and silver quarters. Gleaming copper pennies. I will dust the jars of gilt-wrapped chocolates on the counter. Will straighten, on the far wall, posters of smiling young men raising their beer mugs to toast scantily clad redheads with huge spiky eyelashes. (I have never visited the store—my in-laws don't consider it proper for a wife—but of course I know exactly what it looks like.) I will charm the customers with my smile, so that they will return again and again just to hear me telling them to have a nice day.

Meanwhile, I will the store to make money for us. Quickly. Because when we move, we'll be paying for two households. But so far it hasn't worked. They're running at a loss, Somesh tells me. They had to let the hired help go. This means most nights Somesh has to take the graveyard shift (that horrible word, like a cold hand up my spine) because his partner refuses to.

"The bastard!" Somesh spat out once. "Just because he put in more money he thinks he can order me around. I'll show him!" I was frightened by the vicious twist of his mouth. Somehow I'd never imagined that he could be angry.

Often Somesh leaves as soon as he has dinner and doesn't get back till after I've made morning tea for Father and Mother Sen. I lie mostly awake those nights, picturing masked intruders crouching in the shadowed back of the store, like I've seen on the police shows that Father Sen sometimes watches. But

Somesh insists there's nothing to worry about, they have bars on the windows and a burglar alarm. "And remember," he says, "the extra cash will help us move out that much quicker."

I'm wearing a nightie now, my very first one. It's black and lacy, with a bit of a shine to it, and it glides over my hips to stop outrageously at mid-thigh. My mouth is an O of surprise in the mirror, my legs long and pale and sleek from the hair remover I asked Somesh to buy me last week. The legs of a movie star. Somesh laughs at the look on my face, then says, "You're beautiful." His voice starts a flutter low in my belly.

"Do you really think so," I ask, mostly because I want to hear him say it again. No one has called me beautiful before. My father would have thought it inappropriate, my mother that it would make me vain.

Somesh draws me close. "Very beautiful," he whispers. "The most beautiful woman in the whole world." His eyes are not joking as they usually are. I want to turn off the light, but "Please," he says, "I want to keep seeing your face." His fingers are taking the pins from my hair, undoing my braids. The escaped strands fall on his face like dark rain. We have already decided where we will hide my new American clothes—the jeans and T-shirt camouflaged on a hanger among Somesh's pants, the skirt set and nightie at the bottom of my suitcase, a sandalwood sachet tucked between them, waiting.

I stand in the middle of our empty bedroom, my hair still wet from the purification bath, my back to the stripped bed I can't bear to look at. I hold in my hands the plain white sari I'm supposed to wear. I must hurry. Any minute now there'll be a knock at the door. They are afraid to leave me alone too long, afraid I might do something to myself.

The sari, a thick voile that will bunch around the waist when worn, is borrowed. White. Widow's color, color of endings. I try to tuck it into the top of the petticoat, but my fingers are numb, disobedient. It spills through them and there are waves and waves of white around my feet. I kick out in sudden rage, but the sari is too soft, it gives too easily. I grab up an edge, clamp down with my teeth and pull, feeling a fierce, bitter satisfaction when I hear it rip.

There's a cut, still stinging, on the side of my right arm, halfway to the elbow. It is from the bangle-breaking ceremony. Old Mrs. Ghosh performed the ritual, since she's a widow, too. She took my hands in hers and brought them down hard on the bedpost, so that the glass bangles I was wearing shattered and multicolored shards flew out in every direction. Some landed on the body that was on the bed, covered with a sheet. I can't call it Somesh. He was gone already. She took an edge of the sheet and rubbed the red marriage mark off my forehead. She was crying. All the women in the room were crying except me. I watched them as though from the far end of a tunnel. Their flared nostrils, their red-veined eyes, the runnels of tears, salt-corrosive, down their cheeks.

It happened last night. He was at the store. "It isn't too bad," he would tell me on the days when he was in a good mood. "Not too many customers. I can put up my feet and watch MTV all night. I can sing along with Michael Jackson as loud as I want." He had a good voice, Somesh. Sometimes he would sing softly at night, lying in bed, holding me. Hindi songs of love, *Mere Sapnon Ki Rani*, queen of my dreams. (He would not sing American songs at home out of respect for his parents, who thought they were decadent.) I would feel his warm breath on my hair as I fell asleep.

Someone came into the store last night. He took all

the money, even the little rolls of pennies I had helped
Somesh make up. Before he left he emptied the bullets
from his gun into my husband's chest.

"Only thing is," Somesh would say about the night
shifts, "I really miss you. I sit there and think of you
asleep in bed. Do you know that when you sleep you
make your hands into fists, like a baby? When we
move out, will you come along some nights to keep
me company?"

My in-laws are good people, kind. They made sure
the body was covered before they let me into the
room. When someone asked if my hair should be cut
off, as they sometimes do with widows back home,
they said no. They said I could stay at the apartment
with Mrs. Ghosh if I didn't want to go to the
crematorium. They asked Dr. Das to give me
something to calm me down when I couldn't stop
shivering. They didn't say, even once, as people would
surely have in the village, that it was my bad luck that
brought death to their son so soon after his marriage.

They will probably go back to India now. There's
nothing here for them anymore. They will want me to
go with them. You're like our daughter, they will say.
Your home is with us, for as long as you want. For the
rest of your life. *The rest of my life.* I can't think about
that yet. It makes me dizzy. Fragments are flying
about my head, multicolored and piercing sharp like
bits of bangle glass.

I want you to go to college. Choose a career. I stand
in front of a classroom of smiling children who love
me in my cream-and-brown American dress. A
faceless parade straggles across my eyelids: all those
customers at the store that I will never meet. The lace
nightie, fragrant with sandalwood, waiting in its
blackness inside my suitcase. The savings book where
we have $3605.33. *Four thousand and we can move
out, maybe next month.* The name of the panty hose

I'd asked him to buy me for my birthday: sheer golden-beige. His lips, unexpectedly soft, woman-smooth. Elegant-necked wine bottles swept off shelves, shattering on the floor.

I know Somesh would not have tried to stop the gunman. I can picture his silhouette against the lighted Dewar's sign, hands raised. He is trying to find the right expression to put on his face, calm, reassuring, reasonable. *OK, take the money. No, I won't call the police.* His hands tremble just a little. His eyes darken with disbelief as his fingers touch his chest and come away wet.

I yanked away the cover. I had to see. *Great America, a place where people go to have fun.* My breath roller-coasting through my body, my unlived life gathering itself into a scream. I'd expected blood, a lot of blood, the deep red-black of it crusting his chest. But they must have cleaned him up at the hospital. He was dressed in his silk wedding *kurta.* Against its warm ivory his face appeared remote, stern. The musky aroma of his aftershave lotion that someone must have sprinkled on the body. It didn't quite hide that other smell, thin, sour, metallic. The smell of death. The floor shifted under me, tilting like a wave.

I'm lying on the floor now, on the spilled white sari. I feel sleepy. Or perhaps it is some other feeling I don't have a word for. The sari is seductive-soft, drawing me into its folds.

Sometimes, bathing at the lake, I would move away from my friends, their endless chatter. I'd swim toward the middle of the water with a lazy backstroke, gazing at the sky, its enormous blueness drawing me up until I felt weightless and dizzy. Once in a while there would be a plane, a small silver needle drawn through the clouds, in and out, until it disappeared. Sometimes the thought came to me, as I floated in the middle of the lake with the sun beating down on my closed eyelids, that it would be so easy to let go, to drop into the dim brown world of mud, of water weeds fine as hair.

Once I almost did it. I curled my body inward, tight as a fist, and felt it start to sink. The sun grew pale and shapeless; the water, suddenly cold, licked at the insides of my ears in welcome. But in the end I couldn't.

They are knocking on the door now, calling my name. I push myself off the floor, my body almost too heavy to lift up, as when one climbs out after a long swim. I'm surprised at how vividly it comes to me, this memory I haven't called up in years: the desperate flailing of arms and legs as I fought my way upward; the press of the water on me, heavy as terror; the wild animal trapped inside my chest, clawing at my lungs. The day returning to me as searing air, the way I drew it in, in, in, as though I would never have enough of it.

That's when I know I cannot go back. I don't know yet how I'll manage, here in this new, dangerous land. I only know I must. Because all over India, at this very moment, widows in white saris are bowing their veiled heads, serving tea to in-laws. Doves with cut-off wings.

I am standing in front of the mirror now, gathering up the sari. I tuck in the ripped end so it lies next to my skin, my secret. I make myself think of the store, although it hurts. Inside the refrigerated unit, blue milk cartons neatly lined up by Somesh's hands. The exotic smell of Hills Brothers coffee brewed black and strong, the glisten of sugar-glazed donuts nestled in tissue. The neon Budweiser emblem winking on and off like a risky invitation.

I straighten my shoulders and stand taller, take a deep breath. Air fills me—the same air that traveled through Somesh's lungs a little while ago. The thought is like an unexpected, intimate gift. I tilt my chin, readying myself for the arguments of the coming weeks, the remonstrations. In the mirror a woman holds my gaze, her eyes apprehensive yet steady. She wears a blouse and skirt the color of almonds.

The Heart of a Woman

by Georgia Douglas Johnson

How do you think Hana would describe her life? Consider her experiences throughout Picture Bride *as you read this poem.*

The heart of a woman goes forth with the dawn,
As a lone bird, soft winging, so restlessly on,
Afar o'er life's turrets and vales does it roam
In the wake of those echoes the heart calls home.

5 The heart of a woman falls back with the night,
And enters some alien cage in its plight,
And tries to forget it has dreamed of the stars,
While it breaks, breaks, breaks on the sheltering
   bars.

Acknowledgments

(continued from page ii)

Susan Bergholz Literary Services: "No Speak English," from *The House on Mango Street.* Copyright © 1984 by Sandra Cisneros. Published by Vintage Books, a division of Random House, Inc., New York, and in hardcover by Alfred A. Knopf in 1994. Reprinted by permission of Susan Bergholz Literary Services, New York. All rights reserved.

The New York Times: "A Migration Created by Burden of Suspicion" by Dirk Johnson, from *The New York Times,* August 14, 1995. Copyright © 1995 by The New York Times Company. Reprinted by permission of The New York Times.

Janice Mirikitani: "For My Father," from *Awake in the River: Poetry and Prose* by Janice Mirikitani. Copyright © 1978 by Janice Mirikitani.
"Breaking Silence," from *Shedding Silence* by Janice Mirikitani. Copyright © 1987 by Janice Mirikitani.
Reprinted by permission of Janice Mirikitani.

Doubleday: "Clothes," from *Arranged Marriage* by Chitra Divakaruni. Copyright © 1995 by Chitra Divakaruni. Used by permission of Doubleday, a division of Bantam Doubleday Dell Publishing Group, Inc.